IN THE GLOW

OF THE

PHANTOM

PALACE

MICHAEL JACOBS

IN THE GLOW OF THE PHANTOM PALACE

TRAVELS FROM GRANADA TO TIMBUKTU

PALLAS ATHENE

The mosque in Fez, from Edmondo de Amicis' Morocco

CONTENTS

V

CHAPTER TWO

LAST DAY IN PARADISE p. 50

Granada and its *vega*—A visit to the Islamic tower at Gabia la Grande—A view of the *vega* at dusk—Granada's modern outskirts—Days in the House of the Rich Moor—The arrival of Autumn—The wars of Granada—Alcalá la Real—Loja—The Narváez Gardens—Montefrío—Moclín—The fall of Granada—The site of Lorca's execution—Lunch at the 'Fountain of Tears'—A thwarted passion—The author's departure from Paradise

CHAPTER THREE

LOST WORLDS p. 69

Setting off to the Alpujarra in a battered jeep—The Moor's Sigh—The bridge of Tablate—Jan Potocki and *The Manuscript Found at Saragossa*—The mountain district of the Alpujarra—The spa town of Lanjarón—Cádiar and 'The Fountain of Wine'—Aben Humeya, leader of the morisco uprising of 1569—Searching for the olive tree of Aben Humeya—The legend of Aben Humeya, and the birth of Spanish romanticism—The isolated hamlet of Las Canteras—An ill-advised climb by car up to the ruins of the castle of Juliana—Thoughts of Gerald Brenan—A night in Yegen—Echoes of Bloomsbury—A Yegen scandal—The source of the River Andarax—Boabdil in Exile—Boabdil's 'Palace'—The baths at Alhama de Almería—Off the road in the Sierra de Gador—Boabdil at Adra—A mountain walk to the mysterious Mezquita—A night in a mountain inn—The Dalai Lama and 'The Place of the Clear Light'—Trespassers on the roof of the Sierra Nevada—The route of the snow-porters—A warm welcome in the Venta Bienvenido

CHAPTER FOUR

A LABYRINTH OF CAVES p. 99

The route into exile of Leo Africanus, from Granada to Almería—Lost in a forest—Arrival at La Peza, forgotten village on the 'Royal Route'—An eroded landscape pitted with caves—The decayed spa at Graena—Moorish caves—The mosque at Cortes—Exploring the Cave of 'Tía Micaela'—The elusive baths at Huenaja—The *mihrab* at Fiñana—Granada's Ayers Rock—A thermal pool near Zújar—José Saramago and *The Stone Raft*—The converted cave dwellings of Galera—A night in a cave—*A Spanish Kama Sutra*—Brenan's sexual legacy—Don Juan of Austria and the suppression of Galera's moriscos—Between *'Trivásicos'* and *'Belmontes'*—Huéscar, the Nasrids' easternmost stronghold—Huéscar and the War with Denmark—The ancient thermal pool at Fuencalientes—Sequoiahs in the Sierra Sagra—Puebla de Don Fadrique—Last lunch in the Kingdom of Granada—The Man from Orce

CHAPTER FIVE

MOORS AND ASIATICS p. 117

By bus across the Murcian border—Ibn Arabi, the Murcian mystic—A baroque spectacle at Caravaca—Christ and the castle of Monteagudo—The city of Murcia—The fantastical Casino—The hidden Moorish city—Post-modern Moorish—By the banks of the Segura, the Murcian Nile—The waterwheels of La Nora and Alcantarilla—The baths of Alhama de Murcia—Up the Valley of the Ricote—The spa at Archena—An oasis of orchards and palms—Ricote, the Moriscos' final home—La Venta del Sordo—Further up the Segura—The museum at Cieza—Medina Siyasa—Into the land of the *Asiático*—Exotic Cartagena—The camels of

CHAPTER SIX

EXILES IN THE ORIENT p. 147

CHAPTER SEVEN

TO TIMBUKTU p. 217

The clothes market in Fez,
from Edmondo de Amicis' Morocco

ILLUSTRATIONS

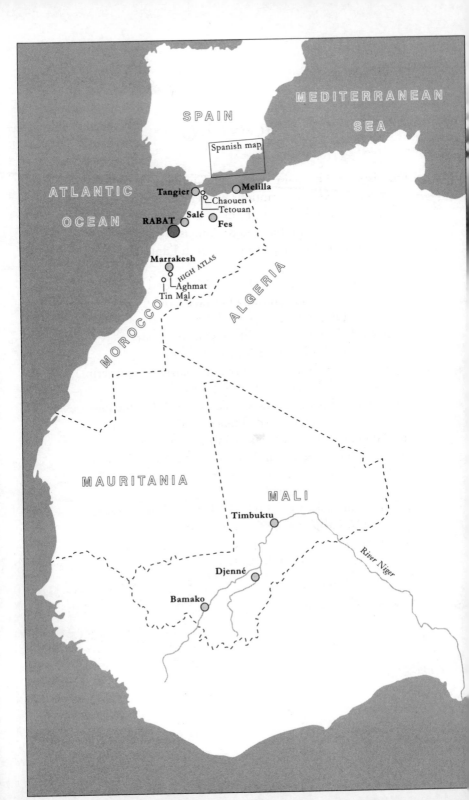

MEDITERRANEAN SEA

SPAIN

Monteagudo
Murcia
Archena
Alcantarilla
Ricote
Cieza
Mula
Baños de Mula
Alhama de Murcia
CARTAGENA

Caravaca de la Cruz
RESERVA NACIONAL DE SIERRA ESPUÑA
Cuevas del Almanzora

Puebla Don Fadrique
Huéscar
Orce
Galera

SIERRA DE LA SAGRA

Zújar
Jabalcón
Baza

Sierra Alhamilla
ALMERÍA

Alhama de Almería
Fuente Victoria
Dalias
Adra

Guadix
Cortes y Graena
Lacalahorra
Huéneja
Fiñana
Fereira
Laújar de Andarax

La Peza
Válor
Yegen
Cádiar
Mecina Fondales
Bubión
Capileira

Trevélez

GRANADA
Monachil
Pto. del Suspiro del Moro

Moclín

Santa Fe
Las Gabias
La Malá
Dúrchal
Lecrín
Lanjarón

Montefrío

Loja

Alhama de Granada

Cómpeta

Cantaríján

MÁLAGA

TO ALL MY
FRIENDS IN
GRANADA

NOTE TO THE READER

This book was commissioned in 1994, under unusual circumstances that have been incorporated into its narrative. I had been asked by the newly-founded Granadan institution El Legado Andalusí to write a travelogue that would help them in their monumental task of promoting Andalucía's Islamic heritage. From the beginning, my interest in Islamic monuments was matched by a fascination with the way in which Spain was succumbing increasingly to a mania for things Moorish. I became absorbed by the paradoxes inherent in a Spain in which the neo-Moorish was flourishing at a time when so many aspects of the country's genuine Moorish past were falling into decay.

The more I studied this phenomenon, the further I entered that twilight area between fact and fiction that has always enticed travel writers, especially those who have explored the land vaguely defined as the Orient. The very style in which my book came to be written was intended as an ironic commentary both on the world of Moorish pastiche and on the sensual, romantic imaginings of so many of my fellow travellers to Islamic Spain.

Though the places featured in this book are very much real and have all been visited by me, the linking narrative contains a considerable amount of fictional embellishment. I leave the reader to decide what is true and what is false, bearing in mind the saying that fact can be stranger than fiction. Furthermore, I should point out that my fantastical-seeming vision of a world being rapidly taken over by an ersatz culture appears to be even truer today than it was in 1994. Not even in my more susceptible moments would I have predicted that by the end of the millennium an Arabian magnate would have begun work on an exact, life-sized replica of Granada's Alhambra, or that a discotheque inspired by the latter would have been opened in Marbella in between a mosque and the palace of Saudi Arabia's king.

The Court of Lions in the Alhambra, illustration by Gustave Doré for de Amicis' Espagne

FOREWORD

IN THE HOUSE OF THE RICH MOOR

This is the Granada that travellers still dream about. The modern town has suddenly vanished, replaced by tilted white houses, stepped alleys, miradors, cypresses, hidden gardens, and a mountain stream rushing between dense greenery and the giant ruins of a horse-shoe arch.

From the grounds of a large villa on the lush slopes of the Alhambra hill, I watch the summer sun rising from behind the palace battlements until eventually a dazzling brightness is cast over the Moorish honeycomb of the Albaicín. I am in an Andalucían paradise, with its proverbial jasmine-scented air, cool fountains, and luxuriant profusion of box-hedges, citrus trees and pomegranates.

Here, in surroundings that appear to parody a thousand sentimental visions, I sit waiting in the villa once known as that of the 'Rich Moor'. I am waiting for its owner.

Intoxicated by the world around me, I begin to picture him as a powerful sultan, to whose splendid court I have been brusquely summoned from a grey and distant London. And as I day-dream under the shadow of the Alhambra, I share for a short while the delusions of Washington Irving, Richard Ford, Théophile Gautier and the many other romantics who have thought of Granada as the gateway to the Orient.

The Orient of the romantic imagination – a realm dreamt up by a tamed and industrialized West – was not only a land where the medieval and ancient past had miraculously survived into modern times, but also a place dominated by extremes of violence and sensuality. Washington Irving, enclosed within the then neglected walls of the Alhambra, invented a tale of a terrible massacre merely on the basis of the red staining on a marble basin. Other writers, inspired by the overwhelming richness of the Moorish plaster-work, have filled the Alhambra's halls with lovesick courtiers and olive-skinned beauties.

It was the supposed sensuality of the Orient that appealed most strongly to romantic travellers to Andalucía, most of whom, according to the cynical critic Mario Praz, were intellectuals suffering from acute sexual repression. The few among them who had seriously studied the Islamic culture of Spain would certainly have relished the fact that the inhabitants of Al-Andalus seem to have enjoyed a greater social and moral freedom than their counterparts elsewhere in the Islamic world. And they would have delighted in the numerous Hispano-Arabic poems that exalt the pleasures of wine and love: poems evocative of 'ambrosial liquids', or of lives 'spent in dissipation and wantonness', or of penises 'making tents out of trousers', or of dancers slipping out of robes 'like buds unfolding'.

Love, ecstasy, paradise, the Alhambra: all became synonymous concepts in the eyes of many a romantic traveller. Edmondo de Amicis, the Italian author of that sentimental classic *Cuore*, brought 19th-century descriptions of the Alhambra to a delirious, gushing climax when he described the building's architecture as expressive not of 'power, glory and grandeur', but rather of 'love and voluptuousness, love with its mysteries, caprices, expansions, and its bursts of gratitude to God; voluptuousness with its bits of melancholy and silence.' 'There is thus,' he added, 'a strong link, a harmony between the beauty of this Alhambra and the souls of those who have been in love at sixteen, when desires are dreams and visions.'

My brain is softening like that of de Amicis, and as I continue waiting in the House of the Rich Moor, the sensual Oriental fantasies of my romantic predecessors become increasingly confused with personal memories of a Granadan love affair. Was it really under the star-shaped openings of the Albaicín's ruined Moorish baths that I first held hands with the woman whom I came to call 'the Moorish Queen'? And did we really kiss under a full moon on the Alhambra hill? As I try and look back today on these romantic memories, I become ever more conscious of the absurdity and unreality of being in love in a town whose identity has been so distorted by the amorous dreams of Orientalists.

Middle-aged scepticism, combined with the attitudes of a traveller in a post-modern, post-colonial age, have begun to sharpen my vision of the outwardly little changed and persistently exotic Granada that lies before me. This is an age in which the romantic utterances of past travellers have grown stale with endless repetition, and in which Orientalism – thanks to the likes of Edward Said – has lost its glamour to become merely a reflection of the westerner's desire to appropriate and colonize the East. And I am visiting a Granada at a time when so much of the European past is being either mysteriously forgotten or else turned into a pastiche.

The 'fabled Alhambra', which dominates the view to my right, bears little relation to the neglected ruins that began to attract foreign travellers from the late 18th century. Reconstructed, over-restored, and reduced to a rigidly designated tourist trail, with arrows and glass barriers, this place which was already being described in the 1950's as a 'glorified gazebo' now seems at times as much of a sham as the hundreds it has spawned.

And as I direct my attention southwards, to the glowing labyrinth of the Albaicín, my head is filled less with romantic notions of the lives once led there by the Moors and their gypsy successors, than with thoughts of gentrified villas, neo-Moroccan tea-rooms, video-recorded sunsets, and the former hippies who have romantically taken on, like a coating of Islamic plasterwork, a Sufi identity.

It is only when I look downwards, towards the so-called Paseo de los Tristes, that I encounter a significant anomaly in this world slowly being transformed into a Moorish showcase. For it is there, in perhaps the most beautiful spot in all Granada, that the Albaicín comes suddenly to an end amidst huge and inexplicable mounds of rubble and cans.

Poised in between the Alhambra and the wasteland below me, I sit waiting in a villa which had itself been left to ruin until its recent drastic transformation involving the entire rebuilding of its upper level, the bringing in of mudéjar ceilings and a plethora of neo-Moorish lanterns, and the laying out of Moorish-style gardens that smell like an overdose of air-freshener. As if in a counter reaction to the genie's lamp, this villa, formerly of the 'rich Moor', and before that the property of one of the greatest of Spain's military leaders, the 'Gran Capitán', has become, prosaically, a place for receptions and business functions.

The arrival of a mobile phone brought to me by the housekeeper helps further to awaken me from my dreams, but only for a moment. I am told that the Sultan is on his way.

The Sultan is growing in my imagination, so much so that the real person and the fictional identity I have invented for him have become indistinguishable. I have heard many stories about him, about his origins as a lawyer, his rapid rise to power, and his present position as the organizer of the World Skiing Championship of 1995 – the event with which Granada hopes to attract some of the international attention of which it had felt deprived during Spain's much publicized celebrations of 1992. But what interests me most about the Sultan, and what brings me back to this town of romantic memories, is his passion for travel literature, and his overriding obsession with Andalucía's Moorish past.

The Sultan has plans for Andalucía that will far outlive the two weeks of the skiing championship. He is devising a series of cultural routes comparable to that of the Pilgrim's Way to Santiago de Compostela – a series of routes that will awaken the interest of Spaniards and foreigners alike in the untold riches of Spain's Islamic heritage, and that will bear names such as the Route of Ibn Battuta, of Leo Africanus, of the Almoravids, of Ibn-al-Idrisi, and of the Caliphate. And he will promote these with conferences, exhibitions, and a multitude of publications, one of which will be an account of a journey undertaken by someone automatically perceived in Spain – merely through being British – as a 'romantic traveller'.

The Sultan is apparently a romantic himself, fascinated by his renegade ancestors, and passionate about Morocco, a land where he feels more at home than in many parts of his native Spain. Perhaps, I am beginning to wonder, he is even a reincarnation of the last of the Moorish rulers of Granada, Boabdil, whose tears on being exiled from his kingdom in 1492 have been endlessly described in romantic travelogues and history books.

The enemies of the Sultan are drawing in on him, and there are rumours that he too will finally flee to Morocco. The disillusioned, financially straitened Spain of the 'post-92 years' abounds in suspicion, intrigue, envy, economic scandals, tales of corruption and imminent falls from power.

Suddenly he is in front of me, a short man whose rounded, unmistakeably Jewish face melts into the warmest of smiles before slipping back instantly into a distracted melancholy. I talk to him, but his eyes are elsewhere. Eventually he nods, a contract is agreed to, he disappears into a patio.

From the upstairs gallery, I look down upon a patio which is filling up with small groups of people, courtiers, emissaries, fellow devotees to the cause of Spain's Islamic past. The Sultan is moving restlessly between them, a gentle despot, lonely among his acolytes, but with a commanding presence and a soft voice which rises occasionally into a bark. I retreat into a room to plan my journey through the byways of al-Andalus.

The moments spent contemplating one of the most hackneyed views in Europe have finally led my mind to wander beyond the famous Islamic monuments of Southern Spain. Hidden away in my upstairs room, I dream neither of the Alhambra, nor of the Alcázar of Seville, nor of the Mezquita of Córdoba, but rather of the ruinous and less familiar Islamic world which lies beyond all the mindless praise and stale visions of a now redundant Orientalism. It is in the more poignant and neglected monuments of Spain's Moorish past – fragments of castles, mosques, baths, waterworks – that I hope to gain a deeper knowledge of the Islamic culture of Spain, and perhaps even a closer understanding of the attitudes towards this culture of the Spaniards of today. At heart I am longing to experience something of the freshness of response and acute sense of pathos that must have been felt by the earliest of the romantic travellers to Andalucía.

The journey which is forming in my mind avoids the traditionally smiling and perpetually festive western half of Andalucía, and covers instead the great wildernesses and arid stretches of the provinces of Granada, Almería, Murcia and Cartagena – an area featuring some of the most African-looking parts of Spain, as well as the last places in the country from whence the Muslims were expelled. And it is a journey which I envisage undertaking on my return to Spain in the autumn, when this part of Andalucía comes fully into its own, with the first falls of snow on the Sierra Nevada. I associate this area with the autumn in the same way that Seville is always linked with the spring, for I know of no other part of Spain which so fills me with a sense of loss. Loja, Baza, Alhama de Granada, Huéscar, Guadix: these and many other names are redolent of the last days of Islamic Spain, and have for me the added nostalgic ring of being places that I once visited with the 'Moorish Queen'. Notions of lost love and of a lost civilization ultimately merge together as I plan my journey through what I and many others before me have seen in terms of a lost paradise.

The idea of a lost paradise is one which lies at the back of so much travel writing, and has engendered quests for little-spoilt enclaves to which authors can give a mythical, arcadian identity. But it is also one of the most recurring themes in the literature on Southern Spain, a part of the world which has been endlessly described as a paradise spoilt by incompetence, greed, and, above all, by the expulsion of its Islamic population. British travellers of the past, confronted by the Alhambra and other Moorish remains, have spoken of an Islamic paradise destroyed by a fanatical Catholicism. Today the biases of Protestantism have been succeeded by those of the western liberal conscience, with authors such as Juan Goytisolo even suggesting that the eroded devastation of so much of eastern Andalucía was one of the tragic consequences of the Christians' neglect of Islamic irrigation systems.

The desire to believe in a lost paradise has in any case been stronger than the desire for historical objectivity, as is particularly evident in the writings on Islamic Granada, whose fall in 1492 has been the subject of glamorous fictions from at least the 16th century, and has recently inspired a whole spate of popular novels ranging from such a poetic achievement as Amin Maalouf's *Leo the African* to the politically correct sentimentality of Tariq Ali's *Shadows of the Pomegranate Tree*.

In pursuing myself the idea of a lost paradise, my vision has finally to extend beyond the frontiers of Spain, and into the Maghreb, where so many exiles from this paradise ended their lives, and where countless traces of al-Andalus are still to be found. And as my projected journey gradually expands in its scope to take in this Islamic Spain overseas, my mind turns to the many pioneering world travellers closely connected with al-Andalus: spies, merchants, geographers and pilgrims, of whom the most famous was Ibn Battuta, whose relentless wanderings took him to almost every part of the known world.

It was above all with Ibn Battuta that travel literature went beyond mere scientific description and developed into something both more entertaining and more profound. He was the master of the Arabic literary genre known as the *rihla* – a traveller's tale which has as its basis one of the five prerequisites of Islam: the journey to Mecca. The idea of a travelogue as a picaresque and semi-fictional ramble has its origins in the rihla, which also did much to reinforce the idea of travel as a spiritual quest.

As I continue my imaginary journey through some of the more forgotten corners of al-Andalus and into what was once perceived as the heartland of the Orient, an obsession with a lost paradise merges with that other vision which once offered travellers the prospect of some ultimate, if elusive goal. A vision of the East.

Night has finally come, and the Sultan has invited me to his private cave in the Sacromonte. I do not know what to expect, and am greeted with suspicion by a jacketed man with greased-back hair who stands at the gate like the bouncer of some night club frequented by gangsters. The Sultan is eating, I hear, but he will not keep me long. A whisky is put in my hand as I wait in the courtyard, glancing occasionally at the floodlit Alhambra, now more unreal than ever.

In the courtyard there are Moroccan and gypsy faces mingling among dark and huddled groups. From the depths of the cave come the sounds of a multitude of diners, talking in diverse tongues in a Babel-like cacophony.

Eventually they emerge into the courtyard, dressed in suits and ties, some immersed in serious talk, others laughing and slapping shoulders. They come from far and wide; emissaries, I speculate, from France, Germany, Italy, Romania, Russia, Britain, Japan. Who are they? I want to ask, but there is no time, for the next moment, so unexpectedly in this heartland of flamenco, there arrive what appear to be balalaikas and Russian folk costumes. The Sultan is smiling at my bewilderment, and continues to do so as the balmy night air of the Sacromonte is disturbed by songs about pine-forested mountains and rosy-cheeked maidens.

They return again into the cave, and I am instructed to follow them. The dinner tables have been spirited away, and chairs laid out against the whitewashed walls. I find an empty seat between an Algerian writer and an overexcited Catalan who tells us with his hand against his heart that his whole being is imbued with the spirit of al-Andalus, and that the Andalucíans themselves have turned their back on their Islamic heritage, and have failed to acknowledge that they too are the descendents of the very Moors whom their priests and history books have always spoken of as an alien race. The Algerian nods politely, and even fails to be roused from his indifference when, minutes later, my interest in the identity of the motley crowd around us is answered by the ominous acronym 'F.I.S.'.

What possible connection can there be between my suited neighbours and the Islamic fundamentalists currently terrorizing Algeria's intellectual community?

But, once again, my wonderings are interrupted by events, for suddenly there have appeared guitars, rebecs, lutes, castanets, and a beautiful, dark-haired gypsy girl who has begun to move her arms with such a languid sensuality that for a moment expectations are raised of her tight, polka-dotted dress falling like the petals in an Islamic poem. A famous Albaicín singer with his hair drawn back in a bun, a drug-addicted male dancer, two plump and elderly gypsy women, a trio of serious young Moroccan musicians, all in turn have their part to play in a spectacle which veers from pure flamenco to pure Moroccan but wavers mainly between the two, in a plaintive, eastern-sounding compromise whose exuberant conclusion brings a hint of emotion to the Japanese emissary's face, flushes the features of the Russian, and has others dragged on to the floor to imitate what appears one moment to be a Turkish belly dance and another a Sevillana swirl.

'We are in an early phase of experimentation,' one of the Moroccans tells me, as he launches into an explanation of the Sultan's interest in uniting flamenco with traditional Moroccan music. 'The rhythms are almost identical,' he continues, but while he talks my mind is ever more distracted by thoughts of Oriental delusions, of the transforming powers of the imagination, and of the curious coincidence that the Islamic world's most active terrorist movement should share its acronym with the Fédération Internationale du Ski.

The Moorish spell under which I have been held has been momentarily broken, but returns with greater force than ever once the skiing delegates have left and the musicians have started playing only to the Sultan's most intimate circle.

Curro Albaycín, celebrated singer and poet of the Sacromonte, mesmerizes us all as his powerful voice wails out a recitative evoking the last days of Islamic Granada.

But it is another and rougher voice, breaking out suddenly from the audience, and grabbing the heart through its spontaneity and deeply felt emotion, that will eventually eclipse the memory of the whole Hispano-Moorish charade with which the foreign delegates have been wooed.

It is the Sultan's voice.

The words are of loss, and pain, and exile, and broken hearts, and once they have reached their harsh and poignant conclusion, and the Sultan has thrown a mischievous smile in my direction I realize that the sentiments are those of the travellers' tales that are being woven in my imagination – tales of empty landscapes, forgotten monuments, oriental dreams.

CHAPTER ONE

ALAS FOR MY ALHAMA!

It is a Saturday afternoon in late September, and I am being driven around an empty port looking for a ship called the *Ibn Battuta*.

The Málaga to which I have just arrived almost resembles the Islamic town praised by the geographer Umar-al-Malaqi for its tranquility and 'limpid air'.

I had flown in earlier in the day in a plane largely occupied by retired couples, and had later had lunch in a beach-side restaurant where the main animation had been provided by waiters trying noisily to sell, as in an auction, portions of food to the last of the midday eaters.

Listening to the exotic cadences of the waiters' shouts; staring out across a near deserted beach to a horizon so clear that Africa had been visible in my imagination: all this had inexplicably encouraged a sentimental urge to begin my oriental journey by paying homage to the greatest of Islam's travellers.

After a period of nearly ten years settled peacefully in the Moroccan town of Fez, Ibn Battuta set off in 1359 on what were to be the last travels of his life. Born and brought up in Tangier, his wanderings had begun with a pilgrimage to Mecca in 1326 and had later taken in Persia, East Africa, Syria, Anatolia, Southern Russia, Afghanistan, Pakistan, India, Sri Lanka, the Maldives, Sumatra, China, the Persian Gulf and Sardinia. Now he intended to make his way through what was left of al-Andalus, and afterwards, on his return to Morocco, to head south over the desert to the fabled Timbuktu.

A young writer and scholar whom he was to meet in Granada, Ibn Yuzayy, would later record all of Ibn Battuta's wanderings in a massive chronicle that reveals little of the man's personality other than a compulsive attitude towards travelling, a squeamishness in the face of violence, and delusions of grandeur that belied a relatively modest social and intellectual status. The great intellectual achievements of which Ibn Battuta so often boasted did not accord either with his having had to find someone else to write up his memoirs, or with his being – according to the celebrated Andalucían judge Abu'l-Bakarat al-Balafiqi – a person whose extensive travels had only led him to possess 'a modest share of the sciences'. And though he loved to emphasize how he had been the guest of princes, kings, sultans and other lofty figures, he had to share for most of his travelling life the fate of the vast majority of his fellow Muslim wayfarers by staying at hostels for the poor and depending heavily on the charity and hospitality of those whom he met on the way.

In contrast to the merchant Marco Polo – who visited countries that few Christians had ever seen before – Ibn Battuta limited his travels almost exclusively to lands where the population was dominated by members of his own religion. He probably regarded himself as a citizen less of Morocco than of the so-called Dar al-Islam, or Abode of Islam, within whose cultural boundaries were thousands of pilgrims who, like him, travelled vast distances not just to fulfil the hajj to Mecca and Medina, but also to receive the blessing and wisdom of the venerable holy men associated with the mystical branch of Islam known as Sufism. Practical motives were also behind many of his more ambitious journeys: it was in the remoter outposts of the Islamic empire that he hoped perhaps that his modest talents as a lawyer would be best appreciated. He served as a *qadi* or judge in India, Ceylon and the Maldive Islands, and was even employed by the Sultan of Delhi to head what turned out to be an unsuccessful diplomatic mission to China. Only with his visits to Spain and Timbuktu does his travelling seem to have been in any way supported by his own country. The powerful Merinid ruler, Abu'l-Hasan 'Ali, was anxious to extend his territories, and probably entrusted Ibn Battuta with the task of assessing the political situations in those lands with which he sought an alliance.

Ibn Battuta started his Spanish tour at Gibraltar, which had recently resisted a long Christian siege that had only been terminated after the Castilian king Alfonso XI had fallen victim to the Black Death. Ibn Battuta referred to the rock as the 'Citadel of Islam', but it was a citadel which now guarded a small and ever more threatened fraction of the original al-Andalus.

It was in the neighbouring port now known as Tarifa that the story of the Islamic occupation of Spain had begun, over 600 years previously. A reconnaissance trip led in 710 by an officer called Tarif had resulted in the taking of this port and the consequent Islamic annexation of Spain's southernmost tip. This was followed the next year by a full scale expedition mounted by Tariq ibn Ziryab, who made his base in Gibraltar and from there proceeded within a few years to win over most of the peninsula.

The smallness of Tariq's original forces, the ease with which they took over the country, and the rapid assimilation of Islamic religion and customs by Spain's indigenous population, have strengthened present-day romantic notions of a close affinity between the Spaniards and the 'Moors'. Such details seem at first to suggest that there was a strong African element in Spain's ethnic make-up long before the so-called 'conquest', and that the idea of a ruthless and bloodthirsty victory by an alien power was an absurd exaggeration put forward by Arab and Christian fanatics from the eleventh century onwards. However, these conclusions conveniently ignore the considerable financial advantages offered to those Christians who converted to Islam, as well as the indisputable fact that the invasion of Spain was in keeping with an Islamic expansionist policy that had made enormous headway since the death of Muhammad in the sixth century.

Spain, under its Moorish occupants, became the most scientifically advanced European country of the early Middle Ages, as well the continent's most important centre of learning. But the relative lack of documentation dating from the first centuries of Moorish rule have undoubtedly given rise to romantic interpretations of early Islamic Spain, for instance the notion that the place was a haven of religious tolerance. What are certainly untrue are popular conceptions of the Spanish 'Moors' as a cohesive and harmonious racial group. The word 'Moor', though probably derived from the north African country of Mauritania, is a blanket term covering the many different races that made up Spain's Muslim population, most notably Arabs, Berbers, Syrians, Egyptians, Yemenis, and Christian converts. This exceptionally complex racial mixture, in combination with the many different factions and sects that made up each of the different races, helped in the early eighth century to transform the al-Andalusi capital of Córdoba into a city as disturbed by infighting as Beirut in the 1980's.

A relative degree of stability was gradually achieved during the rule of the Umayyads, who came to power in Córdoba in 756 and pronounced themselves Caliphs less than two centuries later. By the tenth century, Córdoba had become the most important city in the world after Damascus, with a cultural life very distinct from that of the East, and an architectural legacy which would be enormously influential throughout Islamic Spain and the Maghreb. But, at the beginning of the eleventh century, the Umayyad dynasty was to collapse as quickly as it had risen, leaving al-Andalus as a series of small kingdoms or *taifas*, whose instability was reflected in the lives of such future exiles to the Maghreb as al-Mutamid, the poet-king of Seville, and the remarkable autobiographer 'Abd Allah, last Ziri king of Granada. The intense rivalries between the various courts gave rise to some of the most outstanding poetry in the history of al-Andalus, but it also created the right conditions for the take-over of the country by two successive waves of fanatical Berbers, the Almoravids and the Almohads.

The fundamentalist beliefs of these two tribes from the Maghreb in turn hastened a Christian backlash against Islam which would lead by 1248 to the winning over of much of Muslim Spain. Al-Andalus might not have survived at all had it not been for the cunning and dogged persistence of Muhammad Ibn Nasr who, from having founded a small state in Jaén, managed both to establish the Nasrid dynasty in Granada, and to hold on to this kingdom through a policy of cleverly balancing allegiances between the Catholic king Ferdinand III and the Marinids in Morocco. The support of the Marinids – which was also sought by Ibn Nasr's son and successor, Muhammad II – seems to have provoked an increasingly hostile attitude towards the Muslims who had stayed on in Christian lands, and to have led growing numbers of them to take refuge in the kingdom of Granada. However, for nearly two and half centuries, this kingdom would be little disturbed by the Christians, who were both happy to receive its tribute money, and deterred by its wildly mountainous terrain and proximity to Africa.

Nasrid Granada was not the paradise which has so often been imagined in romantic literature. Though left largely at peace, it must had much of the tense, volatile character of a place under siege, being isolated from the mainstream of Islamic culture, overcrowded with Muslim refugees, fractured by a network of tribes and competing tribal élites, and in flagrant defiance of the laws of Islam by having to pay taxes to a Christian state. It was neither a particularly prosperous place, nor self-supporting in foodstuffs, having to export to the Maghreb specialized crops, sugar, raisins, figs and almonds, in return for such staples as cereals and olive oil. As the distinguished Moroccan scholar Ibn Khaldun noted in the 1360's, the Christians had 'pushed the Muslims back to the seacoast and the rugged territory there, where the soil is poor for the cultivation of grain and little suited to growing vegetables'.

Ibn Battuta, with his habitual luck in seeing Islamic kingdoms at their best, visited Nasrid Granada during perhaps its most relaxed and optimistic period. There were promising developments in Morocco, where the Marinids, under Abu'l-Hasan 'Ali, had united the Maghreb and were encouraging hopes of an Islamic reconquest of Christian Spain. Meanwhile, in Granada itself, the arts and sciences of al-Andalus were undergoing a final flowering under the successive leaderships of Yusuf I and Muhammad V, who were responsible for the building of the Alhambra's courtyards and adjacent halls – structures that might have lacked the originality and wealth of materials of the great monuments of Umayyad Córdoba, but that were none the less a stunning synthesis of the architectural achievements of Islamic Spain.

The prospect of being welcomed at the court at Granada was probably the main motivation behind Ibn Battuta's Spanish visit. After leaving Gibraltar, and making an arduous detour to see a cousin in the mountain town of Ronda, he hurried as fast as possible to

Granada, following at first a well-defended coastal route which passed through Marbella and Fuengirola. Narrowly escaping an attack from Christian corsairs, he arrived at Málaga, the main port of the Nasrid kingdom, and a place described by him as one of the most beautiful cities of al-Andalus.

From the jetty, the main impression of Málaga is of a baroque cathedral tower squeezed between tall modern blocks arranged against an ochre backcloth of barren peaks. Of the Islamic town renowned not only as a port but also as a centre of dance and music, the sole survival is the hill-top castle or *alcazaba*, which, even from a distance, looks like a model in papier-mâché.

I fail to see the *Ibn Battuta*, but find instead a loquacious old sailor who remembers the days when the arrival of this ferryboat from Morocco had never failed to excite.

'The *Ibn Battuta* is here! The *Ibn Battuta* is here!' was apparently a shout which had once echoed through the streets and apartment rooms of Málaga.

The ship is no longer there. I discover that it has recently been taken out of service, but its memory has been preserved in the name of the ferryboat which crosses from Algeciras to Tangier. The name sounds like the sequel to a Hollywood film – *Ibn Battuta II*, 'The Floating Palace'.

The Moorish Queen is smiling as the sailor tells me all this, smiling at the romantic ridiculousness of my having wanted to see the ship in the first place. She has collected me at Málaga airport, and is driving me in the footsteps of Ibn Battuta to Granada. Our affair has been over for several years, but I'm still in love with her. Unfortunately she has brought along her current boyfriend, the 'Usurper'.

The persistence of my love has convinced her of what she had always thought when we had been together: that I am a hopeless romantic who considers her less as a real person than as some distillation of Andalucían womanhood based on prototypes such as Carmen or the sensual dancing-girls portrayed in Orientalist canvases. I argue inwardly that what I like in her is her intelligence, spontaneity, warmth and sense of humour; but it is also true that I overlook what many would consider physical imperfections – skinniness, scrawny hair, exceptionally narrow face, weak chin and prominent hooked nose – in my desire to picture her esse ntially as a dark, olive-skinned, exotic beauty.

The sailor continues to talk, my mind wanders, and the Moorish Queen, recognizing my distracted look, decides it is time to go. We get back into her car – an ageing Russian-made landrover with the words 'Please Clean Me' scrawled in the thick layer of dust on the back window. No sooner are we all in than the Usurper and I are out again on the jetty, giving the car a push start. Will we ever make it to Granada?

Ibn Battuta travelled along the coast for another thirty kilometres, then headed inland to Vélez Málaga. But the Usurper, a hedonist from Aragón, is less interested in faithful historical recreation than in the possibilities of a lively coastal resort. We miss the Vélez turning, and steadfastly remain in a world inescapably associated with mass tourism, unplanned property developments and retired foreigners. I want to forget about all this and find some Islamic justification for our detour. But an enormous effort of will is needed to think of our present route as that of Ibn al-Idrisi, the famous Córdoba-trained geographer whose name is now being used to promote what is generally known as the Costa del Sol.

Nerja, our destination for the night, has outwardly little to warrant an inclusion in an Islamic journey. Marbella, Fuengirola, Torremolinos, Torre del Mar, Almuñecar, Salobrena, and many other of this coast's popular resorts all retain the ruins of their Moorish castles, albeit either over-enthusiastically restored or else neglected to the extent of being tucked away, like unwanted gifts, behind the highrise blocks. But Nerja has no traces whatsoever of its insignificant Moorish past, and little even to remind the visitor of its days as a quiet fishing village unmolested by outsiders until the arrival of the foreign hordes in the late 1950's.

The strangeness of the personal situation in which I now find myself, and the growing sense of unreality that inevitably develops in those who travel obsessively, have made me see even Nerja in a new and exotic light.

I stand perplexed as the sky turns a dark orange, and an international convention of motorcycle riders swoops around the palm-fringed Balcony of Europe like an evening roost. The Moorish Queen presses herself against the Usurper before taking pity on me and joining her free arm with one of mine, and leading the three of us into a festively-lit street partially filled with newly-arrived pensioners and the sad leftovers of the summer crowds. We pass through a plasterwork Moorish arch and enter a place called the Discoteca Boabdil.

The discothèque's interior, dripping with arabesques and plastic gold fittings, is flooded with a mysterious blue and red light, and ringed with crimson wall seating that has been made to resemble the lines of cushions in a Bedouin tent. Kissing male couples dominate the smoky gloom and induce the odd suppressed giggle from a pair of fat Scandinavian women, who sit endlessly protracting the remaining lager in lipstick-stained glasses.

The lights dim, the room goes silent, and then suddenly, in a burst of recorded song, a burly man with hairy arms sweeps in dressed with outrageous pink and silver extravagance, miming all the time the words of a famous *copla*. Laughs and cat-whistles from the crowd accompany a performance that is later interrupted by a rapid stream of high-pitched repartee.

'Señores and Señoriiitas,' he squeals with barbed emphasis on the latter word before turning his attention to the two Scandinavians, now apoplectic with laughter. 'We have here tonight two real Señoritas...'

The drag show continues, tarnishing ever more the image of Spanish machismo. In the meantime I am becoming ever more confused as to the real sexuality of the Usurper, who maintains throughout the performance an enigmatic smile and ends up by tentatively placing one of his hands on the Moorish Queen's knee and the other on mine.

By now the entire repertory of Spanish popular folk music seems to have been exhausted, and we have moved on to an Orient evoked by three men with exposed navels wriggling their hips in imitation of some slave dance by Cecil B. de Mille. A climax is reached, the audience returns to its dancing and embracing, and I am left thinking about the spirit of pastiche informing not only the performance I have just witnessed but also the neo-Moorish decoration of the room I am sitting in. A spirit in which the dividing line between tackiness and fantasy is as ambivalent as the sexuality which surrounds me.

The Usurper's hedonism is catching. Waking up the next morning to another luminously clear day, we put off once more our journey in Ibn Battuta's footsteps. We go instead to the beach.

The car has a temporary new lease of life, though, as we leave the main road and descend steeply down a wild headland, we hesitate for a moment about the consequences of having to start it up again once we have reached the bottom.

Our concerns soon vanish as we turn a bend and are offered a vision of what the whole coast must have been like at the time of the Moors – a virgin expanse of bleached ochre mountains falling down into a crystalline sea. Far below us is the isolated beach of Cantariján. The only sounds are those of the cicadas.

The beach's silent occupants are few and naked. Most of them are elderly German couples who lie motionless like stranded corpses, or else stroll listlessly looking at pebbles. Rolls of dimpled, painfully pink flesh, wrinkled penises, varicose veins, lined, leathery skins, threadbare pubic hair like the exposed coils of an old sofa, and flaplike breasts shrivelled in the sun – these could all be details from a Vanitas painting by a Baldung or a Dix.

The Moorish Queen takes off her clothes to reveal a body as yet untouched by Time. Wandering among the Germans on her way down to the water she provides the necessary complement to the surrounding *memento mori*. A reminder of youth and beauty.

By the late afternoon we are finally on our way towards Granada, having been punished for our hedonism by spending nearly an hour trying to start our car on an uphill slope. The Usurper, unaccustomed to undue exertion, is pale from his efforts. I shock him further by proposing that we stay the night in a thermal hotel outside Alhama, half-way to Granada.

'It'll be like a mortuary,' he says.

'Good,' I reply. 'I could do with a few more corpses.'

I'm using irony as a way of coping with a growing jealousy and agitation that have now given me a reason for stopping at Alhama that has nothing to do with the fact that Ibn Battuta did so.

'According to this leaflet,' I note, '"the waters of Alhama are very beneficial for those suffering from stresses to the nervous system."'

We take the short, steep road from Nerja to Frigiliana, a white-washed village of unmistakeably Moorish appearance, but today so excessively tidied up as to appear like the cover of an estate agent's brochure. Dubious stories of the village's Moorish past are written up on ceramic plaques on every street – surely the legacy of the neat, heritage-minded mentality of the foreign settlers who now fill the place.

After Frigiliana our car comes at last into its own. It is meant to cope with 'every terrain', but it has never been entirely happy on the asphalt, and only now bursts into life as it battles with the rutted dust track we are following. Perhaps, like us, it has been heartened by the views down to the coast, which are getting ever more spectacular as we continue to climb up the barren, herb-scented slopes of the Sierra de Tejeda.

We are in the Axarquía, a district that had once been almost exclusively inhabited by the token Muslim converts to Christianity known as the 'moriscos'. The high and remote village of Cómpeta, to which we are now driving, had been a morisco stronghold, with its own king, at the time of their first uprising. The difficult drive to the village from the coast encourages hopes of finding some unspoilt medieval survival. Continuing to struggle up the winding track from Frigiliana, we almost convince ourselves of the certainty of being met on arrival by direct descendants of moriscos who have managed to hide away undisturbed in this barely accessible mountain lair.

We stop in the village square to try the famous local wine. We have passed at least three foreign-owned estate agencies, and are now sitting at an outdoor bar listening to voices that suggest a local population equally divided between Scandinavians and British.

Leafing through the pages of a local English-language newspaper, I discover that mediocre English pop groups I think have long been extinct have resurfaced as local residents contributing to Cómpeta's 'thrilling night life'.

'We're a young and with-it set,' I am assured by an elderly Englishman at the table next to us.

The man and his wife, momentarily stirred by the arrival of newcomers to the village, shake off their sullen expressions to give me a breathless, unsolicited account of their sad story.

They hate the Spanish and their greasy food, they are only here for the sun, they really want to be in Nerja, and are just biding their time in this claustrophobic village where the coast is too far and the streets induce chest pains. They had been happily married and living in Worthing for nearly forty years. Then they had sold their house and everything they possessed and bought a villa at Nerja that had yet to be built.

'Now we have nothing,' the wife mumbles almost inaudibly, leaving the rest of their story to my imagination. They sink back again into silence, then say goodbye and leave.

The light begins to fade, and the effects of the wine lead me into making a comparison between the Islamic conquest of Spain in the Middle Ages and the foreign invasion of the coast in the twentieth century.

'In the late twentieth century tribes from England, Germany and Scandinavia began settling in the coastal towns and villages of Cádiz, Málaga, Granada, Almería, Murcia, Valencia… Within a few years they had spread beyond the main coastal roads and were penetrating ever further into the interior, to Cómpeta, Gaucín, Grazalema, the Sierra de Huelva, the Alpujarra… By the second decade of the next millennium most of Andalucía had come under their domination.'

Then I toy with notions of conquest and exile and the indivisibility of the two in the case of Spain's present invaders, but the indifferent looks of the Usurper and the Moorish Queen put a halt to the brilliant flow of my argument. They have had enough of Cómpeta, and have come round to thinking that even a thermal resort would be a livelier destination than this.

We set off once more on a winding road, skirting the Sierra de Tejeda until we reach a point where the range is split by a deep cleft. The sun is setting over the tiniest strip of distant sea, but we turn our backs on this and are soon enclosed by steep, rocky slopes. Crossing this ancient pass, we leave behind the province of Málaga and enter a more neglected world. We have rejoined at last the route of Ibn Battuta.

The road we are on had been for many centuries the main line of communication between the coast and Granada, but the creation of important thoroughfares to the north, west and east had progressively reduced it to a quiet and meandering side-road.

We encounter no other car as we drive through the penumbral gloom, appreciating even under these conditions the classical beauty of a countryside in which sparse rolling fields are picturesquely scarred with ravines and rocky crags, as in a sombre landscape by Poussin.

The darkness is falling rapidly, and the arrival of the night is competing with the sudden appearance of stormclouds that are rolling in from the north, threatening the first of the autumn rains. The clear, silvery grey skies are soon obscured by blackness, exaggerating the emptiness of a landscape whose only signs of human life are the pale and distant lights on the hill in front of us.

Sadness and loss – these are the emotions perennially associated with the place we are approaching; a place that had once been one of the greatest towns in the kingdom of Granada, but that is remembered today chiefly as the subject of a medieval ballad.

The ballad's simple refrain – in the translation of Lord Byron – slips from my lips as we reach the outskirts of the village.

'Alas for my Alhama!'

He had been away at the time, at a sister's wedding at Vélez Málaga. Now he had lost his honour and everything that he had held dear. His wife and sons had been killed, and his beloved and famously beautiful daughter Fatima had been taken captive by the Christians and given the name María de Alhama.

This, reputedly, was the gist of a speech given by the governor of Alhama immediately before his head was cut off and strung up over one of the gates of the Alhambra. His fellow Muslims were punishing him for not having been present when his town was sieged by the Christians in 1482 – a siege sparking off the final stage of the bloody war leading to the collapse of Muslim rule in Spain ten years later.

Alhama had always been thought of by the Moors as an impregnable citadel, but it stood in the middle of a kingdom which by 1480 was becoming increasingly vulnerable in the face of a Christian Spain strengthened under the united rule of Ferdinand and Isabella.

The Nasrids, under their unpopular ruler Abu'l-Hasan 'Ali, were economically and politically worse off than ever, and could no longer rely on any military support from the Maghreb, which was itself passing through a period of exceptional weakness. Matters were made considerably worse by growing internal opposition to Nasrid rule, most notably from the notoriously rebellious Abencerrajes of Romantic fame. Finally, if legends are to be believed, the state was further debilitated by a harem feud within the royal household: Abu'l-Hasan 'Ali is said to have aroused the violent jealousy of his nobly-born first wife Aisha by falling in love with a Christian captive, Isabel de Solis, known as Zoraya after her conversion to Islam.

Tensions mounted in Granada in the late 1470's, with various skirmishes made into enemy territory by both Christians and Moors. Rodrigo Ponce de Leon's attack on Garziago in 1477 – an incident in which three hundred and fifty Muslims were killed – was followed by a successful Granadan raid on Ciezo resulting in the taking of two thousand Christian captives. Two years later the redoubtable Rodrigo Ponce de Leon captured the village of Montecorto, which was then immediately retaken by the Muslims, who further boosted their confidence by seizing the nearby castle at Zahara.

The Moors, despite the weakness of their kingdom, were clearly endowed with an army which made up in fighting spirit what it lacked in numbers. It was as a demonstration of its strength that in April 1478 Abu'l-Hasan organized in Granada a massive military parade lasting for several days. Ominously, however, on the last day a violent storm broke out that caused the destruction of buildings and bridges through severe flooding and mudslides. This disaster put an additional strain on the kingdom's finances, to which Abu'l-Hasan responded by raising taxes and retrenching on military expenditure. He appears also to have suffered some sort of nervous breakdown, which led him in the following years – according to the hostile author of the *Nubdhat al'asr* – to neglect his army and 'give himself up to pleasures and amuse himself with dancing-girls'.

In the meantime, Rodrigo Ponce de Leon, still incensed by the Muslim actions at Montecorto and Zahara, was planning his most daring retaliation. Early in 1482 he was finally able to put this plan into action, and set off with his troops towards Alhama, accompanied by a Christian who had spent four years as a prisoner there. By the dawn of February 28th, he had arrived within half a league of Alhama, after having accomplished the remarkable feat of leading his troops undetected on a two days' forced march across difficult, mountainous terrain.

The town was taken completely by surprise, the main defences being unmanned owing to the governor's absence at Vélez Málaga. Sixteen men scaled the walls of its castle, and found only a solitary duty on guard, whom they stealthily killed before doing away with his sleeping colleague. They captured the governor's womenfolk, and then opened the castle gates to let in the bulk of Ponce de Leon's forces.

The inhabitants of Alhama, though so poorly prepared for any fighting, desperately resisted the Christian invaders, and eventually managed to block their entrance into the town by gathering in the narrow street on which the castle's portal opened, and firing from there a continual hail of missiles. The Christians, not knowing what to do, and terrified by the possibility of the imminent arrival of Muslim reinforcements from nearby Granada, were forced in the end to ram down from the inside a whole section of the castle wall.

The Muslim men continued to shoot incessantly at them, while their women and children poured pitch and oil, and threw objects from every roof and balcony.

The fighting continued throughout the day and night until finally the remaining townsfolk attempted a last-ditch defence in the mosque, from which they were soon driven out after their attackers had set fire to it. An estimated four thousand women and children were taken prisoner, while more than a thousand Muslim corpses were counted in the town's streets.

At this point of the story, the exact intentions of the Christians on capturing the town become unclear. Did they hope to hold on to the place, or did they wish simply to run off with a large booty?

Alhama was a notoriously wealthy town, greatly favoured by the Nasrid kings on account of its thermal springs, endowed with thriving cloth manufactories, and entrusted with the safe-keeping of the whole of the kingdom of Granada's public taxes on land. These were reasons enough to justify a raid purely for booty, and yet the town was so deep in Muslim territory that an army returning with the spoils of victory could hardly have hoped to have come back unscathed. None the less the behaviour of the Christians does indeed suggest that they were motivated by a largely greedy and vindictive spirit. If they had not intended to evacuate the town immediately, it is difficult to understand why they had scattered wheat and flour all over the ground, and set fire to great jars of oil and honey – goods that would have been difficult to take with them but immensely useful in the case of a lengthy residence here. Furthermore, the following morning, when Abu'l-Hasan finally arrived from Granada with his troops, they reputedly discovered – according to an Islamic chronicler – that the Christians had brought their prisoners and booty outside the town, and had already hitched up their horses to leave.

Whether leaving the town or not, the Christians seem to have behaved in a way that confirmed Islamic notions of Christian barbarism: the troops from Granada were confronted on arrival with the shocking sight of the piles of corpses that the Christians had thrown over the walls to be avidly devoured by carrion and dogs. Abu'l-Hasan immediately ordered the dogs to be shot, an action that led one contemporary to observe that 'not even the city's dogs could remain alive'.

The Christians meanwhile returned to the battlements, and prepared to defend the defeated town with some of the furious determination that the Muslims now showed in trying to recapture it. The attackers rushed at the walls from every angle, and kept up a relentless siege that would probably have decimated the Christians had it not been for the arrival several days later of Christian reinforcements led by the Duke of Medina Sidonia. Abu'l-Hasan lost much of the remaining respect of his people by deciding to retreat, and though he would try again to retake his beloved Alhama, he was eventually distracted from this objective by the news that a large Christian army was marching towards Loja.

Fernando del Pulgar, secretary to the Catholic Monarchs, and chronicler of the gruesome events befalling Alhama in 1482, was moved by the plight of the town's Muslim inhabitants to ask why 'it had pleased God to show his wrath so suddenly and so cruelly against them'. In the end he found his answer in what might seem at first a most unlikely source – the thermal baths that gave the town its Moorish name.

'We discovered that very close [to Alhama] there are baths in a beautiful building where there is a natural hot spring. Thither men used to resort, both from the town itself and from the surrounding region in order to bathe. These baths were the cause of a certain softness in their bodies, and of excessive pleasure, from which there proceeded idleness and other deceits and evil dealings that they inflicted on one another in order to sustain the ease to which they were accustomed.'

There are rumbles in the night sky, but the rain holds back, as we drive through the lower half of Alhama and out again into the darkness, searching for the Hotel Balneario.

Over a kilometre outside the town, we follow a stream as it plunges into a narrow gorge, from which we emerge as if from some magical tunnel into an elegant park, with hedges, an ivy-covered bridge, and bosky avenues that disappear into the night. In a gravel forecourt illuminated by the yellow glow from wrought-iron lamps, smart cars are parked outside a large nineteenth-century building.

The hotel, to our surprise, is almost full, but two rooms are finally found for us on an upper floor. The guests have all mysteriously vanished, with the exception of three elderly men who sit staring at us in a large lobby that confirms the Usurper's worst fears – worn imitation leather armchairs, stale smells, heavy curtains, a funereal silence.

The Usurper and the Moorish Queen retreat for a while into their room, while I try and distract myself with a visit to the spa facilities in the basement. A young nurse in white accompanies me.

Photographs of a water-filled Moorish chamber have lured me on the tour, but the likelihood of ever reaching this chamber, if such a place should even exist, begins to recede as the nurse leads me through bland, white-tiled rooms steeped in the atmosphere of an old-fashioned clinic. I am shown and explained hydrothermic stress cures, respiratory cures for the 'cleansing of the nasal passages', ozone bubble baths, and a Dada-like shower contraption that fires pressurized water sprays from every angle ('very effective for the nerves', the nurse assures me).

Almost everything I see is the result of recent revamping, though there is the odd quaint detail – marble tubs, blue and white tiling – evocative of the aristocratic spa that had been built in the 1850's over the by then seriously decayed Moorish baths.

At last, when I am least expecting it, we arrive at the one survival of the original building. It is shielded by a glass door and comes as such a complete contrast to the modern, antiseptic surroundings that I almost feel as if I am experiencing a vision – a sensation enhanced by the steaming up of my glasses as soon as the nurse opens the door, 'as a special favour'.

Other Moorish baths in Spain are all in brick, but this one is in stone, and as such probably dates back to the time of the Caliphs, when more expensive materials were favoured in the construction of buildings. The effect created is of a mosque lost in a subterranean, Stygian world, whose waters come up to the capitals of two giant horse-shoe arches supporting a sturdy, octagonal vault. An Orientalist imagination would doubtless have filled this chamber with bathing beauties, but the room was in fact never intended for this purpose, and was simply a water container built directly over the spring. The Moors used instead two adjacent rooms, one of which was reserved for women, the other for men, according to both Ibn Battuta and the Egyptian scholar Abd al-Basit, who passed through Alhama in 1465. François Bertaut, a French diplomat who travelled through Spain in 1659, described the thermal complex as comprising three vaulted rooms, the first of which (the women's bath) he found so steamy and oppressive that he had to move on to the second, which he thought even more unbearable, though not as much as the room with the spring, where 'the water was far too hot for bathing'.

I put a hand in the water, and find it sufficiently temperate to encourage me to want to bathe there. 'You can't,' the nurse abruptly says. 'It's a national monument.' She closes the door and walks with me upstairs, back again into the modern equivalent of the large infirmary that had been attached to the baths in Berthaut's day.

'But where is everyone?' I ask the nurse.

'At evening mass,' she replies.

The chapel is a modern building, and I enter it at the point where the priest is blessing the wine and the host. Over a hundred faces turn in my direction as I sheepishly try and look for somewhere to stand near the door.

The gathering I have interrupted is something straight out of the Franco era, but as seen through the grotesque, distorting vision of a Buñuel. The elderly congregation, exuding wealth and conservatism, gives an overall impression of jackets, ties, black jerseys and blue-rinsed hair but, looking more closely, there are also crutches, missing limbs, Zimmer frames, surgical collars and bandaged arms. I look away, but the presence of age and infirmity is recalled by the sudden sound of a dry racking cough at the back, which in turns acts as a signal for a multitude of irritated throats to release phlegm and relieve itching.

I concentrate on the architecture, and note with amused curiosity the Moorish-style lamps that decorate this Christian place of worship. But the greatest irony of all becomes only apparent to me as the priest lifts up the host into the air, and frames it against a mural brashly painted above the high altar – a mural representing the surviving part of Alhama's Moorish baths.

Did the artist ever consider the inappropriateness of painting for a chapel an aspect of Islamic culture that Pulgar and other Catholics had considered symptomatic of moral decadence?

'The historical memory is short', the Usurper later suggests when he and the Moorish Queen meet up with me in the hotel's dining-room.

For a while the three of us continue talking on the subject of Moorish baths, but my thoughts on the subject are disrupted by the strain of trying to hide my mounting jealousy and sexual frustration behind a polite and friendly façade.

The tension in the air is exacerbated by the room we are in – a vast hall with giant piers and loudspeakers that relay messages to a clientèle so decrepit that we ourselves have become objects of fascination. Our fellow diners, so unusually for Spain, are virtually silent, and both their ears and eyes are directed on our table, where I sit self-consciously sipping an insipid, lukewarm broth while resisting the temptation to pour it over the Usurper's head.

The Usurper's whole life is an attempt to avoid not only undue exertion but also conflict. He remains calmly eating, long after I have finished, and tries to ease my impatience with a slight smile, but succeeds only in aggravating it. The Moorish Queen, sensing my mood, feels that the time has finally come to leave the dining-room. She reminds me of our appointment in the village with one of her father's friends – the former mayor.

As we try once again wearily to start the car, the moribund atmosphere of the spa resort is unexpectedly disturbed by a lively group of youths, who appear from the undergrowth behind the bridge, and run laughing to help us. The car's engine soon stirs into action, and I sit back relieved, experiencing a sudden sense of freedom, while also wondering what our young helpers had been doing down by the water.

I have a strange feeling they are following us, and keep turning round once we have parked the car at the top of the village and start walking across the by now empty main square. Only after we are inside one of the bars do I begin to relax, under the influence of a drink, a friendly environment, and the welcome presence within our incestuous group of the former mayor and leading member of the local Andalucían Socialist Party, Ricardo Cortes.

Ricardo is a modest, quietly spoken man in his early forties who hides a gentle humour behind his distinguished bearded face. His initial shyness disappears as he reveals his passion for his town, and his enticing plans for us for the following day.

'Tomorrow,' he promises, 'I shall give you all the documentation you need, then we'll have lunch in a place I'm sure you'll love, where they do excellent goat with garlic, and an orange salad, which of course is purely Moorish.'

I have mentioned my interest in Alhama's Moorish past, and he has responded by teasingly referring to me as 'Washington Irving'. He is also intending to take me after lunch the next day on a 'Moorish tour' which will include the 'Moorish cemetery', the 'Moorish prison', the 'Moorish quarter', the 'Moorish castle', and – the 'ultimate of Moorish thrills' – a descent into Alhama's gorge by way of the excitingly named 'Ladder of Hell'.

He won't have another drink, he says, he must be getting home, in any case he has gout, and shouldn't be having alcohol. But he stays talking with us, and drinking, and soon he is offering to accompany me to Morocco.

He loves Morocco, it's his favourite foreign destination, and, 'like many Andalucíans', feels a special affinity with its people. He has many Moroccan friends.

'When we get to Tetuan,' he continues, 'we'll go and stay with Mustafa. He was living in Alhama for several years.'

'An immigrant worker?' I suggest.

'No, he's from one of Tetuan's leading families, but he's so lazy that the only place he could get to study engineering was at our small village college. His father was a good friend of the director.'

'He was almost crying,' he adds, 'when he had to leave Alhama, said that it was his true home, and that his ancestors must have come from here. Every day he went to the baths.'

Ricardo is still talking about the Baths after we have dissuaded him once more from going home, and have moved on to another bar for a 'penúltimo'.

'Many other Moroccans used to visit our baths, for sentimental reasons, especially during the years of the Protectorate. The imam of Tetuan was a regular guest at the spa during the 1950's.'

'As a child,' says Ricardo, digressing slightly, 'I remember when Franco passed through Alhama, accompanied, as always by his Moroccan Guard. "The Moors are returning, the Moors are returning," everyone was whispering.'

The next moment we are in a nearby discothèque, enjoying another penúltimo, and continuing our conversation about the baths.

'On autumn nights,' Ricardo tells us, 'the young people here have the habit of going down to the Hotel Balneario to lie in the hot water that flows into the river from the spring. They tend to go when the discothèques close, sometimes coming all the way from Granada in the early hours of the morning. The most popular period is after the hotel has shut down for the season, at the beginning of October. But even tonight you'll probably find someone down by the river.'

Ricardo conjures up hedonistic scenes that correspond to my notions of what the Moorish baths must originally have been like. But the idea of such scenes taking place just outside the stuffy Hotel Balneario is at first difficult to believe. Then I remember the youths who had helped us with our car.

As if in tune with my thoughts, the youths suddenly enter the discothèque, and give me a smile. Later, when we finally say goodbye to Ricardo, I am sure that it is their car which is following closely behind ours, as we descend from the village towards our hotel. But, when we turn off into the gorge, the noise of this other car fades into the distance.

It is four-thirty in the morning, and a Swiss-registered van is parked among the trees and bushes on the near side of the bridge. In the darkness, we tread nimbly over undergrowth and slippery rocks on our way down to the river, where we are greeted by a scene both sensual and infernal.

A channel of hot water rushes furiously into the river, ejecting clouds of steam into a sky fleetingly lit by a crescent moon. Naked bodies, like lost souls, are visible in the steamy blackness: a woman soaping a man's back, another slipping out of her underwear, a couple lying embraced in the water.

I recall how François Berthaut, neglecting to wash in the baths themselves, did so instead in the river outside, where he relished the sensation of dipping simultaneously into boiling and freezing water. We follow his example, and experience the same pleasure.

The Moorish Queen and her lover undress, and disappear giggling behind a rock. I lie some distance away, in a shallow pool where the pleasantly warm combination of the two waters flows soothingly over my limbs.

I barely remember how I get back to my hotel room, and am mainly conscious of falling soon into a deep sleep in which the events and conflicting emotions of the past two days are distilled into a vivid dream centred on images of Moorish baths.

In my hands, as I sleep, are the memoirs of 'Abd Allah, the last of Granada's Ziri kings.

'It is said that sexual intercourse is one of the best remedies for melancholy because of the momentary pleasure it affords. So also is a session at the bath for it fills one with pleasure.'

The words of the Moorish king, written in 1090 from his exile in Morocco, touch on an aspect of Islamic culture that would later be transformed by western dreamers into visions of naked or scantily dressed women langorous in a steamy, marbled setting. The romantics may have given an exaggerated sensuality to the world of the *hamman* or Moorish bath, but the central position in Islamic society they accorded it is borne out by the reality, not least by the sheer number of public baths said by Islamic chroniclers to have existed by the tenth century: between 300 and 600 baths were claimed for Córdoba, and between 1,200 and 27,500 for Baghdad, a city with an estimated population of only 60,000.

The Muslim passion for hot baths, inherited from the Greeks and Romans, and shared by the Jews, reflected at its most obvious level the sophisticated outlook of a civilization which recognized the importance of relaxation and believed that a healthy mind needed not only a healthy body but also a clean one. Massage was a prerequisite of a visit to the baths, as was the deep-pore cleansing of the body with the soapy stone known as the *tafl*. As for the water itself, this was described in a treatise on hygiene by the Loja-born scholar, poet and visir, Ibn al-Khatib, as having 'the same effects as wine, notably happiness and pleasure, which is why so many people sing when they bathe'.

To the sense of physical and mental well-being derived from a visit to the baths should be added the spiritual necessity of going there, for, as an inscription in the baths in Granada's Albaicín reminds us, the body is a mirror of the soul, and thus 'outer stains suggest inner ones as well'. Washing in water symbolizes redemption and purification in many cultures, but in Islam it is an essential preparation for any religious act, which is why there are always pools and baths in the vicinity of mosques, and why women must traditionally come to the hamman on their wedding day.

In between these two extremes of hygiene and salvation is the purely social aspect of bathing, for this is an activity thought of in Islamic countries as an important social ritual, in which men draw up business deals, women size up the bodies of prospective daughters-in-law, everyone lies around gossiping, and all elements of Islamic society are united under conditions of exceptional intimacy that bear out the famous Arab proverb, 'naked we are all equal'.

The steam is rising in my dream, and I am lying pampered and dazed under a barrel vault whose red paint and multitude of star-shaped openings convey an incandescent celestial scene. Mixed bathing has been banned since the days of the emperor Hadrian, but in my somnolent, sensually aroused state men and women are sharing the baths at the same time, oils and perfumes are annointing the blur of bodies, hair is being plaited, make-up applied, pubic hair trimmed, and pale olive skins soothed, pummelled, soaped and kneaded.

The heat is intensifying and becoming unbearable, the steam is obliterating my vision, the light is beginning to fade, I am finding it difficult to breathe, and I want to get out, but the doors have been locked and the openings bricked up. It is the year 1074, and the cruel Sevillian king al-Motadid – who uses his enemies' skulls as flower pots in the Alcázar garden – has entrapped a group of conspirators in the baths of his palace.

Cold water is poured over me, and I feel a sudden rush of fresh air from a crack in the wall. The centuries pass, my vision sharpens, and the baths are now ruins in the middle of desolate open country. A Catholic priest is wandering in the distance.

The fashion for Moorish baths survived the collapse of Islamic Spain, but not for long. Already by 1501 the town hall of Granada was dealing with complaints that there was always a great influx of men into the baths during the hours reserved for women, thus confirming the notions of immorality and degeneracy held by the likes of Pulgar. But what finally led the Church to take action against the practice of public bathing were its associations with Islamic ritual ablutions, and the fear that the supposedly Christian moriscos were profiting from the intimacy of the baths to maintain the religious customs of their forefathers.

From the time of Charles v's visit to Granada in 1527, ever more restrictive bathing regulations were introduced, beginning with the exclusion of all but 'old Christians' from the baths, and proceeding to the closure of these places at night, on Sundays, and during Holy Week, the insistence on royal permission for the construction of new baths, and the refusal to allow repair work on ones that fell into disuse. That these measures were barely effective in stamping out Islamic customs is evident from reports, made as late as 1554, that the baths were still being used for the celebrations surrounding the preparation of a morisco bride, and for the chanting, on Thursday and Friday nights, of the *zala*, or Islamic prayer.

Inevitably, in 1566, it was decreed by the Synod of Granada, that 'henceforth there shall be no more artificial baths in the kingdom of Granada, and that the present ones shall be closed, abandoned and pulled down, and that no-one of whatever status or background shall use the said baths, or bathe in them'. This was one of the final acts of provocation that would lead, two years later, to the second of the morisco uprisings, and the consequent expulsion of the moriscos first from Granada, and then from Spain itself.

The bath culture of Spain had been virtually dead for over a century and a half by the time visions of Islamic baths began to loom large in the burgeoning Orientalist movement. An English aristocrat, Lady Mary Wortley Montagu, greatly influenced the Western imagination with her description of the naked beauties she had seen in the Turkish baths at Sofia – a description which would later inspire Ingres' *Le Bain Turc*, with its hot-house eroticism.

Islamic baths became the ultimate symbol and cliché of a civilization perceived by the West in terms of pagan abandon and sybaritic sumptuousness. And in Spain they lived on in the minds of travellers such as De Amicis, who was so profoundly affected on entering the baths of the Alhambra that he began sadly to reflect on how drably pedestrian was the modern Western world when compared with the intoxicating brilliance of the Orient.

'Don't think of that,' his companion told him. 'Think rather of how much that was beautiful and lovely these tubs have seen; of the little feet that played in the perfumed water, of the long hair that spread over their edges, of the great languid eyes that looked at the sky through the holes of the ceiling...'

The sun breaks through a slit in the curtains, then disappears, shut out by the fiercely moving clouds.

I leave the Moorish Queen and her lover sleeping in their room, and stroll through the empty park along an avenue of elms whose leaves are already dying. At the park's furthest end, at the point where the river escapes into the wilderness, the sounds of shouts and laughter alert me to the presence of another hotel, smaller, more modest, hidden away as if it were an embarrassment to its wealthier relative. A touch of normality amidst the encompassing surrealism.

My travelling companions are still in bed on my return, and I set out alone and on foot in the direction of the village. The effects of my dream are by now wearing off, and as I peer over the bridge at the spot where we had bathed, I no longer find magic, but instead concrete pipes, a discarded wooden box, the remains of an orange foam mattress.

The gorge, under the yellowish glare of this heavy, unsettled day, has the quality of a worn prop, as do the ruins of the one-arched Roman bridge that has been placed at its entrance as if by a landscape gardener striving after the Picturesque.

I meet up with Ricardo in his office, where a pile of pamphlets, maps, photos and xeroxes are waiting for me on his desk. He starts talking about earthquakes.

'Yes,' he says, responding to my expression of surprise. 'We're in the middle of an earthquake zone. The worst was in 1884. It knocked down many of the older houses. Some of the rubble was used for the foundations of the new town below; much of the rubble's still there.'

He grins, and hands me over an old sepia photograph showing the old town lifted up on its great wave of rock but shaken so badly that its disintegrating crest seems about to be thrown with enormous force into the unexpectedly grand chasm over which the town's southern side is perched.

'Then there was the earthquake of 1987, not nearly as bad of course, and no casualties, but everyone was terrified. They were all thinking about what had happened a century earlier.'

I wonder, as he continues telling me this, if he is preparing me for the shock of discovering that one of the most historically and artistically important towns in the whole province of Granada is also today one of the most sadly maintained.

In any case he is keen not to confront me with the reality of present-day Alhama until he has plied me with the most diverse facts about its history. And when he finally proposes that we go out into the town, his intention is not at first to take me to any church or Moorish monument but rather to the town's library.

On our way to the library we pause for a moment outside a modern white house.

'That's where your colleague Théophile Gautier stayed,' Ricardo says with a smile. 'Of course the house itself is new, but it marks the site of the Posada de San Diego, an old inn which was pulled down very recently. Gautier arrived here at two o'clock in the morning, and had to sleep on a brick bed in the most terrible heat.'

Gautier's stay in Alhama occupies only a couple of paragraphs in his *Voyage en Espagne*, but I am now told that a whole book has recently been written about it. Ricardo shows me this as soon as we reach the library.

The book, entitled *Alhama, as Seen by a Foreigner*, turns out to be a glorified reissue of an article written in 1945 by one Inocente García Carrillo, a local scholar and 'employee of the Postal Service'. Appreciations of the life and work of this distinguished local figure occupy nearly half of the book, while the other half is largely taken up by discursive footnotes. Entirely missing is any attempt to address the one important issue connected with the French writer's stay at Alhama. Why was it that Gautier was one of the very few Romantic travellers to visit a town whose history, baths and ballad gave it such an obvious romantic attraction? Ricardo diverts me with a mounting pile of other publications, which the friendly librarian obligingly photocopies for me, until finally a break is called for lunch. We pick up the Moorish Queen and her lover in a bar named after its owner, Paco Moyano.

Paco, a man of monk-like appearance with a large bald patch that suggests a tonsure, greets me with a warm and almost saintly smile. But his big dark eyes, framed by the blackest and thickest of eyebrows, have a hint of underlying mischief.

39

His face seems familiar to me, and I know why after seeing, behind the counter, photographs of him in the company of an elderly friend of mine who runs one of Seville's best-known flamenco centres, the Carbonería.

Paco is a local celebrity, a singer who has had his own group and has performed with some of the greatest flamenco artists. He lived for many years in Seville, supplementing his singing with researches into Andalucían folklore. Settling back again in his home town of Alhama, he instituted here an annual Flamenco Festival, which has been abandoned this year owing to lack of municipal support.

He is a frustrated lover of his home town, to which he refers in a proprietorial manner, and as if he were a party to secrets that no-one else knew.

'On no account,' he gently insists, as I go off for lunch with Ricardo and my two companions, 'should you tour the town this afternoon without me. I'll be waiting for you all in the library at five.'

We eat at an inn a few kilometres outside the town, near the shores of a large, artificial lake hidden by reeds. The unpredictable sun shines long enough for us to sit outside, and I place my chair with a view towards the distant mountains of the Sierra Blanquilla. 'I thought you'd appreciate them,' says Ricardo. 'They're mentioned in Irving's *Tales of the Alhambra*.'

'Ah! Mister Irving has finally come,' says an impatient Paco after we arrive light-headed at the library, nearly an hour after the appointed time. He himself gives the impression of having been drinking, for his eyes are more mischievous than ever, and he is pacing restlessly while tapping the ground with a newly acquired stick. He lets out a large sigh when the librarian tells him that she has still to finish photocopying for me the eighty-odd page *Alhama and her Mother* – a book of anecdotes relating to local devotional images of the Virgin.

'I can't understand the point of all this documentation,' he moans after he and I step out on to the balcony of the library. 'Why can't we just hurry up and look at the town?'

The balcony hangs over the town's rocky ledge, at the bottom of which a diminutive river fringed with green flows meanderingly between giant cliffs. The cubist white blocks of abandoned mills add foreground interest to a composition whose classical austerity is enhanced by the cloud of dark smoke rising in the distance.

'In Spain,' says Ricardo, who has crept up behind us, 'we always choose the most beautiful sites for our rubbish dumps.'

The three of us continue staring at the landscape, which is soon entered by a goatherd leading a line of goats along the narrowest of paths on the far side of the gorge.

'Beeeeeehhhh!! Beeeeeeehhhh!!' shouts Paco, surprising us all, and causing the librarian momentarily to abandon her photocopying.

The din of the goats becomes suddenly louder.

'You see!' Paco triumphantly exclaims. 'They are answering me back. "Come on down!" they are saying. "Come on down!"'.

When we finally set off, we are joined by Paco's girlfriend, who is chuckling to herself, as if in anticipation of some huge joke that Paco is to play on us.

At first he is deadly serious, even as we pass next to the town's privately owned and comically remodelled castle, a medieval pastiche of the turn of the century.

Beyond this we enter the heart of the old town, a small loop of streets with the beauty of a stage set. Gautier, walking through these empty seats in the full heat of the afternoon, was reminded of Africa, a continent he had still to visit. Yet the monuments and architectural details that attract the attention are those evocative of the early years of the Christian Reconquest – the coats of arms marking the homes of the Christian nobility, the ogee-arched façade of the so-called 'House of the Inquisition', and the echoing, aisleless interior of the parish church of the Encarnación, one of the most important gothic churches in the whole kingdom of Granada.

Traces of the Moorish town are harder to find, and need the knowledge of Ricardo or the imagination of Paco to be able to identify them.

A stony, thistle-strewn field enclosed by a battered brick wall is referred to by Ricardo as 'the Islamic cemetery'. He lived as a child in the house attached to this, and remembers a horse-shoe arch now hidden behind the modern plasterwork. We knock at the door, and the old woman who answers this merely smiles bewildered as

Ricardo questions her about the arch, and the Islamic gateway that had reputedly stood on this site.

We are on the edge of the town, in a semi-wasteland, where ruined old buildings and crumbling modern ones stand among rubble and rubbish. The 'Cano Wamba', a worn sixteenth-century fountain bearing the crests of the Catholic Monarchs and Charles V, marks the frontier between the picturesque and the desolate. On the latter side of the divide is the shell of the baroque church of Las Angustias, whose very name is expressive of its present condition.

'The building was always thought of as a victim of Marxism,' explains Ricardo, 'but it was in an even worse state after forty years of Franquismo.'

'And worse still after ten years of Felipismo[1],' adds Paco, who has finally livened up with the prospect of our imminent descent into the gorge.

Inside, I tread carefully over piles of refuse and detritus, and stand warily under the ominously cracked barrel vault of the apse. At my feet a newly discarded kerosene can lies over the burnt remains of a camp-fire.

From the church, our path begins descending into what Ricardo calls 'the Moorish Quarter', an area where rockface and masonry become almost indistinguishable. The mangled, rusting remains of a bicycle are sprawled over some rocks to our right.

'We're going back in time,' comments Paco. 'We have already reached the pre-Indurain era[2].'

Ricardo, trying to maintain a residual seriousness, talks about the labyrinth of galleries and cellars that the Moors tunnelled out of the cliff we are walking down. These had been linked to some prehistoric caves to form a secret escape route connecting the castle with the river – a route that Abu'l-Hasan had been forced to block up to prevent the besieged Christians from trying to smuggle in supplies.

---

[1] A reference to Felipe González, Spain's Socialist prime minister from 1982 to 1995.

[2] Miguel Indurain, Spain's most famous sportsman of the 1990's, was the three-time winner of the Tour de France.

Paco, leaning on his stick like an old man, has taken over as leader, and is soon directing us with an expressive gesture through what looks like the narrow entrance to a cave. Ricardo brings out a torch.

'Some of the cellars,' Ricardo tells us, 'were used by the Moors as granaries, others as dungeons.'

The massive domed space we have entered had been the town's main prison, and it was here that the forces of Ponce de Leon had discovered the Christian prisoners whose chains were among those later hung from the outside walls of the Toledan church of San Juan de los Reyes. Originally the only entrance was from the now partially blocked skylight, from where food and captives had been lowered.

The swarming insects, and the strong smell of urine and excrement, succeed immediately in repelling the Usurper, who decides to wait for us outside. I suggest that the former prison has now become Alhama's main public toilet.

'The cave today is used,' Paco enigmatically replies, 'for special purposes by our dear friends José, Carmen, Paquito and Pepe.'

'Junkies,' Ricardo explains.

The face of Paco's girlfriend is now locked in a permanent grin, and Paco himself is becoming increasingly excitable as we leave the prison, and reach the first of the rock-hewn steps popularly known as 'The Ladder of Hell'.

'They were possibly carved by the Moors,' Ricardo informs us as Paco leads the way with a loud and unexpected burst of song.

'Orpheus descending,' Paco comments, 'but don't worry, we're not going down to hell. We're going instead to the Fuente de la Teja, a very special spring.'

He looks behind him in the direction of the Usurper and the Moorish Queen, whose hands are now permanently entwined.

'I shouldn't think our young lovers will be needing its waters.'

At the bottom of the steps, he waits for us to cluster together so that we can all hear the remarkable story of the Fuente de la Teja.

'The waters of this spring,' he begins in the exclamatory style of an old troubadour, 'were once famed throughout the kingdom of Granada. Their aphrodisiac properties had been recognized as far

43

back as the Romans. On the merest sprinkle, desires were aroused in the most stubborn virgins, limp penises became positively Priapic, dogs were set on heat, and multiple, mutual orgasms could be maintained continuously for nearly twenty-four hours.

'The fame of the waters finally reached the ears of the great Cleopatra, who immediately rushed over on her yacht to Sanlúcar de Barrameda, where, barely pausing to savour the local *manzanilla* and *langostinos*, she commandeered an air-conditioned limousine to drive her to Alhama.

'She is said to have spent over five days lying in a jacuzzi filled with the spring's waters, which she described as having the texture and temperature of warmed ewe's milk with a frisson of champagne. Unfortunately Anthony wasn't around at the time, and she had to satisfy her...'

Ricardo, in a final, pedantic bid for historical truthfulness, interrupts to point out that the Moors, for some unknown reason, neglected the Fuente de la Teja in favour of the hot springs of the present Balneario.

Paco, by now having second thoughts about descending to the very bottom of the gorge, thinks it better to agree with him. 'Its special properties,' he suggests, 'were probably worn off by Cleopatra's voracity. In any case I don't think it's worth going all the way down there.'

I look disappointed.

'It's best to leave these things to the imagination,' Paco consoles me.

We climb back up the hill by a different route, and it is not long before Paco is pointing to a cave on the far side of the gorge with an enormously wide opening.

'A Martian landing-base,' he says.

His hitherto silent girlfriend turns now to talk to me.

'Why don't you put details like that in your book?' she asks with a smile. 'The information you find in books is usually false anyway, so you'd be better off inventing good stories.'

I agree with her, and she continues in a more philosophical vein. 'The imagination grasps the truth in a way that fact-finding scholars can never do. I pity those poor pedants who spend their whole lives researching a handful of topics and have nothing to show for themselves other than a few pebbles from the beach.'

I assure her that the account of my Spanish Islamic journey will be a largely fictional one.

She seems pleased, and offers to lend me a favourite book of hers on flamenco.

'It's far better and more truthful than all the other books on flamenco put together. It's written by a gypsy, and there's not a single fact that hasn't been invented.'

This conversation brings our tour of Alhama to a suitable conclusion. We all retire to Paco's bar, and the three of us who are following Ibn Battuta to Granada decide to try and reach the Nasrid capital this very day. We celebrate our last moments in the town with a few more drinks, and are slightly light-headed when we finally leave the bar to go back to our hotel to collect our luggage.

Are miracles happening, or is the imagination already gaining the upper hand?

The group of decrepit old men who sit on permanent guard outside the Balneario, as if sadly counting their last hours on earth, appear to have discarded their crutches, glumness and age, and are pushing our car with the energy of young men as we make our final clumsy departure from the hotel. We give them a large cheer, and fall laughing on our seats, breaking the nocturnal silence with a long and defiant hoot of the horn. The old men cheer back.

The rain, which has held off since the early spring, makes its belated appearance shortly afterwards, falling with such torrential abandon that the Moorish Queen brings the car to a sudden halt.

She opens the door, and throws her closed eyes ecstatically towards the sky.

'A miracle!' she shouts. 'A miracle!'

We continue travelling through the night, as Gautier had done on his way to Alhama. The lights of Granada will soon be visible, and

I think I can identify in the darkness the characteristic profile – likened by Gautier to 'a bishop's colossal mitre' – of the hill known to the Moors as Aben Abides. From its summit, now scarred by disused strontium mines, the Catholic king is said to have finalised his plans for the conquest of the Nasrid capital.

The rain has stopped, and the Moorish Queen has changed her clothes and dried off, but the combined effects of sea and river bathing, and the recent plunge into the rain, have brought out an insatiable desire for water. When she realizes we are entering La Malahá, she begins unsettling the Usurper by recalling enthusiastically some more Moorish baths in the vicinity.

'In the small hours, when we left the discothèques,' she says, thinking back to her adolescence, 'we never used to make it as far as Alhama, but we often went to the baths near La Malahá. They're completely isolated in the fields, and there's this pool with a ruined Moorish structure on one side. One night a group of us were lying under its vault, and the moon suddenly appeared above one of the star-shaped openings. It was a magical moment. Shall we go there now?'

The problem is the place isn't sign-posted, and she can't remember exactly where it is. It is late on a Monday night, there's no-one in the street, and the first two bars we pass are closed. La Malahá, the flourishing Moorish town known for its silk industries, its salt flats, and its vast water tank or *aljibe*, has now almost half the population it had in Moorish times. Tonight it looks like a ghost town.

We are at the far end of the village, and on the point of continuing towards Granada, when we catch a glimpse of the lurid pink lights of the Pub Aljibe.

The large, inhospitable room is an uneasy cross between a bar and a discothèque. There are flashing lights, music, an amorous young couple, billiard players and a pair of elderly drunkards propped up against a counter displaying a stale tortilla and the congealed remains of a Russian salad. The bored-looking barman makes no attempt to serve us.

'We're back in the land of *la malahafolla*[1],' I punningly respond, refering to the most stereotypical characteristic of the people of

---

[1] From the slang term *malafollá*, literally 'bad fuck'.

Granada – a dour, bloody-mindedness that is sometimes said to be a legacy of the Castillian settlers who moved into the area after 1492.

The Usurper is not amused, and is preparing to leave the place when the barman finally asks us what we want. We have a beer while listening to the man's directions to the thermal spring.

'There's nothing special about them,' he adds unsolicited.

'Aren't there any Moorish ruins?'

'Not as far as I know.'

'But isn't there some large vaulted structure?'

'Yes, it's about twenty years old, part of a projected thermal resort which was abandoned when the waters became contaminated.'

'Contaminated?'

'The mine workings, chemicals, that sort of thing.'

'Do people still bathe there?'

'I don't.'

He pours himself a beer, and continues talking, revealing more of the rather negative outlook on life to be expected from someone tainted with malafolla. The world for him is a place in terminal decline, torn apart by drugs, crime, and corrupt politicians – he seems to imply that the state of the baths at La Malahá is a reflection of all this.

'I wouldn't go there even in daylight, but you'd be mad to go there now.'

'Why's that?'

'Well, first of all you're likely to get lost once you get off the main road. But that's not the real problem.'

'Which is what?'

'Bad people. They go there to fuck, inject themselves, you know what I mean. You could find a knife at your throat, or a syringe.'

He invites us to a room upstairs, where we stand looking out of a window.

'Every night at this time of the year, there's always the odd, suspicious light down by the baths. Look, look over there, can't you see those lights?'

We see nothing, and make our excuses and leave. The Moorish Queen is the first to speak once we are out on to the street.

'Let's go and find the baths then,' she says, having clearly not paid the slightest heed to the barman's words of warning.

Even I am hesitating, but the Moorish Queen's wishes are always respected, and we are soon following the barman's directions, turning off on to a dust track once we have reached a large industrial warehouse over a kilometre from the village.

The track splinters into several others, and after a while we are unsure as to whether we are on a track at all. Wondering whether we are driving over ploughed fields or a huge construction site, we go in circles until finally a distant farm building triggers off a memory in the Moorish Queen.

The building is deserted, and my heart is pounding after we get out of the car, and walk around to the spot where she thinks the pool might be.

There is a pool, but the water is stagnant and cold. Beyond is another and larger pool, protected by trees, and with tepid water. Then a third pool, also tepid, but still no sign of anything resembling a ruined vault.

'We're getting closer,' she claims, as we walk further and further away from the car, lessening our chances of beating a hasty retreat. A fourth pool, grander than the other three, looms in front of us, steaming slightly. At one end is an ugly modern brick construction with large openings in the ceiling.

'That's it,' she says, but then hesitates after staring longer at the building. Could this really be the Moorish structure she had once imagined?

'Let's go,' orders the Usurper, who by now has finally had enough, and is suffering slightly from the early morning cold.

The Moorish Queen obeys, for she too is getting cold, and tired. Or has she sensed, like me, some sinister, lurking presence, in keeping with the village's evil-sounding name?

A rabbit rushes out in front of us, causing me a start. We return quickly to our car. We begin driving back towards the village. The route ahead is blocked, another car has appeared as if from nowhere. My heart is beating faster. There are shadowy figures who appear to be waiting for us. They're the youths from Alhama, I'm sure of it. They've been following us, of course they have. I'm panicking, I know what's going to happen, I've seen it too often in films.

Knives are going to be brought out, bodies will be tied up. There'll be torture, and worse.

'No!' I shout, managing to transmit my fears to the Moorish Queen, who swerves into a deep ditch and makes a drastic manoeuvre that manages remarkably to get us in front of the other car.

Finding our way at last to the main road, she turns round to me.

'Have you gone completely paranoid?'

'Yes,' I sheepishly reply, before escaping into my own thoughts.

I close my eyes, and soon begin to slumber. I imagine myself as Ibn Battuta nearing the promised paradise of Granada.

CHAPTER TWO

LAST DAY IN PARADISE

The Greeks called it a *paradeisos* and the Persians a *pairidaeza*. These ancient words denoted an enclosed garden, which is how Paradise has always been imagined.

The Romantics pictured Granada as a terrestrial paradise, not least because of the wealth of 'enclosed' or 'paradise' gardens that the Moors had created here – the sweet-smelling, water-cooled and cypress-shaded oases that lie hidden within the town's hillside villas or *carmens*, attaining their sensual apotheosis in the grounds of the summer palace of the Generalife.

But the images of paradise formed by earlier travellers to Granada were inspired less by these than by the vast enclosed garden comprising the fertile valley or *vega* in which the town is set.

Ibn Battuta felt no need to praise the beauties of the Alhambra and the Generalife, but instead registered wonder at the vega itself – a valley which the Moorish genius for irrigation had transformed into a vibrant picture of natural abundance.

'The surroundings of Granada,' he wrote, 'are without equal in the whole Universe... Gardens, meadows, orchards, castles and vineyards surround the town on all sides.'

The vega comes into view shortly after leaving La Malahá, but it's three o'clock in the morning, and I am sleeping. Later that day I am given another opportunity to see Granada and its bucolic setting from the same road from which Ibn Battuta had first glimpsed them.

The Usurper has set off for his home in Aragón, and the

Moorish Queen has returned to her flat in Granada's Realejo. I have left my luggage in the House of the Rich Moor, and have taken a late afternoon bus to a village lying halfway between La Malahá and Granada.

The village of Gabia la Grande has grown into a featureless commuter town, but in the middle of its nondescript whitewashed buildings is a quiet little square guarded by an Islamic tower of the fourteenth century.

The tower, a simple structure with bare plaster and tiny openings, is attached to a Flamenco Club, a member of which pulls up in his car as I arrive here on foot from the bus-stop.

When I ask him if I can climb up to the top of the tower for the view, he hesitates for a moment.

'It'll be a bit difficult at present,' he says.

I anticipate being given one of the standard excuses for not being allowed in – the key is not available, the stairs are in too dangerous a condition, and permission is needed beforehand from the Club's president. But I am wrong.

'The door to the tower has become so warped that we haven't been able to open it recently. But you can always have a go if you want to.'

Inside the Club's bar, he obtains for me a key of venerable size and antiquity – a key similar, I imagine, to the ones that Muslims of Spanish descent are said to have kept from their ancestors' homes in Granada. He points me in the direction of the door, and wishes me luck.

After much twisting and turning of the key, and a few shoves from my elbow, the massive oak door gives way amidst clouds of dust and broken cobwebs. A ceramic plaque next to the door informs me that 'The Great Captain captured this fortress on Tuesday the 26th of April, 1491, taking as prisoner thirty of its defenders'.

I am unprepared for the jewel of Islamic architecture awaiting me. The tower's austere exterior has obeyed the strictures of Islam by offering no hint of the ornamental wealth that is increasingly revealed as I climb the darkened stairs into a large room where a frightened bird rushes out through a broken window.

The room's stucco decoration has largely been hidden by a

recent coating of white plaster, but sporadic restoration attempts have uncovered a sufficient amount of the original wall to show crafts-manship equal to that of the Alhambra.

Then I look down towards the floor and find I am standing on Islamic tiles, whose brilliant blues and reds are brought back to life as I clear off a layer of dust and dirt with my hands and my spit. Engaged in this, I notice around me heaps of a brittle, calcinous appearance. Approaching them I discover the skeletons of birds.

The bird cemetery extends to the floor above, as does the stucco-work. There is also an Islamic wooden beam ceiling, and a large impressively carved door which has been temporarily laid against a wall covered in graffiti. Huge letters spell out the words PAQUITA IS A WHORE as well as the names of a myriad of lovers and other visi-tors. Among all the scrawled Pepes, Carmens, Manolos and Pilis, one inscription in particular attracts my attention. The brevity of its message is sufficient for me to picture a sad and solitary Muslim paying homage to the monuments of his forefathers: 'Mohammed Ali, May, 1974'.

Remembering the original purpose of my visit, I climb up on to the roof, to observe the views across the vega. I have delayed too long downstairs, and already a faint moon is appearing over the grey-ing scene. The darkening profile of the Sierra Nevada highlights the fading greens and yellows of a valley which, even under the bright-est sunlight, would surely be difficult to think of as a paradise. Modern, heavily built-up areas have inevitably affected the landscape, but even in medieval times Granada had sprawled well beyond its official boundaries, with numerous villas, farmyards and satellite conurbations speckling the garden of the vega. The real and funda-mental change to the scene that Ibn Battuta had described is the disappearance through erosion of the rich, bosky carpet which had once covered all the slopes of the enclosing hills and mountains.

'All of it is lovely,' wrote the sixteenth-century Venetian ambas-sador Andrea Navagero, contemplating the surroundings of Granada, 'all extraordinarily pleasing to behold, all abounding in water, water which could not be more abundant; all full of fruit trees – plums of every variety, peaches, figs, quinces, clingstone peaches, apricots, sour cherries and so many other fruits that one can barely glimpse the sky for the density of the trees.' But a hint of the vega's dramatic decline over the following centuries is also given by Navagero, who, as early as 1525, is lamenting the way so many houses and gardens are going to ruin 'because the Moriscos are declining in number rather than increasing, and it is they who work and plant this land with the multitude of trees which one sees here.'

The poet García Lorca, brought up in the heart of the vega at the beginning of this century, was still able to perceive his surroundings as a paradise, but he was also to give new meaning to the notion of an 'enclosed garden' by stressing the exclusive, inward-looking and ultimately moribund nature of such a place. He called Granada a 'closed paradise', and, in his famous 'Ballad of the Three Rivers', evoked the enclosed, isolated character of the vega by comparing the navigable Guadalquivir (which runs through Seville) with the two rivers that descend into the vega from the Sierra Nevada:

> For the sailing boat
> Seville has a passage,
> Through the waters of Granada there row only sighs

The poet's final home, the Huerta de San Vicente, had itself comprised a little world of its own within the greater enclosure of the vega. Until as late as 1989, when it was acquired by the Municipality of Granada, it had remained an oasis of repose and tranquility against all the odds. The tower-blocks of one of Spain's ugliest ring-roads had come to overshadow it and block its views of the Alhambra; coachloads of tourists, oblivious of its existence, had begun drawing up besides the neighbouring flamenco travesty of the Sala Neptuno. But it was not until 1989 that its character was irreversibly lost – thanks to the municipality's decision to transform its cultivated fields and enchanting orchard into an ugly public park commemorating the poet.

Lorca, obsessed with the theme of Granada's decline after the Moorish occupation, notoriously referred to the town's present-day inhabitants as 'the worst bourgeoisie in the world'. The philistinism of these people was in complete contrast to what he saw as the poetry-loving sophistication of their Moorish predecessors – a contrast epitomized by the extremes of ugliness and beauty so characteristic of Granada today.

Few of the famously beautiful towns of the past, such as Rome and Florence, can be proud of their modern quarters; but Granada is special in showing that a sense of beauty is not necessarily developed by those who grow up under its shadow. The same people who had happily let the Alhambra and the Generalife fall into ruin until the 're-discovery' of these places by foreign travellers, seem still determined to destroy what is left of their town's beauty.

For Ibn Battuta, approaching Granada on the Alhama road, the town must have seemed from a distance like the jewel on the vega's crown – a jewel brandishing the white pearl of the Alhambra. From the tower of Gabia la Grande, the view today of Granada is dominated by a chaos of ring-roads and high-rises engulfing the supermarket complexes of Hipercor and Continente, and the massively pretentious Palacio de Congresos. The Alhambra itself is an incidental detail almost lost next to the orange-ochre, neo-Moorish bulk of the Hotel Alhambra Palace.

Eventually, as the ugly and the beautiful are all obscured by the night, I descend through the bird cemetery into the Flamenco Club, wondering as I do so what other rich seams of the Islamic past I am likely to uncover beneath the most unpromising of surfaces.

In the Club's dark patio I learn something more about the tower's history from another of the inscriptions on a ceramic tile, this one dedicated 'To the anonymous person of long ago who began the tower; to those who enlarged and enriched it during the Arab occupation; to Don Pedro López de Horozco El Zagal, to whom the Catholic Monarchs conceded it by Royal Decree for his part in the Reconquest; and to those who, from that time onwards, have taken it upon themselves to maintain it, in particular its previous owners, Don José Blanco Reta and Dona Mariana Teresa L. Rubio Olivar.'

I am noting down these emotive words when the man who had given me the key to the tower comes up to ask my opinion of the building. I use the term 'magnificent'.

'Yes,' he agrees, 'but its condition is very poor; very poor.'

The tower, he goes on to tell me, had had its top lopped off by Juana La Loca, and had later been incorporated into an eighteenth-century palace, the present owners of which live in Madrid, rarely come here, and loan the building to the Club for a minimal rent. There are no plans for restoration.

He takes me into a room where a group of old men are playing dominoes. The walls are lined with photographs of the flamenco artists who have performed here.

'Do you know something about Spanish history?' he asks.

'A bit,' I reply.

'Well, in that case you probably know that our country was occupied for several centuries by the Moors, and that they stayed in Granada much longer than they did anywhere else.'

The point of this historical digression is finally reached.

'The fact that Granada was more profoundly influenced by Moorish culture than any other part of Spain explains why flamenco music here is so great and pure. People say that it's better in Seville and Cádiz, but that's not true at all.'

I do not want to contradict him, but have to express my disbelief at what he tells me next, after we have moved back into the patio.

'The tower,' he insists, 'was Spain's first "National Monument".'

To prove his point he stops in front of yet another plaque, and reads out an inscription recording that the 'tower was declared a National Monument on June 6th, 1922'.

'If not the very first,' the man continues, 'it was one of the first.'

I think back to the birds and the skeletons.

From the ruined tower of Gabia la Grande I escape into the ivory tower of the House of the Rich Moor.

Here, as the days pass, I slip back ever more into a world of unreality. I have been given the mirador as my bedroom, and sleep every night under a crafted mudéjar ceiling, surrounded by a panorama embracing the Alhambra, the Albaicín and the Sacromonte. Shortly after sunrise I take a walk through the gardens up to an isolated bench, where I can enjoy looking at the Alhambra in the knowledge that no-one will disturb me. The caretaker's wife brings me breakfast on the terrace, after which I might stroll across to the Albaicín to sit reading in the Carmen de Chápiz, a sixteenth-century mudéjar villa which has recently been transformed into a Centre of Moorish Studies. Yusuf, the bearded Moroccan librarian, displays the smiling serenity of a contented Sufi mystic as he places on my desk volume after volume on the history and culture of al-Andalus. After absorbing myself in this bygone Islamic world I sometimes have lunch in the neighbouring Carmen de la Victoria, where guests of Granada's university can indulge their own paradise fantasies in terraced gardens overlooking the Alhambra and the Generalife. Cloudless days seem now to have returned for ever, but, with the arrival of the autumn, the hill facing the sunlit gardens of the Carmen de la Victoria is cast in a permanent shadow.

Every day I return after lunch to the ever colder House of the Rich Moor, where I try and read before generally falling asleep, lulled by a Moorish lethargy. I share the large house only with the caretaker and his family, but occasionally the peace is disturbed by members of the Sultan's circle. There are meetings connected with the world skiing championship and with the organization promoting Spain's Islamic culture, the 'Legado Andalusí'. There are also 'Gastronomic Days' presided over by the elegantly beautiful Sultana and by a man whose meticulously cultivated moustache gives him the appearance of some ceremonial sword bearer from the days of the Ottoman Empire. From time to time women from the court harem boost my growing reputation as a post-modern Irving by visiting me in my mirador retreat, where they gasp astonished at the sight of a romantic writer in his environment. They do not throw me peanuts, but come instead bearing canapés and gin and tonics.

My thoughts remain with the Moorish Queen, whose love I hope to rekindle now that the Usurper has left. I still have the keys from several years back to her Realejo flat, and jokingly compare these with the proverbial keys kept by exiled Moors to their Granadine homes. But she does not let me use them, telling me that she does not want her place turned into a 'rotating harem'. Neither can I tempt her with the ultimate romantic prospect of the double bed in my Moorish mirador. The mudéjar ceiling has no appeal for her, nor does the view from my window of the floodlit Alhambra. She is not a dreamer like me, she says.

Trying to console myself, I deepen my researches into Islamic Spain, and increasingly seek out the company of other dreamers.

The more I read the more aware I become of the number of major works by al-Andalusi poets and scholars that are as yet unavailable in translation. Much of the time I am forced to turn to the brief commentaries on these by modern scholars, from whose pedantic and often turgid writings I sometimes come away carrying with me only the odd, incidental detail: for instance, that the Granadine word for villa – *carmen* – has nothing to do with passionate, sultry women, but is derived instead from the Arabic word for cedars, *karm*.

My own training is that of an academic historian, but I am now developing an ever more sentimental and imaginative attitude towards the study of the past. Historical novels, such as Amin Maalouf's *Leo the African*, or Antonio Gala's fictional memoirs of Boabdil, *El Manuscrito Carmesí*, come to enthuse me more than do most of the strictly factual accounts of the period. They transport me back to fifteenth-century Granada, to where I go again when a lively Moroccan historian, Khalid Kamal, arrives from Marrakesh to present the Sultan with some coins that could have been held by Boabdil himself.

Khalid Kamal is an historian of immense erudition who enlivens his historical works with fictional elements, and talks anecdotally about the great figures of al-Andalus as if they were personal friends. He is unconnected with the university world, from which I myself try and keep my distance, increasingly attracted as I am by a world beyond that of conventional scholarship.

Suitably, my main link with Granada University is with some-one who confounds the academic stereotypes – a professor of English who has joined the outer fringes of the Sultan's circle through being commissioned to write for him on those numerous British travellers who have journeyed through Andalucía under a Moorish haze.

Whereas Khalid Kamal brings past figures into the present, my university friend Juan Antonio Díaz transposes present ones into the past, thus changing me into one of the travellers he is studying. He offers his services as my Boswell, and together we enter a world veering between history and actuality, fantasy and reality, earnestness and parody.

Elegantly bearded, like some dandy adventurer of the last century, he cultivates a playful image that makes it difficult to take seriously anything he says. He is constantly relating the most farfetched of stories; and though these always turn out to have a basis in truth, I none the less remain sceptical when he tells me one day about Mahmud Zakari, the 'leader of the Andalucían community of Timbuktu'.

'He's been spotted in Granada,' he claims. 'You must try and see him. He and his fellow Andalucían Moors are still the kings of Timbuktu. He'll show you the key to the house of his Granadine ancestors. He's probably come here to reclaim the place.'

But other friends of mine confirm that this man is indeed in town, and that a huge force of Andalucíans led by the Almerian renegade Yuder Pacha had conquered Timbuktu in the sixteenth century, and established there an Andalucían quarter, which still survives.

I become excited, and make persistent attempts to track down the mysterious Mahmud, eventually locating the phone number of a neighbour of his in the Albaicín. Mahmud is never at home, he is away on a trip, he'll be back later, you should phone tomorrow, I'll tell him you rang. But the days pass, and I still can't find him, until one evening the neighbour confesses that Mahmud has now left Granada for 'a very long while'. Perhaps he's returned to Timbuktu, perhaps he's in the Almerían village of Cuevas de Almanzora, birthplace of Yuder Pacha. The neighbour does not know. 'You'll meet him one day,' he adds enigmatically.

Even without seeing Mahmud, the very knowledge of his having been here helps further to take me away from the provincial reality of present-day Granada. Combined with my dream-like existence at the House of the Rich Moor, my shared fantasies with Juan Antonio, and my encounters with Khalid Kamal and other international members of the Caliph's circle, this knowledge makes it easier for me to imagine the Granada described by Ibn Battuta – a town of illustrious and exotic personages, where you could find travellers from places as far away as Anatolia, Persia, Samarkand and India.

Ibn Battuta, though never managing an audience with the Nasrid Sultan, received gold coins from the Sultan's mother, and was welcomed into the homes of many notables, including that of the eminent jurist Abu'l-Kasim ibn'Asim, whose garden was the setting of the Moroccan traveller's most memorable and significant moments in Granada.

In the garden of the Carmen de la Victoria, relaxing after an alcoholic lunch with Juan Antonio and his university friends, I am suddenly reminded of that other garden where Ibn Battuta had found himself surrounded by the greatest poets of the age.

Ibn Battuta, regaling this brilliant company with the tales of his great exploits, made the most profound impression on the twenty-eight-year old Ibn Yuzayy, then employed in a secretarial post in the Nasrid government. The two men would meet again in Fez, where Ibn Yuzayy, with the aid of imagination and a pruning hand, would bring Ibn Battuta's wanderings to their literary fruition.

Over one hundred years after Ibn Battuta's visit to Granada, the Egyptian traveller Abd al-Basit would still be describing Granada not only as a terrestrial paradise, but also as 'one of the most important and populous cities of the West', 'a meeting place of illustrious people, poets, scientists, artists… some of the greatest figures of our age'. But there is also a word of warning. 'The infidels,' he notes ominously, 'are closing in, and have already taken the greater part of this land of al-Andalus.'

My own days in Granada, cocooned from the real world, cannot last for ever, but the imaginary garden in which I am enclosed becomes ever more difficult to leave. In preparation for my departure, I make repeated forays into the vega, charting unintentionally the infidels' advance on Granada.

My longest excursion takes me to Alcalá la Real, which the Christians captured as early as 1341, thus securing for themselves a place of vital strategic importance at the northern approaches to the vega. The largely rebuilt town is dwarfed by the ruins of the enormous citadel, crowned by the twin summits of a Renaissance church and a Moorish keep. I have been here several times before, but it is only now that I pay any attention to the small plaque placed just beyond the massive main gate, and commemorating the 'scholar and poet Ibn Sa'id'. I wonder how many visitors to the citadel are aware that the Alcalá-born Ibn Sa'id was the author, in 1243, of the earliest anthology of Hispano-Moorish poetry? And even among those who have read this book in its English or Spanish versions, how many know that it forms a small and relatively unimportant part of an as yet untranslated and exceptionally lively treatise on al-Andalus?

Unread plaques such as the one at Alcalá serve as sad reminders of the enormous forgotten wealth of Spain's Islamic culture. A few days later I come across another one at the town of Loja, which guards the western entrance to the vega, and was the birthplace in 1313 of Ibn al-Khatib, who excelled as physician, philosopher, poet and historian, and even rose to the rank of vizier before arousing widespread jealousy and being exiled to Fez.

The plaque to him at Loja stands behind the town's small and ugly main square, at the entrance to a narrow street which climbs steeply through the cramped and sorry remains of the citadel. Adjacent to the plaque is a dreary modern block of flats which in itself encloses glamorous memories, at least for the Loja-born friend who accompanies me around the town: he remembers how he and his schoolmates stood underneath one of its balconies, waiting to catch a glimpse of the baker's sensationally beautiful daughter. Later, this same friend takes me across the river Genil to his brother-in-law's restaurant, from the terrace of which, suspended between gardens and chalets, Loja appears at its best, rising above fields and framed against barren peaks.

But the intimations of paradise evoked by early travellers entering the vega at Loja are not felt by me until after lunch, when my
friend drives me to an isolated estate, a few kilometres west along
the valley. My friend has promised me one of Granada's most
hidden and rewarding treasures – a luxuriant garden, one of the finest
in Spain.

The side-road, following at first the Genil, soon runs out of sight
of the new Seville to Granada motorway, and wanders among olive
trees and rolling, cropped fields. Then it peters to an end in a
dusty forecourt, alongside a firmly closed gate, behind which, in
shocking contrast to the surrounding dry earth, bursts a jungle of
date-palms, cedars, monkey-puzzles and other exotic greenery.

The garden is open to the public, according to my friend, who
has not been here since his childhood, but there is no way of
checking this, for the place is not promoted anywhere, or even
mentioned in any guide-book. From the upstairs window of an
adjoining white house there appears a surly old caretaker, afflicted
apparently by a heavy dose of malafollá. The garden is closed, he
insists, and can only be seen on Wednesday mornings from nine
o'clock to ten – an hour, my friend retorts, when no-one is likely
to come here.

'The owner makes no exceptions,' the caretaker says sharply, closing the window behind him.

We walk around the railings, and stumble across the owner's
daughter, who invites us inside. But the caretaker intercepts her, and
tells her off for doing something her father would not approve of.
An argument ensues, the daughter rings her father in Granada, she
finally has her way, but is shaking and ashen-faced. The peace of the
garden soon calms us all down.

It is not a Moorish garden, but has some of the attributes of one
– secretiveness, jasmine, privet-hedges, narrow channels of water.
Designed by the landscape-gardener of the royal park of La Granja,
near Segovia, it was commissioned in 1789 by the local political and
military hero, General Narváez, whose tarnished bronze statue in
Loja's main square is now almost as ignored as the nearby plaque
to Ibn al-Khatib.

The owner's daughter gives us until dusk to enjoy the freedom of her garden, allowing time for us to note the weeds, pavement cracks, unclipped trees, and other signs of Nature struggling to defeat the fragile human order. I am tempted in the end to think of the garden as a last and poignant enclave of the paradise that was the vega. A paradise whose fate was finally decided by the events that took place in Loja in the early 1480's.

In July 1482, when Abu'l-Hasan abandoned his attempt to recapture Alhama and rushed to the support of Loja, he did so knowing that the latter was strategically the more important of the two towns. Arriving in Loja to find the place being valiantly defended by the redoubtable 'Ali al-'Attar, he was able to assist in the routing of the Christians, who fled, leaving behind their artillery and siege equipment. A great moral victory was scored for the Muslims, but the effects of this were to be short-lived.

Abu'l-Hasan's son, Boabdil, profited from his father's absence by rebelling against him in Granada, and apparently was supported in this both by the Abencerrajes and by his mother, who still resented her husband for favouring the Christian slave Zoraya. Division within the Nasrid family fatally weakened Islamic resistance to the Christians, and was fully exploited by the latter. When the Christians captured Boabdil at Lucena in 1483, they thought it best to release him and set him up as the puppet emir of Guadix, to the east of Granada.

Abu'l-Hasan died in 1485, and his more radical and bellicose brother al-Zaghal was proclaimed sultan in his place. Boabdil, after being defeated by his uncle's troops at Almería, fled to Castille, but was reinstated in eastern Andalucía by the Christians, who by now had occupied Ronda, and the whole coastal strip up to Málaga. After taking the Albaicín quarter of Granada, Boabdil decided to seek peace with his uncle, and in so doing so incensed the Catholic Monarchs that they embarked on an all out assault on the vega.

Loja finally fell in the spring of 1486, and was immediately followed by Colomera, Montefrío and Moclín. I make trips to all these last places, enjoying, ironically, an October day of exceptional warmth at the beautiful small town of Montefrío (the 'cold mountain'), where an eagle's nest of a Moorish castle now competes as an attraction with such Christian innovations as a spectacularly domed neo-classical church, and the excellent local pork products.

The weather changes overnight by the time I reach Moclín. The temperature has plunged in the dramatic way for which the autumns here are famous, and a light covering of snow has fallen over the Sierra Nevada.

Moclín, like Colomera and Montefrío, lies on one of the now little-used side-roads that straggle the vega between Granada and Alcalà. Its citadel, with its well preserved ring of walls, was described by the historian Pillement 'as one of the most important Islamic castles in Andalucía'. Ferdinand referred to it as 'the key to the vega'.

A bus-load of pensioners from Granada coincides with my arrival here, on a late Sunday afternoon. They have neither the strength nor the will to go further than the Christian sanctuary which stands near the citadel's entrance and contains the much venerated image of the Cristo del Paño. But I climb over rocky slopes to the very top of the ridge to appreciate a view of overwhelming dimensions.

The light is perfect. Last night's clouds have disappeared, and the wind and the cold have given the sky an icy blue clarity. From this extreme distance the worst aspects of the modern vega have become wholly incidental to a microcosmic landscape reduced to foreground ochres, a vast central oasis of green, and a floating white backcloth of Himalayan mystery and luminosity. The sun sets, pale pinks turn to an intense crimson, and the snows of the Sierra lose all contact with the earth. Under these conditions, it is hard not to give in to the romantic temptation of imagining Boabdil crying at the loss of such beauty.

Boabdil, taken captive again after the Christians had occupied Moclín, was released a second time, and given another chance to be a puppet to the Catholic Monarchs. Remaining in Granada after al-Zaghal was finally forced first to withdraw and then to capitulate to the Christians, he was soon secretly negotiating the inevitable – the peaceful surrender of his town. The Catholic Monarchs entered the Alhambra on 1 January, 1492, and the following day were presented the keys to Granada by Boabdil. They were dressed, curiously, in Moorish costume.

I spend my own last days in Granada as a participant in an 'international conference' on the British Hispanist and lesser Bloomsbury associate Gerald Brenan, the international element being provided by myself and a trio of British writers whom the local papers are calling 'the new Bloomsbury'. My friend Juan Antonio has organized everything, including a coach trip into the vega which has us all arriving late and in an inappropriately merry state for the opening of an exhibition devoted to the researches of Brenan and others into Lorca's death.

On another occasion Juan Antonio suggests we all have lunch near the spot where the poet was executed by nationalists at the start of the Civil War.

The place of Lorca's execution is situated high in the hills behind Granada's Charterhouse, and has famous views over the vega. The supposed actual spot is marked today by a solitary olive tree – the one human touch in a formal commemorative park imbued with some of the totalitarian spirit of Franco's Valley of the Fallen.

Beyond the boundaries of the park is the mineral water spring whose bubbles gave to the fountain it once fed the Moorish name of Ainadamar, the 'Fountain of Tears'.

Described by Ibn Battuta as one of the vega's loveliest corners, the fountain and its surroundings were greatly favoured in Islamic times. The wealthy built villas here, and poets were repeatedly inspired by the fountain's waters to write about love and its loss.

Ibn al-Khatib, who himself possessed a villa in the area, wrote about how the fountain 'overflows with water which is channelled along the road, and enjoys a marvellous situation, blessed with pleasant orchards and incomparable gardens, a temperate climate and the sweetness of its water, in addition to the great prospects it commands'.

In some of the poems quoted in Ibn al-Khatib's historical treatise on Granada, there are various lines referring to nights of love spent beside the fountain, and to the way in which the mere sight, sound and smell of its waters bring back memories of love, sad and passionate.

Another poem, written by the fourteenth-century Almerían-born scholar and poet, Abu'l-Barakat al-Balafiqi, claims that the women who live near the fountain are so beautiful as 'to make every Muslim abandon his faith for that of love'. Elsewhere this poem evokes how the fountain's 'water moans in sadness like the moaning of one who, enslaved by love, has lost his heart'.

The Moorish villas of Ainadamar have today gone without trace, replaced by a bosky picnic area, bungalows and a rustic-style bar and restaurant. As for the mineral spring, its water is now channelled into an eighteenth-century basin which Juan Antonio insists is shaped like a tear. I stand with him, the 'new Bloomsbury' writers, and a group of young women who have come with us, staring at it for a while, looking for the occasional bubbles that appear among the fallen leaves and flotsam. Then we have lunch at the restaurant.

The biographer Victoria Glendinning, whom in our Bloomsbury confusion we have all variously addressed as Vanessa, Virginia and Vita, is asked by the waiter if she would like to have her mineral water 'with' or 'without gas'.

The waiter is clearly not a poet, for he fails to understand her literary reply – 'with tears'.

Before leaving Granada I have a farewell meal with the Moorish Queen. After a few drinks she confesses that all is not well between her and the Usurper, whose sexual ambiguity and lack of commitment have begun wearing her down. She does not know what to do. Should she go up north and try living with him in his remote mountain village? Should she stay waiting in Granada, where there is increasingly less work for freelance environmentalists such as herself? Or should she give it all up and accompany me on my journey?

The last possibility is only half-serious, but is sufficiently strong as to make her begin battling with her conscience and talking about her enormous love for the Usurper. She proposes a compromise.

She will lend me her battered car so that I can give up once and for all my absurdly romantic idea of having to rely on walking, hitch-hiking and local bus. She realizes I can't drive, but suggests that an English friend of ours in Granada, Harry, should be my chauffeur, and take the car back to her when I go on to Morocco. And, who knows, she adds, she might even come and join us herself when she gets things sorted out with her work and her boyfriend. She smiles insecurely.

She pours out the remains of the bottle of wine, and orders a cognac, and then another. She loses her habitual commonsense and practical nature, and begins toying with my fantasies. She could share my exile in Morocco, we could set up home together in a small village near Marrakesh, perhaps within sight of the mausloeum of the poet-king of Seville, al-Mutamid. We wouldn't need much, a simple mud hut, lots of books, a job teaching Spanish, a Moroccan maid to prepare us endless delicious meals – lamb tajine sweetened with apricots, pastries stuffed with pigeons, marinated meats resting on beds of rice, and mint-flavoured stews dripping over comforting plates of couscous.

Soon she is coming back with me to see my room in the House of the Rich Moor.

She looks out of each window in turn, enjoying the sunset views before sitting down on the double bed and leaning back to wonder at the craftsmanship on the mudéjar ceiling. It has an aphrodisiac effect.

The desires I have repressed since the now distant time of our break-up find at last a renewed response in her. We lie kissing under the ceiling, and clothes are removed. Sapped by emotional deprivation, dehydrated by the effects of the alcohol, and already fantasising about Moroccan deserts, I press my lips urgently to the fountains of her breasts, then slide my head down the dunes of her navel, until finally my mouth comes to rest in a luxuriant oasis of pubic hair. I am murmuring something about paradise, while fighting off the same thoughts of romantic ridiculousness that I had had when I had first kissed her by moonlight under the Alhambra.

I continue burying my head in her body, knowing that to look up at the ceiling or to glimpse the Alhambra through the window would almost certainly succeed in changing my purring sounds of pleasure into fits of giggles.

My reflective foreplay is suddenly interrupted by a knock at the door. I almost rupture myself in my haste to put on some clothes.

Tragedy and farce seem to be inseparable ingredients in romantic love.

The caretaker is waiting outside, and wants to know if the radiator is working in my room. He has been sent by the Sultan's sister who apparently is worried that the mirador might be too cold for me. The sweat from my brow suggests otherwise, and he goes away.

Back inside the room the Moorish Queen is putting on her clothes with an irritated, impatient expression. She can't understand what came over her, says it must be something to do with the Moorish setting, she's normally a very loyal person, she has a wonderful boyfriend, and she doesn't love me in the same way I do her.

She'll still lend me the car, but thinks it better if we never see each other again. She doesn't like long farewells, and insists I stay in the room while she finds her own way out.

Alone in the Moorish room of my dreams, intoxication turns to shock, putting me soon into an even deeper sleep than ever.

The next morning, carrying my luggage, I walk through the paradise garden for a final time. The caretaker closes the large gate behind me.

I leave Granada like the last Moor, sighing.

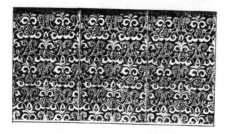

Balconies in Granada, by Gustave Doré, from de Amicis' Espagne

CHAPTER THREE

LOST WORLDS

Harry, twenty-five years old, blond hair slicked back, is laughing at the car. Don't mock it, I say, it's the Moorish Queen's, it'll console me for her absence. But for Harry it's just a joke, won't get us out of the garage. The Alpujarra? Forget about it.

'The ignition's fucked, the gears are jammed, the battery's low, and the electrics are up the spout.'

He pauses, then lets out a whooping sound, bringing his right hand sharply down against his thigh.

'Let's go for it!' he shouts.

He's a risk-taker, loves challenges, danger sparks off a hidden immaturity, turns him into the sort of person who shows off by speeding, talking about sports cars, ignoring traffic lights, taking difficult roads for the hell of it. In any case, he's got to get out of Granada, he's fucked up himself, another love story, a girl called Carmela. He'll tell me about her as soon as we get going. If we get going.

The garage attendant lends a hand with the pushing, while Harry fiddles ever more desperately with the gears and dashboard.

'Yeah, we're off!' he finally exclaims, now that the garage attendant has gone red in the face and I'm on the verge of a coronary. I jump into the car, we climb up the ramp and enter the open air, holding our breath all the time, and praying that none of the traffic lights will be against us.

The morning has already passed, and memories of the House of the Rich Moor have been diffused by the hours hanging around the ugly modern district where Harry has been living since the summer.

Once we have crossed the Ronda, and are more optimistic about the car's chances of making it at least to the outskirts of the town, I ask Harry about the Islamic course he's taking at Granada

University. How can he afford so many days off to accompany me to the Alpujarra and beyond?

'Because I've got fuck all else to do,' he says cheerily, while trying to release a cigarette from his pocket. 'There aren't any more classes until the end of November.'

He's soon changing the subject, for he'd rather talk to me about his amatory pursuits than his academic ones.

'Do you feel like a drink?' he asks, pulling into a service area a few kilometres to the south of Granada, on the main road to the coast. The place is called 'El Suspiro del Moro', 'The Moor's Sigh'.

Behind the service station and the nondescript restaurant and bar where Harry orders his first gin-tonic of the day is one of the most famous landmarks in the romantic topography of Spain. This is where Boabdil, ignominiously leaving Granada after securing a good deal with the Catholic Monarchs, reputedly broke down and wept. The half-blind Boston historian William Prescott was one of the many to recount the story.

'The Moorish king, traversing the route of the Alpujarras, reached a rocky eminence which commanded a last view of Granada. He checked his horse, and, as his eye for the last time wandered over the scenes of his departed greatness, his heart swelled, and he burst into tears. "You do well," said his more masculine mother, "to weep like a woman for what you could not defend like a man!" "Alas!" exclaimed the unhappy exile, "when were woes ever equal to mine!"'

The words 'Suspiro del Moro' are written over the packet of sugar which I pour into my black coffee as I listen to Harry relating his problems with Carmela, a blonde advertising executive.

'I don't know what the fuck she's playing at. I mean we've been seeing each other for nearly three months, and she still won't acknowledge me as her *novio*... I admit, she's been seriously fucked up by her previous boyfriends... I can't go on with all this play-acting... Sent her a letter yesterday... said it's all over... God, I'm dying to see her again...'

He's still moaning as the two of us, lovesick victims of Granadan womanhood, get back into the car and continue along the route described in 1850 by an excited Lady Louisa Tenison as the one 'which Boabdil chose when leaving his house and his kingdom for ever'.

At Mondújar, a few kilometres further south, Boabdil briefly broke his journey, directly under the slopes of Mulhacen, the highest peak in the Sierra Nevada. The mountain is named after a Moorish king whose remains are said to have been placed in a casket at its summit. But Boabdil wanted to pay homage to those of his ancestors who lie buried at Mondújar itself, in a cemetery below the castle.

Harry has another gin-tonic in the bar where we stop to ask if the ruins of such a cemetery can still be seen.

'Whenever a woman fucks me up,' he comments, 'I've just got to smoke and drink.'

Finding out that there's nothing left of the cemetery, we resume our journey, speeding as best we can down the dual carriageway until we turn off past Béznar on to the main road into the Alpujarra. We're concentrating so much on our car that we're hardly aware of having just crossed what had served for many centuries as a natural defensive moat guarding the entrance to the Alpujarra – the deep and narrow gorge of the Tablate.

We pull up to the side of the road with a sudden jolt that succeeds in snapping the winding mechanism of one of the windows.

'Oh fuck it,' says Harry, 'at least we've got here.'

Ignoring the problem, and risking being hit by the frequent passing cars and lorries, we walk back along the road to a site which had played an important role in the morisco uprising of 1569.

From the modern bridge we look down towards a much older one, bearing the dust track that had once been the principal route into the Alpujarra. The moriscos, seventeen days after their leader Aben Humaya had crowned himself king at the Alpujarran village of Cádiar, had pulled this bridge down in the hope of preventing the Christians from entering their kingdom. However, they had not reckoned with the fanatical determination of a Franciscan friar called Fray Cristóbal Molina, who – according to the chronicler Diego Hurtado de Mendoza – showed the Christian troops how they could negotiate the abyss by boldly leaping across it, a sword in one hand and a crucifix in the other. Two soldiers followed his example, with fatal consequences for one of them, but the monk, aided by the other soldier, braved salvoes of arrows to put back the bridge's wooden beams.

Despite the signpost marked 'Moorish Bridge, 14th century', I know that the structure I am looking at was almost entirely rebuilt around 1600. But I prefer to think of it as the very bridge used by Boabdil on exchanging the lost paradise of Granada for what the romantics came to consider as the lost world of the Alpujarra.

The Alpujarra was a place of refuge of such remoteness and isolation as to encourage the not implausible idea that the Moors had been able to stay on there in hiding even after their official expulsion from Spain in 1614. This idea, at its most fanciful, was expressed in Jan Potocki's *The Manuscript Found at Saragossa* (1815), a mad and wildly inventive Gothick novel by a peripatetic Polish aristocrat who reputedly killed himself with a silver bullet fashioned from a melted-down samovar. Potocki set his novel in the Sierra Morena, in the dangerous untamed days shortly before the establishment there of colonies of foreign settlers; but the book's geography is a wholly magical one centred on an eighteenth-century Alpujarra in which 'The Great Sheikh of the Gomelez' is still ruling over a secretive Moorish domain.

Potocki, though almost as intrepid a traveller as Ibn Battuta, was probably no different to the majority of nineteenth-century visitors to Granada in being content merely to imagine what lay hidden on the southern side of the snowcapped Sierra Nevada. The few early travellers actually to have explored this lost world would have found villages of cubical, interconnected houses almost identical to those of the mountainous districts of North Africa inhabited by the Berbers, to whom the Alpujarra had always been a favoured home, particularly after 1492.

The first important travel account dedicated to the Alpujarra was written in 1874 by the Guadix-born Pedro Alarcón, who claimed that the district had been so little visited up to his day 'that there was hardly a map which represented it with any accuracy, and that neither the foreigners who came from London or St Petersburg in search of Moorish associations, nor the Spanish poets who sung of these associations as of a precious heritage, had ever penetrated into that labyrinth of cliff faces and chasms, in which each rock, each cave, each tree testified to an episode in the Saracen domination'.

The Alpujarra remained relatively little known and virtually without roads right up to the 1920's, when Gerald Brenan settled in the village of Yegen. García Lorca, unaware of Brenan's existence, was delighted by how unspoilt the district still was, and by the lack of French and English tourists making 'lyrical journeys' through it. His impressions were mainly based on stays in the small spa town of Lanjarón, a few kilometres uphill from Tablate, and the first place in the Alpujarra to be developed by tourism.

'Lanjarón, Gateway to the Alpujarra' reads the inscription on the modern Moorish gate with the half-open door that confronts Harry and I as we finally approach the town in the late afternoon. This literal-minded monument, as yet unfinished, rises in sorry isolation above a parched traffic island. Nearby is a fountain with Granadan ceramics painted with a faded line by Lorca, who came here frequently to drink from it, listen to the water's 'eternal song', and admire the extensive views over the crumpled, craggy landscape.

'A dream of poets' was how Alarcón described Lanjarón, a town which others have likened to a balcony stretched out on the southern slopes of the Sierra Nevada. From the fountain, where we park our car, we observe the mountainous panorama under a clear light that highlights the landscape's contours and exaggerates the sublime profile of a ruined crag-top castle thrown up above the narrow patch of fields separating the town from a deep abyss.

But the town itself seems from here to contradict the drama and wildness of the setting. Even in the 1920's, before the construction of modern blocks as clean and anodyne as the town's famous mineral water, the contrast between the place and its surroundings must have been a striking one. From this period there survive a spa-house with neo-Moorish towers in brick and tiles, some palm-filled gardens, and a number of grand hotels and residential blocks that would seem more at home in Marienbad or Vichy.

Lorca was a regular guest at the Hotel España, to where I make my way with Harry, wondering as I do so how the poet could have written from Lanjarón that he felt here 'a wind from Africa'. Then suddenly, so incongruous among the spa's frail and grey-clothed

Spaniards, appears a group of young Moroccan women, with colourful silk robes flowing to the ground, and faces half covered by masks. I stare open-mouthed in their direction, astonished by this apparent confirmation of what I had heard about wealthy Moors returning to the favourite haunts of their ancestors. My stare is returned by the proverbial pair of mysterious dark eyes that had lured romantics ever deeper into the Orient.

From Marienbad to Marrakesh: Lanjarón turns out to be the strangest of cultural mixtures. After settling in at the Hotel España, we discover, behind the smart main street, an old quarter in the traditional Alpujarran Berber style – a compact, claustrophobic arrangement of whitewashed stone walls, alleys under painted wooden beams, flat grey stone roofs acting as terraces to the houses above. And, escaping the confines of the town into the dusty fields and olive groves below the castle, we enter a world that the romantic traveller would have known and appreciated.

The sun is setting when we reach the forgotten ruins of the castle – the castle that Ferdinand the Catholic had taken by surprise during the first uprising of the moriscos, in the spring of 1500. Rather than surrendering, the castle's valiant captain – 'a terrible and notorious negro', according to legend – threw himself into the dark void into which Harry, defying history, proudly empties the afternoon's long intake of drink.

Harry, an insomniac, is up early the next morning, and reports back with a tale of low clouds, light drizzle and a cold wind, apparently not from Africa. I am rooted to the warm bed and memories of the Moorish Queen, but Harry is already having his first smoke of the day, and is proposing a breakfast cognac to kick-start our worn bodies.

'Aben Humaya is calling us,' he tells me with a hint of sarcasm.

We have decided today to go on to Cádiar, to search out traces of this near mythical figure who mustered his fellow moriscos in their second and last attempt to prevent the wiping out of their culture. Outside Cádiar are two sites of fundamental importance for anyone undertaking a sentimental journey in Aben Humaya's footsteps – his summer house at Narila, and the massive olive tree under which he was sworn king of the moriscos in 1569.

The prospect of either of these places is not a particularly appealing one as I continue to lie immobile in my bed, depressed by the glimpse through the curtains of low-lying clouds turning Morocco into Marienbad again.

'You're getting worse than the car,' Harry says in another attempt to get me up. This time he's successful, and I'm soon struggling to my feet.

An hour later we're off again at last, with the wind and the rain entering the now irreparable car window after we've forked off at Órgiva on to the road running along the southern side of the Alpujarra. In Moorish times, these southern slopes had been completely forested, but then fires and the ruthless exploitation of timber had gradually left them barren – a process reflected in the change of the Alpujarra from a Moorish district which had prospered through the cultivation of silk to a Christian one falling into growing poverty and oblivion. Perhaps all would have been different had events taken another turn after the coronation of Aben Humaya.

The town where he was crowned, described by Brenan as the 'navel of the Alpujarra', looks especially dreary under a steady drizzle. The rain has driven most people off the streets, into the modest modern blocks that largely make up present-day Cadiar, a town whose outward ordinariness is marred only by the presence in its main square of 'The Fountain of Wine' – an object of fairground appearance which comes into its own during the summer festivities, when wine is distributed freely to everyone around it.

'How the fuck are we going to find this tree?' asks Harry, bringing me back to more practical considerations.

'It says in my guide-book,' I reply, 'that it's in between Cádiar and the village of Narila.'

'Oh great,' Harry retorts, 'Andalucía is famous for its lack of olive trees.'

I try and persuade Harry that Aben Humaya is a local hero, an

Alpujarran Robin Hood whose tree is probably visited by every schoolchild in the vicinity.

'It's bound to be marked,' I persist, while trying to hide my misgivings about the guide-book in question – a work of compendious research and learning put together by someone who shares our mutual friend Juan Antonio Díaz's love of wine and tendency towards fantasy and exaggeration.

'How can you honestly think that such a tree exists?' says Harry, who remains unconvinced even after I show him a rather dark photograph of it reproduced in the guide-book.

'You can see that was taken after a day spent hanging around the Fuente del Vino. In any case, olive trees aren't like sequoiahs; they're unlikely to survive for fifty years, let alone 450.'

'Granted,' I answer back, 'but this is not meant to be the actual tree but only a descendant.'

'I can't believe this,' Harry chuckles. 'You mean to say we're going to be fucking around in this pissing rain looking for a tree that by some extraordinary coincidence has been grown from seeds that can be linked back through a good twenty generations of trees to some original tree associated with a person largely created by romantic novelists?'

I know that at heart Harry is as keen as I am to undertake a sentimental journey rather than a strictly historical quest, and that his cynicism, like mine, is only a symptom of being a romantic in the true, rebellious sense of the term. In many ways we are like-minded historians – debunkers of myths who need also an element of poetry in our history. I find it appropriate that we should be touring the Alpujarra together, for in no other part of Spain is Islamic history so intertwined with romantic legend as it is here.

Julio Caro Baroja, the most clear-headed of Spanish historians, suggested, in the preface to his pioneering study of *The Moriscos of the Kingdom of Granada* (1957), that many of his generation, himself included, had originally acquired their knowledge of the moriscos from reading popular historical novels such as *Los monfíes de las Alpujarras* by Seville's answer to Sir Walter Scott, Manuel Fernández y González. For this reason he claimed in his own book to have adopted a style which was purposefully 'lack-lustre, unromantic, and un-oriental, a style in which metaphor has been banished and that has been influenced instead by the modern tendency towards dry, hard and rather pedantic abstraction'. However, despite having written a book which he thought would be of little appeal to the poet, he was forced also to admit that the material it contained seemed at times straight from one of the stories in *The Thousand and One Nights*: 'We shall, indeed, be dealing with ferocious bandits, prisoners, slave merchants, noble captains, wise astrologers, damsels in distress, caves full of treasures, castles, the crowds of the market-place, farmers, muleteers, pirates…'

Aben Humaya is one of these larger-than-life figures. Known at birth as Fernando de Córdoba y Valor, his elevation to the title of 'King of the Andalucíans' was engineered by his uncle, a native of Cádiar, seat of the Alpujarra's main judge or *Qadi*. Renouncing his Christian name, Fernando assumed an Islamic one (strictly speaking Ibn Umayya) which would call to mind the great days of the Córdoban Caliphate. He also took his full Quranic complement of wives, and, cunningly, chose these from a number of areas corresponding to the political alliances he wished to forge. For his coronation he reputedly seized the crown of a local votive image of the Virgin of the Rosary.

Searching for the olive tree where the great event took place, we take the side-road between Cádiar and Narila, and pull up next to a slightly startled old woman. I put my head out of the window.

'We're looking for the tree of Aben Humaya.'

I try to ignore Harry's suppressed giggle as the woman looks blankly at me.

'Ah,' she eventually replies, 'you mean the tree of the Moor?'

Unfortunately she is not very sure about where it is, and thinks we should ask again in the village.

' You know,' she adds with a smile, ' in all my years I've never actually been to it. My husband says it's much smaller than it used to be.'

We drive on the extra two kilometres to Narila, where we hope, if all else fails, to see Aben Humaya's summer palace. The palace is in fact easy to find, if indeed it is really his palace.

'This can't be it,' says Harry, despite the unanimous agreement that it is by the group of workers mending the road in front of it.

'A Muslim bought it a few years ago,' says one of them, as if to prove conclusively that Aben Humaya must have lived here.

'It can't be more than about sixty years old,' Harry mutters to me in English.

'That's unfair,' I reply, 'I wouldn't be surprised if it dated back at least to the early nineteenth century. Well it's certainly the oldest looking house in the village.'

This is indisputable. The place looks like a war-scarred shell whose façade has been torn off by a landslide or an earthquake. A 'For Sale' notice and a few telephone numbers have been painted in black on a wall with smashed windows; but the pots of geraniums on a balcony crudely divided in two by boarding suggests at least partial occupancy. The workers claim that the owner hasn't been seen for weeks.

A dispute arises when I finally pluck up the courage to ask them about the famous tree. The oldest among them begins giving directions, but is suddenly interrupted by one of his colleagues.

'It's no longer there,' he says.

'What do you mean?'

'It was struck down by lightning.'

'No it wasn't,' says another. 'A tractor drove into it.'

'It's definitely still there,' interjects someone else. 'It's just been badly pruned, that's all.'

The dispute persists, as does the rain, but Harry, as I have predicted, is now almost violently insistent that we try and find at least the site of the tree.

'Just ignore these jokers, let's just get there,' he mumbles, opening the car door. The whole issue has become a wild challenge, which leads him to drive back through the village streets and on to the Cádiar road with manic determination. In a matter of minutes we have reached the unpromisingly modern property in whose grounds we now think the tree or its site might be found. The owner is not in, dogs are barking loudly, the clouds are almost enveloping us, but we continue struggling through a ploughed field until the field falls abruptly in front of us, revealing what looks in the half mist like a large and wizened olive tree.

'That's it!' Harry shouts, but the excitement is short-lived, for two other such trees come simultaneously into view. 'Well, let's say that's it.'

We give up. On this note of anti-climax we walk back to the car.

'And what happened to Aben Humaya?' Harry asks, becoming sensible again.

I tell him that the events after the famous coronation mirrored those of the last years of Nasrid rule in Granada, and that for all the advantages of fighting on their own terrain, the Alpujarran rebels were fatally weakened by dissension among the Muslim leadership. Humaya was assassinated in a coup sponsored by Turkish military experts whom he had enlisted, and his successor, Aben Aboo, was killed by his own men. The scant facts of Humaya's short life were then embroidered by legend – a legend which would have important repercussions for Spanish literature.

It was to this legend that the exiled Granadine writer and liberal politician Francisco Martínez de la Rosa turned to in Paris in 1830 after falling under the spell of Victor Hugo's romantic plays. Inspired by these, he wrote the tragedy of *Aben Humaya, ou la révolte des maures sous Philippe II*, which broke away from the classical model of his earlier works, and was rapturously received by the Parisian public. Though its reception in Madrid six years later would be less warm, its tentative romanticism came to be seen as heralding a turning-point in Spanish drama.

'Under this elusive olive tree,' I pompously suggest to Harry, 'you could almost say that the seeds of the Spanish romantic movement were sown.'

I look at my watch, and realize that our quest for Aben Humaya has occupied only a small part of the morning. We're going to spend the night at the nearby village of Yegen, and we've still got hours to spare. Besides we've been left slightly frustrated by our Cádiar visit and are still hungering for the untamed Alpujarra that had so astonished the likes of Alarcón, Lorca and Brenan. Does such a place still exist?

Harry remembers hearing from an Alpujarran friend about the ruins of an Islamic castle situated high above the isolated hamlet of Las Canteras, about twenty kilometres south-east of Cádiar.

Ostensibly his main reason for wanting to visit this site is that it is a harshly beautiful place which almost no one knows about, but I suspect that he is also motivated by the ultimate challenge that the journey there will almost certainly pose for our car. A distant break in the clouds gives heart to us both.

The Alpujarra becomes progressively wilder, more barren, and less obviously affected by tourism the further east you drive into it. By the time we have reached the unasphalted road leading to Las Canteras, the violently contoured landscape has turned almost uniformly bare and rocky, intensifying the pathos of the few remaining patches of green – patches that glow luridly when struck by dabs of sunlight tearing through the dark, shifting clouds.

Las Canteras, a small group of traditional but unprettified Alpujarran houses stranded above the curve of a nearly dried-out river, is probably representative of what the region must have seemed like to nineteenth-century travellers.

We look for someone to direct us to the castle, and the one person whom we find on the street points to a craggy peak rising high above the other side of the river. I prepare myself for a long walk, but Harry has other plans. The solitary villager nods her shrivelled head, affirming that the track to the castle is accessible by car. 'A car like yours almost made it to the top a few years back, so they tell me.'

This time it is my turn to summon reason, but Harry will hear none of this, and is soon driving the car into the river, and cackling with laughter as we meander through the trickling water, skirting a bank of dense reeds in search of an opening. We finally climb on to the bank and bump and twist over stony ground until what we think of as the track turns into a scar slashed at a steep angle across the slope in front of us. Without a thought as to how on earth we are going to be able to turn the car around, Harry perseveres, Aguirre-like, uphill until we reach a point where he too concedes that the last part of the climb will have to be done on foot.

As we scramble to the very top, rocks become indistinguishable from ruins, and the landscape below us begins to resemble the infernal creation of some Gothick fantasist. The river has entered a deep gorge surrounding us on three sides before being swallowed up to the east by the ominous black mass of the Sierra de Gádor.

A rainbow, like a coda to this cataclysmic scene, hovers over the void, touching on the other side what seem to be the ruins of a further castle.

We identify the castle opposite as that of Escarientes, a place of enormous strategic importance dating back to the first days of the Islamic occupation and guarding the heart of the district Boabdil had secured for himself in a secret deal made with the Catholic Monarchs in November, 1491. The castle of Juliana, where we are standing now, marks the western limits of this district, but has fallen down entirely, or so Harry and I think until we come across, almost at the moment of our departure, a perfectly preserved barrel-vaulted structure which had once served as a water-container. Shepherds, using it as a hut, can be thanked for its near miraculous survival in this bleak and exposed spot.

The descent is as dangerous as I had imagined, and largely carried out in reverse gear, with my legs dangling out of the car's open back door, and my eyes continually gauging the distance between the wheels and the precipice. I am ready to jump off at any moment, and occasionally I give a loud shout.

Badly shaken, in more than the literal sense, we proceed at last to Yegen, having had an inkling of the Alpujarra that Brenan had originally known – a near roadless Alpujarra cut off both from the present and the rest of Andalucía, an Alpujarra in which Brenan, in his search for the village of his dreams, had covered vast distances on foot, slept in beds crawling with bugs, put up with a diet of eggs fried in rancid oil, and succumbed to terrible dysentery.

As we drive towards Yegen, Harry lapses into an uncharacteristic silence, leaving me to my thoughts on Brenan's first encounter with the Alpujarra, in the early 1920's.

Brenan had come here, as he had come to Spain itself, largely ignorant of its history and geography, and unaware of his romantic predecessors. Recently demobilized from the army, and with vague ambitions to be a poet, he was travelling through Spain on a global journey of self-discovery which he envisaged as ending up somewhere in the East. He had been attracted to the Alpujarra by its look of isolation on the map, and would later describe his arduous journey to get here as if he were some colonial explorer investigating reports of a lost world. Looking for a place in which to set up temporary home, he eventually picked on Yegen, a village of no especial beauty but with the appeal of its microcosmic situation in between the snows and greenery of the western Alpujarra and the barren slopes and eroded wastes of the eastern half. Here, with the aid of nearly two thousand books sent out to him from England, he embarked on the task of creating his own private world out of the lost one he had discovered.

Harry is pensive, he confesses, because memories are coming back to him of Yegen, a place where his own love affair with Spain had begun, five years ago. On holiday in Málaga, he had struck up a relationship with another Andalucían woman, and had moved in almost immediately with her. An innocent romantic impulse had led them to opt for a simple life together in Yegen, where they had found a cheap and primitive house for rent. They had not heard of Brenan before, but had had their fill of him, and of each other, after six turbulent months spent in the village. Harry had not been back since.

He is more and more nervous as we approach Yegen, towards the end of the afternoon. Will much have changed? Will his romantic memories be shattered? He feels somewhat relieved after he has parked the car at the top end of the village, and reassured himself that Yegen has remained the same friendly and unassuming place he remembers, with no outward sign of tourism. Only when we reach the small square in front of the fonda where we want to stay does he register a slight disappointment: the stagnant duck pond has been replaced by a fountain reproducing the one in the Courtyard of the Lions in the Alhambra. But his disappointment has an essentially academic basis: he does not mind the kitsch aberration in itself but the fact that it reproduces the monument prior to the recent restoration involving the removal of tiny columns supporting the basin.

The owner of the fonda identifies us as the advance guard of the Brenan party due to be fêted here tomorrow as the climax to the 'international conference' organized by Juan Antonio Díaz. He recognizes me from the summer, when a local newspaper, *El Ideal*, had photographed the participants of a 'Brenan commemorative walk' from Granada to Yegen. A broken foot had in fact prevented

me from taking part in this, but I had travelled by car to Yegen for
both the photograph and the accompanying festivities – a band greeting us at the entrance to the village, a long supper under a pergola,
and a meeting in the village hall at which some elderly inhabitants
had danced the paso doble below banners proclaiming the 'Cente-
nario Gerald Brenan'. 'What a wonderful man', 'so sensitive', 'aloof
but understanding', 'no one knew us better', 'so refined', were
some of the comments the villagers had uttered for the benefit of
outsiders such as ourselves.

Now Yegen is already into its winter hibernation, and, as Harry
and I descend after darkness into the lower half of the village,
there is no one in the streets to assail us with memories of Brenan.
In the one bar we find open, we sit surrounded by unfamiliar and
uninterested faces until the arrival, an hour or so later, of a slight
man whom I know to be the husband of the matronly and calmly-
spoken *concejal de cultura*.

He walks straight up to us, and slaps me on the shoulder, slur-
ring a drunken greeting. His 'spies' have told him that we arrived
at Yegen several hours back; his wife, he says, is very hurt that I didn't
go straight to see her. 'Never mind,' he bawls, slapping me again
and ordering some drinks.

By the time we leave the bar, he is so drunk that his speech is
almost impossible to follow. Muttering non-stop as he accompanies
us part of the way uphill to our fonda, he is endlessly stopping and
tapping me to make sure I'm listening.

'Ssssssshhhhh…' he whispers, hitting me harder than ever, and
breathing his alcoholic fumes right at me. 'Can't you hear the
silence?'

'Ssssssshhhhh…' he repeats. 'There's just the sounds of the
water, nothing more.'

'Ssssssshhhhh…' he goes on. 'There's water everywhere, a
symphony of different water sounds. Listen, over there, over here,
everywhere.'

'The Moors are responsible,' he claims further up the hill. 'They
channelled the streams, dug the pools, made the fountains.'

We are making a short-cut, balancing precariously on the sides
of a raised channel of rushing water on the outskirts of the village.

The sky has cleared, and a crescent moon lights our steps.
A quote from Lorca comes to his wine-reddened lips.
'The eternal song of water. Sssssshhhhh…'

It's a sunny November dawn, and a brilliant after-the-rain clarity has settled over a world which Brenan had first perceived as a paradise. A patchwork of the richest autumnal colours acts as foreground to a landscape that has been transformed into the fantasy of some naïve artist by a broad strip of sky-blue sea floating with its tiny ships above the Sierra de Contraviesa.

Harry and I are standing above the village studying this magical illusion when the bus carrying Juan Antonio and the remnants of his Brenan conference hoots its horn besides us. Soon we are all posing for a photograph in front of a signpost marking the village and listing its attractions. I speculate with Juan Antonio about what is meant by the village's 'morisco cuisine'. We relish with excitement the prospect of a 'sopa de moriscos'.

Before any eating can be done there is a ceremony in the village hall involving Juan Antonio presenting Yegen with a framed poster for the 'Simposio Internacional Gerald Brenan'. Apart from the concejal de cultura there are only two villagers present at this grand occasion – a couple of female school-teachers who mistake me for the locally renowned Lorca biographer Ian Gibson, and realize their mistake too late to prevent me from signing another copy of the Brenan poster.

Three long rows of tables have been laid out, optimistically, outside the Bar Discoteca, alongside ping-pong tables and chicken crates. We occupy only one of them, but are consumed with a gluttony that makes quick work of the delicious and rapidly piling up plates of locally prepared sausages, ham, black pudding and other porcine products that surely cannot fall into the category of 'morisco cuisine'.

At my end of the table, a discussion ensues about Brenan's

attitude towards food. The novelist Margaret Drabble fails to understand why some of the main criticisms in Brenan's Spanish books are directed towards food, especially that of the Alpujarra. The *concejal de cultura* takes a charitable view of the great Hispanist, whom she says was badly looked after by his notoriously mean Yegen housekeeper, who tried to save money for herself by preparing the cheapest meals for him. However, I argue that Brenan was hardly alone in his dislike of Spanish food, and that he was typical of the British middle classes, whose traditional inability to stomach either the food or the baroque architecture of Spain has greatly limited their understanding of this country.

Finding myself at an Alpujarran table with eminent middle-class British writers such as Drabble brings to mind Brenan's description of the 'incongruous and un-Spanish note' provided by the brief presence at Yegen of his Bloomsbury friends Lytton Strachey, Dora Carrington and Virginia Woolf. Yet Brenan himself was essentially little different from these compatriots of his – he too was an unmistakeable product of his social and intellectual British milieu, someone who believed ultimately in the cultural and culinary supremacy of the French, and who could conceive of love solely with the likes of Carrington, even though he was only able to overcome his habitual impotence through an affair with a local girl, Juliana.

My return to Yegen reinforces my view of Brenan as one of the long line of exiled dreamers who have been drawn to the Alpujarra since the time of Boabdil. Furthermore, after Juan Antonio and his group have left, and a winter silence and darkness have descended again on the village, my misgivings about Brenan's relationship with the villagers of Yegen are apparently confirmed.

Harry and I have returned to the Bar Discoteca, where we find a group of young men sneering at the day's festivities. They tell us about the hatred that Brenan had aroused in many of the elder members of the village, and about their own resentment at the amount of attention still given to him by the 'philistine' municipal authorities. They find it ironical that the concejal de cultura should devote so much money to the commemoration of Brenan while most other aspects of the village's culture, life and history are being shamelessly neglected.

'And what member of the community has benefited from today's lunch?' asks one of the men, Pablo, a mason who made his money in Andorra but recently returned to his home village to set up a co-operative dedicated to the restoration of old houses. He hates the idea of the village's old buildings and traditions being gradually abandoned.

But he is particularly upset by the municipality's treatment of his school-teacher wife, Rosita, who has repeatedly tried to have the village publish her historical novel on the moriscos of sixteenth-century Yegen.

'The book is called *Al-Akwat* after the Arabic word for water. It's so good that it came eighth in Seville's prestigious Guadalquivir literary prize.'

Early the next morning, when paying a diplomatic farewell visit to the concejal de cultura, the subject of Rosita and her historical novel comes up again, for the news has already spread about my night-time conversation in the Bar Discoteca. The concejal de cultura is on the defensive, and is anxious to leave us with an impression of Rosita as a likeable but sadly deluded person.

'She's completely obsessed by her novel, can't think of anything else. But what can we do about it? We haven't the funds to publish novels.'

I nod as if in agreement, and feel distinctly furtive and hypocritical when Harry and I later leave the house of the concejal de cultura and walk the hundred metres or so from here to the village school. We have arranged to meet Rosita and have a look at her novel. We have also been promised some 'extraordinary revelations' about the municipality's true attitude towards the village's past.

Rosita, lively and good-humoured, seems far from the neurotic obsessive we have been led to believe. Her problems, in her view, stem from her having been originally from another part of Spain. The villagers, she says, can never fully accept 'foreigners' among them. Brenan, I retort, appears to have done quite well out of his foreign status.

'But Brenan,' she insists, 'never really understood what was going on here.'

After joking about the petty squabbles and jealousies of village life, she presents me with her manuscript. A cursory glance reveals an impressive wealth of historical detail about sixteenth-century Yegen.

'Every name,' she proudly claims, 'is that of a real inhabitant of the time. I got all the names from contemporary documents.'

Her faces lights up when I ask her about the whereabouts of the local archive. She beckons us out into the street and into her car. Our movements are registered by the concejal de cultura, who appears to have lain in waiting outside the school.

Rosita drives us to her house in the upper village, where, closing the curtains, and speaking almost in a whisper, she brings out a numer of vellum-bound sixteenth-century documents.

'This is the archive,' she says, 'or rather what is left of it. A proper building to house the local library and archive was promised for years, but nothing ever came of this. Then, one day, my husband and I came across members of the village council throwing numerous books of local history on to a bonfire – nothing of Brenan, of course, only earlier and much rarer works. Afterwards, when Yegen's town hall was absorbed into that of Valor, we were naturally concerned about what would happen to our remaining archive records. We were assured that these would be safely kept at Valor, but when we went there one day to ask for them, no one could tell us where they were. Only after a considerable search did I find all these documents rotting in an attic. I smuggled them out for their safe-keeping.'

Pausing for a while as I skim through the brittle records, she reads my thoughts with a curt and caustic observation.

'What a strange village this is. We honour the memory of an English fantasist, and destroy our own past.'

There's the prospect of further ruins as we leave behind Brenan's place of exile and head towards that of Boabdil. Crossing from Granada into the bleaker Almería province, we are confronted to the south with the arid and now fully extended Sierra de Gádor, in front of which, on the northern side of the narrowing valley, cower the last of the Alpujarra's woods.

We stop for lunch next to the 'Source of the River Andarax', a popular beauty spot sheltering within the woods that cluster around the small town of Laujar. The brilliant sunshine breaks through the foliage to touch the falling water, conjuring up a momentary vision of cheerful summer picnics. But the inn where we eat is cold and empty, the trees have withered and gone yellow, and the drought-depleted water is barely sufficient to cover up the ugly concrete blocks that channel it.

Boabdil passed the first year and a half of his exile at Laujar, which would also be the capital of the rebel morisco kingdom founded by Aben Humaya. The chapter on Laujar in Antonio Gala's fictive memoirs of Boabdil (*El Manuscrito Carmesí*) concentrate on the bisexual monarch's grief at the death here of his wife Moraima. Little else can be said about Boabdil's stay at Laujar, other than that much of it was spent hunting, according to a report sent to the Catholic Monarchs by the royal secretary, Fernando de Zafra.

Described sometimes as 'the last Moorish kingdom in the Penin-sula', Laujar has a number of old monuments, though nothing directly associated with either Boabdil or the Moors in general. However, a palace claimed to be his is said to be found at the neighbouring village of Fuente de la Victoria, which was known in Islamic times as Cobdaa. Harry and I, trying to forget our experi-ences with Aben Humaya, decide to investigate.

For a good thirty minutes we encircle the rutted streets of this quiet, agricultural community, looking for a building which our increasingly fictitious guide-book refers to as the 'beautiful, well-preserved palace where the last king of Granada, Boabdil El Chico, was lodged during his short stay in this region'. The villagers are sleeping off their lunch, and the only buildings of any obvious age are a parish church of the late eighteenth century and a palace of comparable date and style featuring a tall tower, and brickwork which seems to have been devastated by shelling. Two boys whom we even-tually encounter confirm our worst suspicions about this latter structure. 'Yes,' they say, 'this is Boabdil's Palace.'

We peer through a hole in the broken main door, and glimpse at a small ruined courtyard crammed with pot-plants, tomato crates, egg boxes, plastic buckets, and other miscellaneous bits-and-pieces. We knock on an adjoining door, and are faced with a sturdy, no-nonsense woman. Did Boabdil really live here, we ask?

'El Rey Chico, you mean?' she responds. 'Well, they say he did, but I don't believe it for a minute. Just look at the courtyard. This is a modest place, as you can see. A Moorish king wouldn't have somewhere like this.'

We are convinced by her argument, and are relieved by her commonsense, but she stops us before we can prevent ourselves from wasting any more time in the village.

'But the Austrians were here,' she adds, referring to the Hapsburgs in the same matter-of-fact tone as if she were talking about the Perezes or the Garcías.

There seems little point in asking her why a building unfit for a Moorish king should be fit for a Hapsburg, but we now think it best to take a closer look at the place. She tells us to be careful when climbing the courtyard staircase.

It is difficult to tell whether the building has been charred by fire or made rotten by damp, or indeed whether it has suffered both these fates. The wooden banisters, or what is left of them are half falling off, and the beams of the ceiling stick out like the remains of a barbecued chicken. The floorboards creak, and the door of one of the upper rooms almost collapses as we push it open to reveal, we hope, some sign of an earlier, perhaps even Moorish structure. Instead there is a gaping hole through which we look down on to a store-room containing electrical equipment and giant speakers. The Palace of Boabdil, we now discover, adjoins the local discothèque.

The gentle sigh of Boabdil on leaving Granada seems to turn into a desolate shriek as it echoes across the ever more barren landscape of the eastern Alpujarra. We keep on driving until we reach the district's easternmost limit, where erosion crumbles every surface, and the architecture is reduced to stark, pastel-coloured cubes, covered sometimes in a vomit of patchwork mosaics.

At the busy small town of Alhama de Almería, we find the eponymous baths encased in the art deco Hotel San Nicolás. A marble Roman tub stands in isolation in the courtyard, but there is nothing from the Moorish period, when the waters were praised above all others in al-Andalus for their 'sweetness, purity, and curative properties'. The hotel has just changed management, and the new owner admits he knows nothing about the baths' history. His predecessor, he says, took with him all the documents.

The surroundings of Alhama are not so much steeped in history as strewn with it, uncaringly, as if the landscape were a rubbish dump. The largest neolithic site in Europe, an adjoining ironwork bridge, fragments of Moorish castles, futuristic solar installations, the reconstructed Wild West village of 'Mini-Hollywood' – all have been scattered haphazardly across a bleached wasteland.

We stay here a little longer to pay a final farewell to the memory of Boabdil, whose last days in Spain were spent at the coastal town of Adra. Harry is in one of his restless, reckless moods, and, losing patience with the asphalt road from Alhama, takes a direct route to Adra involving a maze of tracks leading across the Sierra de Gádor. After several wrong turns we succeed in dragging the car up to the platform of aerials at the mountain's summit. The sun has already set, and a deep red glow is shining over the huge sheets of plastic that serve as today's answer to the irrigation schemes of the Moors. This glow helps to guide us down to the Campo de Dalías, and to the now ageing plastic-covered fields that had signified briefly a new and exciting era in the agricultural history of eastern Andalucía. The neon lights of brothels, bars and gambling dens take over as we reach the road again, and drive through the unplanned urban sprawl that grew up in the boom years of 'plastic culture'. We spend the night in Adra.

The fictional Boabdil of Antonio Gala's imagination is unable to heave a sigh as his boat finally pulls out of Adra. I am not surprised. Had fifteenth-century Adra been anything like the tattily modern and slightly sinister town of today, I too would happily have embarked for Africa.

My bad memories of the town date back to the time when I had come here with a hot-blooded Sevillian friend and her unbalanced American partner, a former marine. Their respective temperaments had formed a potentially explosive mixture which had needed only the threatening atmosphere of a nocturnal Adra to ignite. I had left them drinking in the early hours of the morning, and had woken up shortly afterwards to be told by the manager of the hotel that I should be packing my bags as soon as possible, and that neither I nor my companions were welcome any longer in the town.

Eight years after that last visit I still have an irrational fear that someone will recognize me as the friend of that mad couple who smashed up their hotel room in a drunken lovers' quarrel, soon after telling the police that a murderous drug-addict had been chasing them around the streets. The hazy details of what had happened had been relayed to me not by the hotel manager but by a policeman who, during the long wait while my friends sobered up and settled the damage, had directed me to 'Boabdil's Castle'.

The almost non-existent ruins of this castle, flanked by a construction site and grey apartment blocks, had captured my bleak mood on that hung-over morning. I now return there with Harry after an uneventful night, and find there is no castle at all.

Boabdil has vanished from Adra, and I am not yet ready to search for him in Africa. Spain holds on to me through my clinging, masochistic longings for the Moorish Queen, to whom I feel a greater closeness once we leave behind the dust and sleaze of Adra and head back again towards the green, terraced slopes of the western Alpujarra.

By the late afternoon we have parked the car under the distant snows of Mulhacen. The air is exhilaratingly fresh, and the autumnal colours have acquired the unreal, exaggerated freshness of those of a calendar photo. Clusters of long white houses with flat slate roofs and flower-filled balconies sparkle and recede on the steep slopes behind us as we walk through thick grass towards some curious rock formations poised on a tongue of land above the deep gorge of the Trevelez. The site we are aiming for is known, mysteriously, as the Mezquita.

From what I have read I am not sure whether we are walking towards a 'natural fortress' or some genuinely Moorish ruins. My guide-book further confuses the issue by referring to the foundations of a temple dedicated to Minerva – the sole remains of a city which the Greeks are said to have founded while searching for precious minerals.

In the middle of the bushes through which we hack our way, is the serrated profile of an old brick wall which Harry is convinced is Moorish. But, emerging from the overgrown path at the foot of the rock-hewn citadel, there are further walls that turn out at close quarters to be those of abandoned farm buildings.

A young man who has followed our progress through the undergrowth is waiting for us at the top of the citadel to give his own explanation of this site.

He is solemn and slow of speech, and is holding a spiritual guide by the twelfth-century Murcian Sufi, Ibn 'Arabi.

'This is a Sufi hermitage,' he mutters, pausing for us to recover our breath and take in a sublime view in which the savagery of the rocky gorge is offset by the endlessly rolling patchwork of white villages, green fields, and yellowing to red elms and chestnuts that cover the lower slopes of the Sierra Nevada.

'A holy man,' he continues, 'recited from here prayers that would echo throughout the valley, and be taken up by other Sufis positioned in hermitages situated several kilometres away, like the ruined one you should just be able to make out directly in front of you, on the other side of the gorge.'

The stranger's choice of reading-matter, his unnaturally slow and serene manner, and his fanciful sense of history, make Harry and I immediately identify him as one of the many hippies who have settled in this part of the Alpujarra in recent years. However, he tells us that his family are farmers who have owned for generations the plot of land on which the Mezquita is standing. In fact, he has a strong dislike of hippies.

'They say they are spiritual and non-materialist, and yet they spend most of the time wondering how they can financially exploit others.'

When I ask him about the Venta de Los Castaños, an isolated

inn where we hope to spend the night, he implies that the place has been taken over by hippies, and warns us to be careful.

'I haven't been there for years, but I've heard it isn't what it used to be, it's been left to ruin. You'll find some strange people there.'

We arrive at the Venta de los Castaños after nightfall, after taking a long, unmarked drive leading off the road to Mecina-Fondales. There is a disturbing silence and lack of light, but as we nervously approach the door we notice a faint orange flicker between the cracks. A tentative push reveals a large, dark interior, lit only by a blazing fire and two candles placed on top of an old bar counter. An elderly couple, so much more welcoming than the owners we had been led to imagine, beckon us in from the cold.

The season is over, the electricity supply has been turned off, they weren't expecting mid-week visitors at this time of year, the 'most beautiful time of year'. They urge us to sit by the fire on frayed wooden seats that enhance the homeliness of the rustic interior. They ply us with pungent local cheeses, cold glasses of sharp-flavoured Alpujarran wine, and tough home-made sausages that are cooked in the flames. When the candles begin to fade, and the fire dies down, we are handed a small torch and extra blankets to carry up to a musty, freezing bedroom where the glow from the starlit sky penetrates the threadbare curtains.

A sense of spiritual well-being overcomes the physical discomforts of our stay, and seems almost to flood into our bedroom as we open the curtains early the next morning on to a blaze of chestnut trees gilded by the autumnal dawn.

Filled with an unexpected energy, we set off soon after sunrise into the Sierra Nevada, ascending into that world of dreams which has so often enveloped those who have been lured into the Alpujarra.

The Alpujarra is a region malleable to the fantasies of travellers, to some of whom it might appear as a hidden Islamic world, and to others as a lost Tibetan Valley. Islamic dreams give way to Buddhist ones as Harry and I, turning off on to a steep and winding track marked O.Sel.Ling, climb up almost to the last of the trees, towards a spiritual retreat founded in 1982 by Tibetan monks under instruction from the Dalai Lama himself.

Two parked landrovers with German and Swiss licence-plates mark the point from where we have to walk, taking in before doing so a request to visitors 'not to kill (not even the smallest insect), 'not to steal', 'not to lie', 'not to take drugs, alcohol, or cigarettes', and 'not to indulge in improper sexual conduct'. Harry stubs out his cigarette, accidentally killing an ant in the process. He shrugs his hands: we are, after all, only on the start of the road to salvation.

Higher up, a line of prayer flags flutters in the breeze, while a man with exposed chest mutters a Buddhist text as he slowly encircles a freshly painted shrine – an unmistakeable Tibetan gompa. Even without this whitewashed confection, with its tapering gold crown, and dado of coloured deities, the scene in front of us is almost how we imagine Tibet to be like. Ignoring a remote strip of sea to the west, we are left with a succession of mountain profiles rising above a mist of oriental delicacy. Turning round, and continuing to climb towards the gaunt, snow-capped peak of Mulhacen, we pass below simple flat-roofed stone huts that we might once have compared to the dwellings of the Atlas Mountains but that now only serve to heighten our Tibetan delusions.

The name O.Sel.Ling means 'The Place of the Clear Light', a name appropriate to the crispness of this autumnal morning if not to my present state of mind. My exact plans for the coming days, let alone for my future, are far from clear. I look towards Mulhacen in search of inspiration, and am soon devising schemes that throw at least the day ahead into a sharp and exciting relief.

'We're fucking mad, but what the hell,' says Harry, who's been similarly affected by the rarefied air and the sight of the snow-capped peak ahead of us.

We say a prayer for the car and for ourselves, drive all the way to the bottom of the track, and then climb up again on a parallel road, following this time the sharply falling mountain stream which links the showcase villages of Poqueira, Bubión and Capileira with the snows of the Sierra Nevada. At Capileira, the highest of these tourist-loved villages, I stop to phone the Moorish Queen.

'I'm coming with you to Morocco,' she says, making one of my most far-fetched fantasies come true, and saving me from bidding her a dramatic final farewell prior to the near suicidal next stage of my journey with Harry.

She's going to pack her bags immediately, there's no need for us to pick her up in the centre of Granada, she'll meet us at lunch-time at the Venta Bienvenido, a favourite place of mine at Monachil, on the northern slopes of the Sierra. We'll go straight on from there, we'll talk more later, the coins are running out, and she's got to get ready.

I haven't told her how we intend getting to Monachil.

'It's the sort of impetuous lunacy she might appreciate,' says Harry, worried by the sudden way I've put a renewed value on both my life and her car, 'In any case, there's no turning back now.'

Ignoring a sign reading 'Pass ahead closed', we continue climbing up the road from Capileira, one of the highest roads in Europe. We have chosen the direct route out of the Alpujarra – a route which climbs nearly to the summit of Mulhacen and is generally open for only three months of the year. It has snowed little this year, we try and convince ourselves, and much of what has fallen has surely been melted by the recent sunshine.

The asphalt comes to an end six kilometres outside the village, at the entrance to a dark forest. There's a 'No Entry' sign and a warning that the road ahead is dangerous, unasphalted, and only suitable for landrovers. We keep on driving.

The inevitable happens a short distance further on, after we have emerged above the tree level: a barrier has been placed across the road, thus presenting our adolescent, foolhardy scheme with what appears to be an insurmountable impediment. An unconfessed relief tempers my profound disappointment.

But Harry remains unperturbed, and, on the dubious grounds that the barrier is unlocked, feels entirely justified in driving around it.

The need to be at Monachil by lunchtime, the thrill of the ever more sensational views, and the special opportunity of driving across the Sierra Nevada under the most perfect of atmospheric conditions, soon outweigh all my concerns about the legality and wisdom of what we are doing.

The hesitations return only after we have reached the point nearest to the summit of Mulhacen. From here the road turns towards the rival peak of La Veleta, to which it curves its way along the contours of the range, keeping only a short distance from the ridge. Narrow, roughly surfaced, and with nothing to protect you from the sheer drop below, this is never a road for those fearful of heights. But sprinkled as it is now with a light covering of snow and ice, the road becomes truly sublime in the sense that its beauty becomes tinged with a very real terror.

Our main fear up to now has been to have our car break down completely in this inhospitable spot where we've no right to be. But a sudden slip taking us to within inches of the drop gives a more tangible and urgent form to our worries. Harry lights up his fifth cigarette while I try and enjoy as best I can a view that now embraces the whole of the Alpujarra and the sea beyond. Eventually, as the snow deepens, and the threat increases of having to continue on foot, we reach the pass. Harry permits himself a short stop and an exasperated cry of 'Fucking hell!' His hands are trembling.

The snow thickens on the northern side, but the views down to Granada and the vega eradicate the more sinister memories of the last stretch, and cheer us up with the prospect of a speedy arival at Monachil. Such is our new confidence that when we near the well-graded modern road leading to the ski resorts, we reject this in favour of the track used by the Moors for carrying snow down on the panniers of donkeys.

This route is still known as that of 'the snow porters'. Its steepness, and my newly acquired awareness of the dangers of the Sierra Morena climb, make me now understand why the snow that actually reached the market-place in Granada was so expensive. And as I settle into these historical thoughts, I think of the pleasure that snow-cooled drinks are said to have given Boabdil on a hot summer's day. For Nicolás Menardes, the Sevillian author of a sixteenth-century treatise 'on snow and ices', this pleasure was so great as to be 'beyond any estimable price or intellectual explanation'.

I have so often thought of the Sierra in terms of the lofty inspiration it has given to poets and mystics that I am glad now to be reminded of the more practical use to which its snowy mantle has been put. As our car pulls up outside the wonderful Venta

Bienvenido, on the Sierra's built-up lower slopes, I find a comparable bathos in the contrast between the spiritual heights of O.Sel.Ling and the gastronomic pleasures promised by the inn.

The Moorish Queen appears and embraces me in a way which melts the ice that has begun to form in my middle-aged heart. The young wine from Huetor-Vega arrives, as does a welcoming dish of the Venta's smoothly textured and richly spiced black pudding. The eponymous Bienvenido, knowing of my passion for this dish, tells me that the pig has just been killed; a joke is made about the blood going directly from one pig to another. We sit outside, and talk excitedly in this restaurant whose charms are so difficult to convey to the English middle classes, who hate black pudding and expect a country inn to be a simple, quaintly wooden and beautifully situated place rather than somewhere which seems every year larger, plusher, more unpicturesquely modern, and ever more entangled in Granada's expanding suburbs.

By the time I start sipping a local sloeberry liquor distilled by the Navarrese parish priest, my previous thoughts on the antithesis between the physical and spiritual domains have been called into the question. Contemplating my present happiness, I wonder about the respective roles played in this by the drink, the food, the relief on having brought the car back in one piece, my love for the Moorish Queen, and my similarly inexplicable passion for the Venta Bienvenido.

Harry, equally elated, has had a telephone reconciliation with Carmela, and is on the point of rushing off by taxi to see her. The Moorish Queen is looking at her watch and telling me that we've a long journey ahead of us.

Bienvenido loads our car with sausages, wine and bottles of liquor. Is this a suitable state, I wonder, in which to be rejoining the Moors on their road to exile?

The car is given a farewell push, the Moorish Queen turns on the ignition. We head off east.

que hico dios con Abinacer Altamari y Respondio
esta mas alto que yo consetenta grados dijuronte
ques lacausa y entendimos que tuebicia mas
alto quel dixo alcanco esto por lapaciencia quelu
bo consus hijos y mujer y en Resulucion
quelcasarsse es Una cosa quese hace enlacon
formidad de sucostumbre yasimesmo por
lasarca pues lomando dios en muchas ayas
carimas debusagrado Curan desdecipiina
pio delmundo ycomo lomando quiso que
Secunpliesse concuy acausa Seaciecienta
elmundo yqueasi quedase hasta latin del
y Secunple Sudibino querer conelcasarsse yasi
mesmo lodixo cala Allah u çalan guacatan

تناكحوا تناسلوا فاني مكاتر بكم الامم يوم القيامة

como Sidijera casaos y haced Jeneracion porque
Yoacueciento con bosohos las Jentes eldia deluycio
yasimesmo quecon hacerlo y teniendocueçcion
queda sunombre bibo y Se leacueçienmn ابو

CHAPTER FOUR

ᴀ ʟᴀʙʏʀɪɴᴛʜ ᴏꜰ ᴄᴀᴠᴇꜱ

The route we're following has now been officially designated that of Leo Africanus. I'm beginning to think we're on the road to nowhere.

The future author of *The Description of Africa* left Granada shortly after its capture by the Christians. The year of his birth is not known, but he was probably little more than three or four years old when he set off with his family to their exile in Fez. The novelist Amin Maalouf imagines them sailing to Morocco from Almería, to where they would probably have travelled along the ancient route that skirts the Alpujarra to the north – the route that had once been called 'The Royal Route'.

Thanks to my pedantic insistence on following in the presumed footsteps of Leo Africanus right from the outskirts of Granada, we have rejected a dual carriageway in favour of the 'old road' to Almería – a road which has proved so old that a large section has been blocked off for reconstruction, thus diverting us on to a succession of forest tracks, and leading us to our present dilemma of not knowing where we are other than that we are in the middle of a large and dark forest.

This is just like the old days, I want to tell her, recalling not the times of Leo Africanus, but the happy weeks at the height of our affair, when we had driven meanderingly to every corner of eastern Andalucía. But she is not laughing at my navigational incompetence like she would once have done. She bears openly the scars of her recent break-up with the Usurper, she has become impatient, distracted, irritable. I decide not to remind her of our past, and talk only of that other past, the Islamic past, the past which has become absurdly, dangerously entwined with my present life.

In front of us, where the forest begins to peter out, the ruins of a hilltop Moorish castle come to my assistance. By luck we've managed to reach the right road, and are nearing the once busy but now little-visited village of La Peza.

I relay to the Moorish Queen glittering details of the village's past – its military importance during the Islamic period; the visit of Cervantes; the wooden cannons with which the cunning locals caused Napoleon the first setback in his military career. I am merely repeating what a native of La Peza had told me during a drunken evening in Granada. He was shocked that I had never been to his village, 'one of the greatest places on the Royal Route'.

La Peza is undeniably beautiful, so much so that I want to verify what I have heard about its past. The afternoon siesta is still continuing, the library is open only in the mornings, and the parish priest is not at home. I am forced to put my questions to a group of builders enjoying an after-lunch cognac in one of the bars. They display a strong if unruly love for local history, and talk about the past as if they were exchanging gossip about present-day events.

'The immortal Cervantes? Here in La Peza? What joker told you that?'

'Surely you mean that Flemish chap, Münzer,' says someone else. 'Hieronymus Münzer. He was here, in 1499, on his way to Murcia with that diplomatic mission.'

'Then of course there's that famous short story by Alarcón about the cannons,' adds another.

They flit from topic to topic, eventually settling on the Moorish period, when the church was a mosque and the public fountain in front of it a bath house. To round off this conversation one of them accompanies us up to the impressive ruins of the eleventh-century castle, from where we have a view to the east of a landscape pitted with caves and troglodytic dwellings.

'That's where the Moors ended up,' he says, 'the ones, I mean, who wanted to stay and keep their religion. Some of them are still there now; they're easily confused with the gypsies.'

The Moorish Queen is shaking her head once we're back again inside the car. 'You're amazing, you know. I can't understand how you put up with such idiotic people.'

We drive towards the strange, surrealistic landscape to the east, where the remains of lush-green fields and orchards have found their final refuge besides the banks of a weary, shrivelled river.

'Perhaps the man wasn't such an idiot after all,' I am thinking as we arrive at the small thermal resort of Graena, which is situated below a barren cliff blighted by erosion. A group of dark-skinned women, emerging from behind a Moorish arch, are walking towards us, covered in exotic headgear.

My oriental delusions are such that I am convinced at first that these women are Moors rather than a group of elderly patients with towels wrapped around their heads. The reality sinks in once we reach the bath-house, with its neo-Moorish portal of the 1920's and its shabby, grey-tiled interior. There are more old people inside, some drifting around in bath-robes, others sweating it out in a dingy sauna which a young assistant mysteriously insists on showing us.

'The waters are good for rheumatism and old age spots,' he claims, before hunting out for us an article on the baths which had appeared in a local magazine with the arabic name *Wadi-As*.

I read about Bronze Age and Roman finds, about the use of the waters by the Moors, and about the regulations drafted during the rule of the Catholic Monarchs so as to prevent the 'dishonest practices' resulting from the sight of Moorish women bathing in full public view. But the healthy properties of the waters are strongly denied by an anonymous poem bemoaning the place's unbearably dry surroundings and dangerous climate of extremes. So many ill people have come here and died, concludes the author, that the local cemetery is constantly being enlarged.

Caves, like ancient burial chambers, pepper the landscape beyond the narrow green strip in which the modern spa is sheltered. Münzer, during his famous journey of 1499, described the Moors bathing inside the cave from where the thermal spring itself once issued. Neighbouring caves served as the patients' lodgings, supplemented by an adjoining inn, the scant ruins of which include a Latin inscription that reinforces the overall resemblance of the landscape to some neglected necropolis.

When I ask about Moorish ruins, I am told only about the caves, 'where the Moors lived'. It is to find out more about these caves that we leave the spa and drive the four kilometres up to the actual village of Graena, where there lives, I have heard, a Belgian archaeologist who is obsessed by the caves and might well guide us into one of them.

The prospect of entering this great labyrinth of caves that seems to extend all the way from Granada's Sacromonte to the eastern boundaries of the Nasrid kingdom reminds me of the concluding section of Potocki's maze-like and amazing novel, *The Manuscript Found at Saragossa*, in which the hundreds of threads in this tale of tales within further tales all lead at the end to the tale of the Great Sheikh of Gomelez, the morisco leader of a gold-enriched underground domain which has been preparing since the sixteenth century for the eventual reclamation of Spain by Islam. A tale, in short, which takes the romantic traveller's Moorish delusions to their ultimate conclusion.

Other Moorish mysteries, perhaps, are to be revealed to us in the caves around Graena, if only we can find the Belgian archaeologist whose name, we now discover, is Maryelle Bertrand. We have found our way to her home, but she is not there, no one knows where she might be, she keeps to herself, has no real friends in the village, lives alone. She fell in love with the landscape fifteen years ago, bought a house here, has devoted herself single-mindedly to the study of the caves. Nothing else is known about her.

The mystery of Maryelle Bertrand remains unresolved. She is probably away on a conference. Our final enquiries have taken us into the town hall, where a couple of helpful employees make futile attempts to contact her, before giving us photocopies of some of her writings.

I learn from these that the cave dwellings of this part of Granada province – the province with the highest number of such dwellings in Europe – are known specifically as 'Moorish Caves' or '*Covarrones*'. Displaying clear evidence of medieval occupancy, and carved out of the soft rock with pickaxes, they are characterized as much by their strong defensive character as by the variety of uses to which they were put – they served variously and at times simultaneously as watch-towers, hiding-places, full-time residences, granaries, stables, dovecots, and so on. Those of the elaborate medieval complexes that survived erosion were inhabited right up till the end of the eighteenth century, the place of the departing moriscos being taken eventually by the poorest families of the district.

The young mayor appears as I am sitting with the Moorish Queen looking at Maryelle's articles. He agrees with his assistants, it's important we should visit the caves in the company of someone who knows them well, otherwise we might fall through a hole, get trapped, end up like one of the Moorish skeletons that are periodically found in them. In the absence of Maryelle he proposes as a replacement guide a friend of his called Pepe.

We wait for Pepe in the village bar, the owner of which happens to be the mayor – it is one of those villages. On the wall is an old photograph of an attractive sixteenth-century palace that once stood on the site. The feudal lord, the Marquis of Peñaflor, had left the palace to the municipality shortly after selling off the local baths and taking their archives with him to Madrid. The municipality later responded by pulling down his palace. I wonder how they could have destroyed such a beautiful structure, and so recently as well.

'That was before my time,' the mayor defensively says. 'They used to do those things then.'

Pepe, a plump, red-cheeked man with a Figaro-like moustache, comes into the bar to be told by the mayor that he should accompany us immediately to the cave known by the homely name of 'Tía Micaela'.

Pepe nods his head, and comes with us to our car, which he promptly rejects in favour of his own. We drive off fast in an easterly direction, roller-coastering below eroded outcrops that culminate in the far distance with a serrated row of what appear to be giant ant-heaps jutting above the townships of Purullena and Guadix.

We pull up in a cloud of dust at the hamlet of Cortes, where the seventeenth-century tower of the parish church incorporates the distinctive brickwork of the former mosque. The hamlet merges into its eroded surroundings, its houses being mainly built into the rock, and its one, stony street ending in a pile of discarded stoves and other rusted objects that complement the tattered rocky backcloth behind.

The modern cave dwellings have whitewashed frontages and quaint, conical chimneys that push their way through the tufa. Above them, like the scars of an abandoned quarry, are gaping holes belonging to what Pepe describes as 'Moorish Caves'.

'But we're not going there,' he adds, before putting the car once more into gear, and heading off onto a small track which trails down into cultivated fields. He is driving as if in a car chase, and when he makes at least a couple of mistakes rectifies these with abrupt three-point turns that cut deep grooves into the ploughed land.

'You know,' he confesses, 'I've lived all my life in Graena and I've never been on any of these tracks, let alone inside the cave where I'm supposed to be guiding you. This is all quite an adventure.'

At the end of the fields we climb up to a narrow irrigation channel which echoes the contour lines of the crumbling, near vertical slope into which the Cave of Tía Micaela has been hollowed. The car can go no further, and we have to proceed on foot, with Pepe cheerily leading the way, his middle-aged girth belied by a youthful agility and enthusiasm. The Moorish Queen follows close behind, while I struggle a long way down, slipping continually, and lacerating my hands on the thistles that I grab on to while trying to break my falls.

More acrobatics are needed inside the cave, which we enter through a narrow hole that Pepe later reckons to have been the chimney. We ease our way down a sandy chute to a compact lower level illuminated by a small opening and containing what had probably been the sleeping quarters of the dwelling. We tread warily, forewarned by Pepe of the frequently collapsing floors of these multi-level dwellings.

I feel like a burrowing rabit as we bend our backs and descend a rock-hewn tunnel towards the faint, golden glow emanating from the dwelling's lowest and largest level. This floor extends in different directions deep into the rock, and Pepe is confidently able to ascribe which of the respective sections was reserved for humans, livestock and wheat. When I almost fulfil the mayor's prediction of falling into a large hole, he tells me that this must have been the place where the skeleton of a Moorish farmer was found several years back. The bones had been carbon-dated to the eleventh century.

'There's been talk of opening up this cave to tourism, perhaps even turning it into a museum of everyday life during the Islamic period,' he tells us, as we stand at its main entrance, contemplating the sheer descent that now faces us. 'But just think of the problems of access!'

We look down at the distant irrigation canal, which, from above, loops through the inhospitable landscape like a text-book example of engineering.

'To think that's been there since the times when the Moors lived in this cave,' Pepe reflects. 'Why, we even call it by its Moorish name.'

We scramble down to the car, and return to Graena by a different route, enabling Pepe to show us to a fountain which has been pumping water from the Sierra Nevada for 'nearly ten centuries'.

'The best water in the world!' exclaims Pepe as we take it in turns to place our mouths against the ice-cold jet, imagining the pleasure of doing so on a parched summer's day.

'And now for the wine,' he adds.

But the Moorish Queen shakes her head, it's getting late, we've got to be going, it's well past five o'clock, we've only an hour or so left of sunlight.

I'm tempted briefly by the wine, I'm about to suggest we should stay the night in Graena, we're in no real hurry, she's left her job, the whole future stretches ahead of us, a day or two more here, a day or two less there. It doesn't really matter.

But I too am overcome by an irrational impatience, a desire to move on for the sake of it, a hidden hope that the journey will never end, a fear perhaps of the time when the Moorish Queen and I will seriously have to confront our emotions, the ambiguous reality of our situation. The constant worry that the past can never be revived.

In any case I have in mind a place for the night more extraordinary than any mirador under the Alhambra.

Back at Graena, we say a quick farewell to Pepe, and drive off even quicker, as quickly as our car – surely in its last days – will allow.

We drive without stopping through Guadix, with its surrealistic cave district bristling with tufa pinnacles and Gaudí-like chimneys, and its atmosphere that Brenan had found unmistakeably

'Oriental', 'harsh and sordid'. But we continue to avoid the dual carriageway, and to follow instead the route into exile of Leo Africanus.

The road, by now as straight as a runway, rushes us through the flat, mine-scarred expanse in between the forested slopes of the Sierra Nevada and the wrinkled, mountainous desolation to the north. We are in the fiefdom of the Marquises of Zenete, whose former castle at La Calahorra looks from the road like a sturdy childhood toy which has been dropped on top of a slag-heap. Resisting the temptations of the castle's Renaissance interior, we keep on driving, deviating only momentarily to look for some Moorish ruins.

The district is meant to be rich in the remains of Moorish baths, but their existence is denied by the villagers of Ferreira, who suggest we go on to the neighbouring Huenaja, where there is a street promisingly named the Calle del Agua. There we hear of some ruined baths in the house of 'Tía Antonia', but the key to these is missing, and the view through the keyhole merely reveals a tiny cellar crammed up to its barrel-vault with farming implements and hay.

At the ugly small town of Fiñana we uncover at last an exquisite jewel of the Nasrid period within a modest and otherwise unremarkable roadside chapel – the altar has replaced a mihrab, whose filigree stucco panels have survived in all their decorative complexity.

But the rapidly failing light speeds us on, increasing my desire to reach before it is too late the place where I have fantasized celebrating my nocturnal reunion with the Moorish Queen.

We branch away from the road to exile, and drive north to a half-forgotten corner of Granada which projects like a long tongue into the provinces of Jaén, Albacete, Murcia and Almería. The landscape becomes progressively lunar in more than one sense, for, over the whitening rugged terrain, rises the timid outline of a crescent moon. The sun disappears into a reddish-purple glow that settles on the Jabalcón, a European Ayers Rock, ever-changing in its colours, a fluorescent beacon in the near desert beyond Baza.

At an isolated thermal pool near the abandoned spa of Zújar, a group of bathing women are faintly illuminated by lingering traces of red sky that turn the clouds of steam into phantasmal flames. Beyond the pool is a dried-out reservoir, and beyond that, hidden in the growing darkness, is a landscape which the Portuguese writer José Saramago considered less a landscape ('a delightful word') than an 'infernal abode'.

In Saramago's humorously apocalyptic novel, *The Stone Raft*, the whole of the Iberian peninsula becomes detached from the rest of Europe and floats out into the Atlantic – a catastrophe that has been sensed by a solitary, psychic old man who works as a pharmacist in the heart of this landscape which is not a landscape. A landscape that manages to suggest both the end and the beginning of the world.

We drive across this empty quarter in the emptiness of the night until we see the reassuring lights of Galera.

Miguel Rodríguez Gómez, historian of Galera and local entrepreneur, has little in common with Saramago's pharmacist. He is a middle-aged family man who plays the trumpet in the local band and lives in a house which surprises me by its cheery ordinariness, so unexpected in these cataclysmic surroundings.

But he too, in his own way, is a man of vision, putting Galera on the tourist map through his ambitious plans for the multitude of cave dwellings that encircle the village like the seating of a ruined amphitheatre. While the archaeologists of today are busily unearthing important vestiges of the prehistoric and ancient past in Galera's pock-marked cliffs, Miguel is posing problems for archaeologists of the future by converting the more recently vacated caves into luxury holiday homes for tourists.

The Moorish Queen and I shall be the only tourists staying there tonight, he says while instructing us to follow his car. We get out near the top of the cliff and are given a whole range of caves from which to choose. 'All of them different, no uniformity here,' he insists.

'The word "cave" is not synonymous with "slum" as some people in England like to think,' wrote an English visitor to Guadix in 1963. 'There are poor people and better-off people and some quite well-to-do people living in troglodyte colonies just as in any of our council estates.' I wonder what this writer, Penelope Chetwode, would make of Miguel's luxury caves, which 'provide the latest of modern comforts within a traditional rural interior'.

The cave we opt for has tasteful wooden furnishings, a ceramic tiled floor, a large brick fireplace, and the odd plough artfully arranged against the whitewashed walls so as to reinforce the rural element.

'A good choice,' says Miguel, who mentions that a German painter had stayed here in the summer. She had heard about Miguel's caves in Berlin ('the Germans love them'), and had rushed to Galera all the way by taxi from Granada. Galera and its surroundings had proved as enchanting as she had imagined, 'like a painting by Dalí'. She had not wanted to leave; the cave had been 'the home of her dreams'.

Miguel wishes us 'happy dreams', as he hands over the keys, together with a complimentary bottle of local wine and a packet of special biscuits, 'a local speciality'.

I light the fire. Mysteriously this is always a man's job, like lighting a barbecue, some throw-back perhaps to our cave-living ancestors. 'We are in a cave,' the Moorish Queen reminds me, as she warms herself by the nascent fire, a glass of wine in her hand.

The conversation is stilted. I'm realizing a dream but this is not how I've dreamt it. Primeval instincts are being held in check. There are too many uncertainties between us; too much which ought to be said if only we had the courage to say it. The wine is harsh, almost undrinkeable, but we manage to finish off the whole bottle, slowly, squirmingly, as if sipping acid in some dual suicide pact.

The Moorish Queen is the first to break the morbid inactivity, at around two in the morning. She goes off to have a shower, and emerges wrapped in a white towel, looking more Moorish than ever.

I follow her into the womb of the cave, where a double bed covered in sheepskins occupies most of a low chamber, flooded in a lurid orange light such as you might expect in a night club or a brothel. She lights some candles, turns off the electricity, drops the towel. She lies face downwards on the pillow, waiting.

♣

For the past few weeks I have been dipping into a book called *A Spanish Kama Sutra*. 'This is not a pornographic book you've laid your hands on,' warns the editor, Luce López-Baralt, in an opening *caveat* intended to dissuade the sort of reader who might be expecting a different use of the hands in the course of perusing a work with this title. Instead it is a lengthy and very scholarly edition of the first sexual treatise in the Spanish language. I am reading it, of course, purely in the interests of my researches – my researches into Spain's Islamic past.

In my desire to attain a greater closeness to this past, I have begun to explore Moorish attitudes towards the most intimate of human activities. The book to which I have turned reveals for me more about morisco life in sixteenth-century Spain, and its cultural complexities, than most works of social history. Penned during the anonymous author's exile in Tunisia, it forms part of a much larger manuscript expressing the heart-rending dilemma of a morisco torn between the Islamic culture that was denied him in his native Spain and the Spanish culture which maintains a nostalgic hold over him now that he is in Africa. It is written in Spanish, but with the odd lines in Arabic and a sentence structure more Arabic than Spanish: it is no less hybrid a product than those Spanish texts in Arabic script that go under the name of *aljamiado* literature.

Its hybrid nature is reflected also in its contents. *El refugiado de Tunez*, as the author is sometimes known, shows in his work a love of Spanish Golden Age literature: he can recite by heart the poetry of Lope de Vega, Garcilaso and Góngora, and he might sometimes turn to their verses when reflecting on an aspect of sexuality such as jealousy. But he is also steeped in the rich erotic literature of Islam – Nefzawi's *The Perfumed Garden*, and the writings of Asbagh, al-Ghazali and, above all, Ahmad Zarruq. His guiltless approach to sexuality is profoundly Islamic, as are his mingling of the practical and the spiritual, his insistence that women too should lead a full sexual life, and his belief in sexual bliss as a prelude to paradise. Whereas Christian writings on sexuality lay a strong emphasis on chastity, Islamic ones view sexuality as a Quranic obligation. Thus the Tunis Exile puts down in Spanish what could never have been written by a Spaniard of his day: Sex leads to God.

'More soap!' the Moorish Queen is groaning as my quest for guilt-less, God-finding sexual satisfaction battles with a Catholic conscience and a northern upbringing.

She herself has no such complexes, is truly Moorish, which is why she is lying on her front wholeheartedly indulging my fantasy that we are together in a Moorish bath and that I am a strong-limbed black masseur who is slowly soaping and caressing every part of her body, gradually working up to that rousing moment when I am ready to follow the edicts of the Tunis Exile and shout out *bicmi ylahi* ('in the name of God') at the very moment of penetration.

The groaning suddenly stops, she pulls up the sheets. She has been worn out after over half an hour of unproductive foreplay.

I mumble some excuses, I have devoted myself recently too much to the theory and not to the practice, the barrenness of the landscape has finally got to me, I have been blighted by the curse of Brenan – the curse which the discoverer of the Alpujarra has put on all those Hispanists who follow too closely in his footsteps.

'It does not matter,' she murmurs. 'I'm almost grateful in a way.'

I try to snuggle up close to her in the bed, and express some consoling thoughts about the cosiness of being alone together deep inside a cave, far from the rest of world. But she pushes me away. Her eyes are red with tears. 'It does not matter, it does not matter.'

She is shaking off a nightmare when we wake up. The Usurper has been pummelling her in a jealous fit, that's all she'll tell me, for the moment. She retreats into silence, packs her clothes, I wait outside, nervously.

It's only ten o'clock, but the light is already so dazzling that my cave-accustomed eyes need several minutes to adjust to it. When I'm finally able to look directly at the landscape, I begin to imagine the summer conditions, and wonder what Miguel's cave-dwelling tourists manage to do with themselves during their daylight hours.

The magical amphitheatre of caves has become a gigantic dust bowl ringed in the far distance by unwelcoming peaks. 'Soaked in the blood of Moors and Christians' was how Saramago had perceived this environment – a phrase expressive of its nightmarish quality if not wholly appropriate to somewhere so dessicated that it is difficult to think of it as being soaked in anything.

Perhaps there is indeed some truth in the romantic view of this landscape as the consequence of Christian bitterness and hostility. Turning to some historical notes with which Miguel has supplied me, I read about the particular violence with which the Christians suppressed the Galera moriscos who took part in the rebellion of 1570. Don Juan of Austria, furious at losing over 400 of his men in his first attempts to capture the morisco-held town, killed over 2,000 moriscos when he eventually took the place. He spared not a single life, razed every building, and devastated and sowed with salt surroundings that had been praised, first by the ninth-century geographer al-Jacubi and later by the great Ibn al-Khatib, for their meadows, fertility and abundance of water.

The Moorish Queen quietly takes my arm, and places a finger to her lips when I start to speak. We drive into the village for our silent breakfast. There is a dispenser for condensed milk next to the coffee machine.

We are at the eastern extremity of Andalucía, and have already crossed that mysterious frontier separating those Spaniards who prefer their coffee with ordinary milk from those who take it with condensed milk – a legacy of post-war rationing. In the nearby province of Murcia a popular breakfast drink combines coffee, condensed milk and cognac. It is called a Belmonte.

The owner of the bar looks perplexed when I ask him for one. 'Ah!' he finally exclaims after I've described to him the ingredients. 'You mean a Trivásico.'

A single Trivásico proves insufficient to my present needs, and I ask for another one once we have left Galera and entered a bar at the neighbouring town of Huéscar.

'Ah!' says the new barman after I am forced into another

explanation. 'You mean a Belmonte.'

A large and flowing art nouveau façade, a rarity for Andalucía, adjoins the bar and reinforces the fact that we are in an indeterminate border zone between the kingdom of Granada and the Levant – an area which had repeatedly changed hands between the Moors and the Christians.

Huéscar, together with Galera and Orce, were seized from the Moors in 1241 by the Master of the Order of Santiago, Don Rodrigo Iñíguez. He fortified these places heavily so as to form a defensive barrier against the nascent Nasrid kingdom; the Nasrids, under Ismail I, won them back in 1319. Huéscar became the Nasrids' easternmost stronghold, and as such was subject to constant Christian forays led by knights of the Order of Santiago. In 1347 the town was visited by Ibn al-Khatib while accompanying Yusuf I on a tour of inspection of the Nasrids' eastern defences. He found a place whose inhabitants had become so used to constant danger that they 'were prepared for any fate that God had in mind for them'. The definitive Christian capture of the town took place in 1488.

I sit with the Moorish Queen listening to an organ recital in a Renaissance parish church expressive of the spirit of the Christian conquest – a massive structure, gothic in proportions but classical in its detailing, based on the cathedral of Granada. She places a hand on my knee in a gesture of reconciliation.

Our mood is further lightened on our way back to the car when we pass a plaque recording the signing in 1981 of a peace treaty marking the end of a 172-year old war between Huéscar and Denmark. We smile at this historical anomaly of Napoleonic origin which has recently led to the twinning of Huéscar with a town we picture as its geographical and architectural antithesis – the Danish town of Kölding.

When we drive out to the famed Moorish beauty spot of Fuencalientes, we detect a certain Danish influence in the modern transformation of this ancient thermal pool: the addition of a blandly geometrical framework of modernist masonry and anachronistic grass verges has given it the wholesome, Scandinavian look of what could either be a leisure centre or a spanking new sewage farm. But this nordic element vanishes entirely in an adjoining old mill, which languishes parched and in ruins above a landscape pining for green.

The renewed tenderness shown towards me by the Moorish Queen is unlikely to last, but it makes me briefly ignore a sense of foreboding as strong as the fatalism that Ibn al-Khatib had encountered among the inhabitants of Huéscar. I feel once again like a young and happy lover, and try to capture this moment by using my camera's automatic shutter to take a photograph of the two of us embraced among the ruins. A flashing light and rapidly faster beep warn us to finalize our pose; but nothing happens. I remove the batteries, warm them with my hands, try again, but there's nothing doing. The Moorish Queen teaches me a new Spanish expression.

'You're wanking a dead man.'

She tugs my beard with a playful smile edged with pity.

'Where now?' she asks.

'Where God wills.'

She makes God's decision for Him, and drives north towards Puebla de Don Fadrique. We are driving almost for the sake of it, or at least for the sake of driving to the furthest corner of the remotest part of Granada.

Puebla is like a smaller and emptier version of Huéscar, a fragment of a dying, provincial Spain that has been preserved like a stage set. But the landscape is mountainous and green, and, as we turn west towards the Sierra Sagra, we enter a wild verdant territory containing in its midst a refreshing fragment of the New World – a grove of sequoias planted early this century by a visionary landowner who had made his fortune in America.

We lie under their shade, like sepulchral figures, the Moorish Queen holding my hand distractedly. I break the formality of the situation by leaning over to smile into her eyes, we roll over towards each other in the thick grass, laugh for a few moments, fall back into silence.

We are driving in circles, we should be heading east, into Murcia for a few days, then rejoining the path of Leo Africanus as he sails from Almería into his exile in Morocco. But by the early afternoon we are once more in Huéscar, having a late lunch in the tiny and friendly Casa Felipe, which seems from another era in Spanish history.

Standing at the bar while waiting for a table, we drink vermouth and try out a local dish called *remojón* – a winter salad of peeled roast potatoes, salt cod, hard-boiled eggs, pimento, onions. Sitting down, we have lamb chops grilled in a wooden fire, and a traditional charcuterie dish commended by the Nobel-prize-winning novelist Camilo José Cela in an article in the *ABC* – a *relleno* made with pork, chicken, turkey, bread, rabbit, saffron, cloves, cinnamon, eggs, lemon juice, garlic.

She wisely leaves it until after we have eaten the home-made *tocinos de cielo* before telling me what has clearly been on her mind all day.

'Michael,' she begins, in a tone I recognize only too well, in a tone which stops the digestion like a plunge into cold water. I know what she's going to say, I've heard it all before, there's a limit to the ways it can be said. She uses one of them.

'We can't go on like this.'

I can't believe it's over, I can't take her seriously, I can only joke about how inauspicious it was to have come to a place named after the Aragonese home town of the Usurper.

But it's definitive this time, as definitive as these things can ever be, the future is always uncertain. She wants to be back in Granada early tonight, I could take the next morning's bus from Huéscar to Murcia, she'll wait with me until the evening.

I thank her for this last consideration.

The shock, I know, will be largely retrospective, coming to me in my ever more painful moments of lucidity, when I'm lying alone in a Huéscar pension, or enduring an endless bus journey filled with mindless videos.

The restaurant is empty, the owner is waiting for us to leave, I finish slowly the remaining few drops of my cold Belmonte.

The Moorish Queen accuses me of melodrama when I refer to 'our last hours together' as we embark on a final, short trip into the arid wasteland to the south.

Morocco, she says, was a chimera, she should never have got my hopes up, she wants to get away from Granada, but not with me, not with anyone, there's the prospect of a job in Argentina, she has relatives there.

The soap opera of our affair ends where human life on earth began, according to the signpost outside the village of Orce. 'Orce,' it reads, 'home of the oldest human remains.'

The skeleton of 'The Man from Orce' is advertised as one of the exhibits within the 'Moorish' Castle of the Seven Towers, in the very centre of the village. The castle, owing more to modern restoration than to the Moors, projects its crisp cut blocks into the deep turquoise blue of the late afternoon sky. It is closed, leaving us to speculate if its most famous exhibit is still on show in the wake of a recent scientific enquiry.

A culture of falsity is fast engulfing Europe. The Man from Orce is a goat.

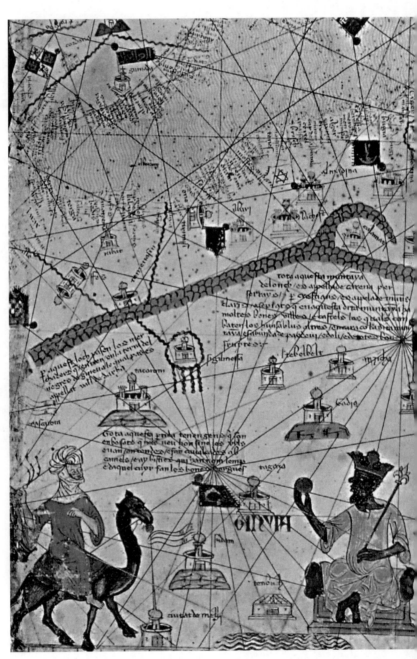

Mansa Musa of Timbuktu, reputedly the richest king on earth, greets the founder of Marrakesh,
Abu Bakr Ibn Umar al-Lamtuni. Granada is visible top left

CHAPTER FIVE

MOORS AND ASIATICS

I am already in an alien land, though I have yet to cross the sea. The kingdom of Granada, steeped in the fame of its Moorish past, has given way to a little known region of ill repute. The border post was a sign marked 'Murcia': it stood alone among empty mountains.

The bus, following its obscure route from Jaén to Alicante, enters what many might call the middle of nowhere. It is almost as empty as the landscape, though not empty enough to suspend the showing of a video involving terrorist plots, designer violence and evil Asiatics.

I retreat from the meaningless movements on the screen into the book I have now exchanged for *A Spanish Kama Sutra* – a spiritual guide by the most famous of Murcia's Islamic figures, Ibn Arabi, a twelfth-century Sufi. His is a mysticism that goes beyond religious boundaries, a mysticism appropriate to the hybrid culture of medieval Spain and which has even inspired a work controversially entitled *El Islam cristianizado*. I am hoping it might have a special meaning for someone such as myself – a Jewish Catholic agnostic.

Ibn Arabi tells me, reassuringly, that 'this world is only a testing ground', and that I should seek in it 'neither comfort nor riches'. But I seem to lack the necessary asceticism to be a true follower of his. In my momentary sadness and loneliness I have begun to dream of nights on the tiles with Murcian friends, soothing Belmontes, delicious local rice dishes made with fish broth, garlic-fried rabbit, or the abundant vegetables from the Murcian huerta. 'Eat less,' I am urged. 'This will leave more room in your heart and will increase your desire to pray and be obedient. You will be more active and less lazy.'

There is hope for me yet, however. To be able to renounce earthly pleasures, Ibn Arabi had to experience them himself: the divine revelations that began coming to him during his student years in Seville would not have happened had they not followed on from nights of indulgence that are deeply familiar to me – nights of music and dancing, bed at dawn, mornings of impoverished concentration that in Ibn Arabi's case made it impossible to attend to his obligatory prayers and ritual ablutions without becoming bored, wanting to sleep, or absorbing himself in thoughts 'about the marvellous night I had just spent listening to an excellent musician declaiming some fine verses'.

Divided between a desire for God and a desire for the low pleasures of the world, Ibn Arabi underwent in Seville a period of uncertainty that the Sufis refer to as *jahiliyya*. He emerged from this as one of the greatest and truest of Islamic travellers – someone whose repeated wanderings throughout al-Andalus, the Maghreb, Egypt, Syria and Arabia were echoed in a constant and complex inner journey that his most recent biographer, Claude Addas, has defined in terms of a 'quest for the red sulphur'.

Though Ibn Arabi, like Leo Africanus, was one of those people of whom it could be said that he belonged to 'no country, no city, no tribe', his roots, strictly speaking, were in Murcia, where he lived until the age of eight. During his childhood years, his native region was an enclave of resistance to the fanatical Almohads known as the Sharq al-Andalus. Shortly after his death in 1240, it would be absorbed by Christian Spain.

A massive symbol of the Christian triumph over the Murcian Moors appears in the bus window as we pull into Caravaca. The driver announces an hour's stop for lunch, enabling me to put to immediate test one of the spiritual recommendations I have gleaned from Ibn Arabi. I take this advice to its extreme conclusion and forsake food altogether. I walk instead up to a fourteen-tower citadel built by the Templars over a Moorish fortress.

Within the stark enclosure is a baroque sanctuary commemorating the miracle that heralded the end of Moorish domination of Murcia – the conversion to Christianity of the Moorish king Abu Zeid after seeing two angels carrying a cross to an imprisoned priest.

The sacristan is on the point of locking up the church when I ask him if I can briefly see this famous cross. He happily delays his lunch to give me a demonstration of how this object is brought out during the annual service celebrating the Moorish departure from the town.

As he cranks a lever, an organ sounds, a large wheel of bells rotates, and the shutters of a neo-gothic High Altar slowly open to reveal a jewel-studded cross. I am left as stunned as if I myself had witnessed some miraculous vision.

Back in the bus-station, talking to one of my fellow passengers, I learn about another side to the festivities surrounding the miracle. He evokes a colourful cavalcade ascending with celebratory splendour up to the castle, a votive image of the Virgin being borne on the shoulders of penitents, a number of large wine barrels being dragged by horses. The wine flows freely, the penitents get drunk, the time comes to go down the hill, they throw the Virgin into the back of a van and sit in the front giggling.

The bus leaves, I drift off into semi-consciousness, I am aware only of endless castle ruins, the ghostly profiles of half-abandoned towns, the brief return of desert-like surroundings that are banished once more as we near the city of Murcia, sprawling in its palm-studded huerta. On a sheer and distant outcrop, standing above the huerta like a Murcian Corcovado, are the compact ruins of the castle of Monteagudo – a Moorish structure so impressive that the Christians have tried to lessen its impact by building on top of it a monstrous statue of an outstretched Christ.

'The Church will never allow us to take it down,' Mariela says in her quiet, serious tone as we sit in her office, looking at a photograph of Monteagudo's Fascist excrescence.

Mariela is an art historian employed by the Junta de Murcia to catalogue the region's monuments. She has now been told by her boss to act as my Murcian guide, and to drive me wherever I want to go – an arrangement which gives a further unreality to the increasingly unexpected course of my present existence.

She is tall and beautiful, with thick, dark hair and a smiling, child-like timidity that makes her at times seem younger than her 38 years. But she is also cerebral and other-worldly, someone whose softly-spoken snatches of humour fail to wipe away a predominant impression of a person who does not engage fully with others, and who has a sadness and maturity born out of loneliness and loss.

Her life seems to have a hidden tragedy of which a clue is given when we collect her son from school and take the lift to the top floor of a central block of flats where the two of them live, apparently alone. There is no mention of a husband, only a framed photograph of the son with a bearded man of intellectual appearance. I do not ask any questions.

The flat has a panoramic view of the city the Moors knew as Mursiya – a city which, by the time of Ibn Arabi's childhood, had begun to outlive its years of prosperity and to suffer from famine, misery and a deranged ruler reputed to have assassinated his sisters, immured his two viziers alive, drowned his sons, and tortured his companions. Though the fertility of Mursiya's surroundings led the twelfth-century author 'Abdallah al-Hijari to describe the city as 'a sister to Seville', it was a reclusive and introverted sister bearing little relation to the bustling, temptation-filled Seville to which the family of Ibn Arabi were eventually forced to move.

Present-day Murcia, as seen from Mariela's window, is also an antithesis to its Andalucían sister: renewed prosperity may have taken away much of the city's former sobriety, but in doing so it has left little of its history and even less in the way of conventional beauty and sensuality. The baroque-fronted cathedral and a handful of grand seventeenth-century buildings have been engulfed by a development comparable to that of the downtown area of some provincial American city. Conspicuously absent is that labyrinth of whitewashed streets and alleys that make it still possible to picture what medieval, Moorish Seville must once have been like.

I cannot imagine the sort of Moorish tour Mariela is planning for my first evening in Murcia. 'We won't be gone long,' she tells her moody son, who is pretending to be engrossed in his computer. He follows us furtively to the door, and eyes me suspiciously as I enter the lift with his mother. We go straight to the Casino.

In a Spain whose Moorish past is either being left to ruin or else restored in such a way as to appear entirely false, the neo-Moorish extravagances of the last century can often be more exciting than the works they are trying to imitate. Pushing open the heavy, glazed doors of Murcia's main social club, we begin our Moorish tour of the city with one of the most breathtaking of ersatz interiors.

The Casino is an Aladdin's Cave of nineteenth-century eclecticism, a wax-polished, oppressively atmospherical world inhabited by a quiet scattering of suited old men and blue-rinse women. We walk down neo-Renaissance corridors, through a marbled Pompeian courtyard, up bronze-banistered staircases, past chairs and sofas in bombastic leather, through a wood-panelled library and billiard room of neo-gothic mustiness, across a gigantic ball-room glistening with chandeliers and gilded rocaille, and – thanks to Mariela – into a women's toilet frescoed by some art deco imitator of Tiepolo.

But we end as we have begun in a room which was added in 1899 and that overwhelms all the others in its fantasy and exuberance – an 'Arabian Hall'. Classical pilasters and draped figures from mythology provide the incongruous framework to a colourfully glazed horse-shoe-arched door through which we pass into a room based partly on the Alhambra's Hall of the Ambassadors but with the stalactite vaulting of its ceiling bursting into the art nouveau detailing of a magnificent glass and metal dome. My eyes do not know at first where to settle amid the writhing ornamentation, but eventually rest on the Nasrid motto so inappropriately interwoven into the fabric of this bastion of gambling and Catholic values: *wa-la galib illa Allah* ('There is no greater conqueror than Allah').

Out again on the streets of Murcia, and sucked into the stream of returning office-workers and early evening shoppers, we continue on a Moorish tour that can surely only decline into the prosaic after the neo-Moorish fantasy of the Casino. From now onwards, the tour will indeed go downhill but only in the literal sense, for Mariela begins promising a vast, Islamic city hidden below the ground.

We go behind the dreary, classical façade of the College of Architects, pay our brief respects to a group of chattering architects at a private view, descend the building's modernist staircase, and enter the basement archive. In between the stacks runs a large section of the city's Islamic wall, which extends for a good fifteen metres before disappearing out of the room into the basement, apparently, of another building, and from there into so many other basements that the complete line of Murcia's Islamic fortifications can almost be reconstructed.

The whole centre of modern Murcia is like an ugly layer of cladding placed above the near intact foundations of Islamic Mursiya. To show me more of this underlying city Mariela takes me from the College of Architects to the similarly pompous and coldly classical town hall, where an archaeologist friend of hers, Miguel de San Nicolás, is currently engaged in some exploratory excavations in a basement room.

Miguel and his three assistants are working late when we arrive at this bare and gloomy 1950's room, to which a dramatic chiaroscuro has been given by the presence of powerful spotlights directed towards some recently-dug holes. Dark-skinned and with a tightly curled white beard and hair, Miguel has an Old Testament appearance which for Mariela is certain proof that his Murcian ancestors must have been Moorish. He smiles distractedly as she tells him this, then immediately starts talking about the work he is now doing.

The present town hall, according to his investigations, stands on a site that has always been at the civic heart of Murcia. Directly below us, illuminated by the spotlights, is the exposed brickwork of a poor people's hospital incorporated within the Moorish alcazar. In one of the holes Miguel and his team had found the skeleton of a man whom they had identified as a mason.

Death is not the equalizer that has traditionally been thought. Modern archaeological technology, Miguel explains with the excited tone of some schoolboy with a passion for gadgetry, is now able to tell from a skeleton such details of a person's past as their profession and social standing.

'Skeletons of scholars,' he says, looking at Mariela and me, 'can easily be distinguished from those of people who have spent their lives working with their hands.'

Miguel, I have been told, is one of Spain's leading archaeologists, and a pioneer in the application of computer technology to his discipline. We move over to the desk on which he has put his

Apple Mac computer. He scans the screen until he stops at a series of coloured diagrams that sketch out the presumed whereabouts and ground-plans of all of Murcia's hidden Islamic sites.

Five Moorish baths and three cemeteries have already been excavated, to considerable international controversy in the case of the latter.

'A number of Islamic embassies wrote to Murcia's town hall to complain,' says Mariela. 'They said that the cemeteries should be left undisturbed, and that we were desecrating the bodies of their people.'

'The town hall's reply,' Miguel takes over, 'was that the cemeteries, though Islamic, were an important part of Spain's own heritage, and that in digging them up we were finding out vital information about our ancestors.'

I ask if any of these sites are on public view.

'No,' Miguel answers. 'We generally bury the sites as soon as we've extracted from them all the information we need. We'll be doing exactly the same here. The only exceptions have been some of the sections of the city's wall.'

He packs up his work to accompany us on the rest of our evening's walk. The one remaining stop is a place called the Bar Muralla.

'We can now combine work with pleasure,' Mariela quietly teases me as we step into a place that looks at first neither pleasurable nor remotely Islamic. We have entered the hotel bar attached to the Rincón de Pepe, the smartest and most famous restaurant in the whole region of Murcia. The near empty bar is luxurious, modern and as bland as the recorded piano music that wafts over the polished, designer surfaces.

'Don't worry, we're not there yet,' Mariela assures me as we walk down a staircase towards the part of the bar normally reserved for late night drinkers. 'When they were laying the hotel's foundations a few years back,' she continues, 'they made this extraordinary discovery. They did not know at first what to do with it.'

We appear to be descending onto the stage set of some post-modern production of a romantic opera. A modern shallow vault of enormous proportions looms in the darkness over a spotlit stretch of fortifications so long and well-preserved as to include two of the original towers.

'The sheer cost of the vaulting,' Miguel notes, 'was astronomical. Only a successful restaurant could afford to display the past in this way. But the place will never recoup its investment. You hardly ever see people here except at weekends.'

We sit down at one of the tables that have been laid out on the ramparts themselves, in between massive blocks of masonry.

A disturbing image comes to me while we're drinking our beer. I am picturing a group of Muslims defending to the death a section of defensive wall that would later become the decorative centre-piece of a post-modern bar.

The following morning Mariela is driving me into the huerta, where Murcia's Islamic legacy, shadowy in the city itself, sparkles under an open sky. These fields around us, sown with fruit trees, cereal crops, vines, vegetables and palms, are essentially Moorish fields, cultivated over what had once been hostile soil barely touched even by the Romans.

The theme of our morning's tour is water. We begin by the banks of the Segura, a few kilometres upstream from Murcia, outside the satellite conurbation of Javali Nuevo. A modest modern dam, replacing a near identical Moorish structure, crosses the river here, and forms the starting-point of the sophisticated hydraulic scheme that the Moors devised to distribute water throughout the huerta.

The water, diverted from the dam into large channels on either side of the river, once flowed underground in tunnels described by the fourteenth-century author al-Himyari as having regular ventilation holes as well as openings through which the accumulated mud could be let out. From these large channels, now exposed, the water branches off into a network of over fifty lesser channels, the present names of which are almost all Islamic in origin.

Mariela, who is telling me all this, talks now about the great wheels or *norias*, so abundant in the Murcian countryside, that lift up the water in the last stage of its journey into the fields.

'Many are still in use,' she says, 'but they are being replaced increasingly by motorized pumps. We're trying hard to conserve those that are left.'

We drive on, across the river, to see one of the largest of Murcia's norias, in a township suitably named after the colloquial corruption of this Moorish-derived word, La Nora. As with all of the surviving norias, only the brickwork framework is Moorish, an ironwork wheel of 1936 having in this case replaced the wooden one that the Moors had used to draw water with the aid of earthenware vessels tied together with rope. Today there is no water to draw – the irrigation canal has been left a stagnant drain, choked with weeds and the detritus of modern civilization.

The same, we soon find, is true of nearby Alcantarilla, where there is an even larger wheel, eleven metres in diameter, adjoining a temporarily closed museum of the huerta. An almost summer sun is blazing once again over a drained canal whose plaintive emptiness, so telling of the drought from which the south of Spain is suffering, seems also to be saying something about the emotional state of the two of us who are staring into it.

A busy main road rushes past the noria, and hurries us on our way west to Alhama de Murcia, where we end the morning in the waterless ruins of this town's eponymous baths. Our guide to these is someone who has undertaken a scholarly study of them – a subject to which he was destined by his name, Pepe Baños.

Alhama is on the edge of the huerta, underneath a bare, bleached outcrop supporting a Moorish castle on its summit and some ancient thermal baths at its foot. Pepe Baños has the key to the latter site, which has been closed for years owing to the incomplete state of the modern superstructure that has been built to protect the ruins and to convert the whole into a small archaeological museum.

Pepe, apologizing for the confusion we are about to see, prepares us beforehand by explaining something of the site's history and layout. He also presents me with a copy of his contribution to an international conference on the theme of Water in Dry Climates: Archaeology and History. His paper concentrates on the use of

Alhama's thermal waters to irrigate the fields, a use first recorded by the thirteenth-century cosmographer al-Quaziwi.

I am scarcely the wiser when we begin to wander around what appears to be an abandoned construction site. The ruins, complex in themselves, have been further complicated by the running out of funds for the modern work on top of them. Roman vaulting and Moorish masonry are at times indistinguishable from the ancient-looking shell of a nineteenth-century thermal building, above which project steel girders and expanses of concrete. From a rickety wooden walkway I take a photograph looking down onto medieval brickwork foundations covered in weeds, planks, breeze blocks and wire mesh.

Pepe hopes I won't be publishing this photograph. I smile and ask him what has happened to Alhama's thermal spring. An earthquake, he says, moved it further down into the huerta, to where the town's present spa is situated.

Mariela and I pass by this spa on our way back towards the Segura. Above the gateway to this modern complex a crucifix hangs over a sign promoting the water from the spring as both health-giving and 'holy'.

The Segura was often likened by Muslim writers to the Nile, ancestral river of so many of the inhabitants of Islamic Murcia. Following the river upstream, we approach the beautiful Valley of the Ricote, which Mariela has described to me as the most African-looking part of Spain.

The gateway to the valley is Archena, birthplace of Murcia's greatest poet, Vicente Medina, and home to a spa whose aristocratic elegance is the very antithesis of Medina's earthy, colloquial evocations of the region's traditional rural life.

The spa is beyond the village, leisurely spread along the Segura at a point where the river narrows to accommodate the encroaching rocky slopes that hem in the valley. Parking our car near an ancient plaque attesting to the site's fame during the time of one Caius Caianus, we stroll along a shaded promenade in between a neo-gothic church and a white classically-fronted building touched with an imperial Russian dignity.

Mariela, who has smart elderly relatives who frequent this spa, is becoming more relaxed as the day progresses.

'They're constantly gossiping and having affairs,' she says of the old and impassive-faced patients who move up and down the promenade with an incorporeal, dream-like manner.

The dream intensifies within the main spa building, where we descend from the cold classicism of the vestibule into an enormous, steamy basement with wide, barrel-vaulted corridors converging onto the neo-Moorish centrepiece built around the thermal spring. White-robed patients slide silently by on wheelchairs, or else sit around like classical statues on marble benches fringed with Moorish-style ceramics. From a copy of the Alhambra's Fountain of the Lions – worn, stalactite-encrusted and more venerable in appearance than the original itself – bubbles out the spring's hot, sulphuric water.

Lunchtime comes, the patients disappear, we return upstairs to wander through emptied rooms where the neo-Renaissance and the neo-Baroque give way to the neo-Moorish and sometimes to a hybrid mixture of the three, as in the grand staircase's octagonal dome, Bramantino-like in its cool geometry, baroque in its theatricality, and exuberantly, overwhelmingly Moorish in its stuccoed, honeycombed and imitation tooled-leather decoration.

A breath of air is needed, so we sit outside at one of the white ironwork tables of a bar arranged among palms and topiary. The strange magic of Murcia is beginning to assert itself, we are entering a wonderland worthy of Alice – at our feet, laid out in black and white marble slabs, is a gigantic chess set with human-sized pieces. Further away, beyond a classical balustrade, runs the now tiny river, its reedy, shady banks erupting on the other side into a dense jungle of palms and other exotic trees. In my imagination I can hear the shrieks of monkeys and parakeets, the mysterious murmur of a hundred hidden creatures.

We leave Archena and continue into the Valley of Ricote, into what is truly at times an Africa within Europe. The oasis loses its jungle-like character, the palms become isolated clumps rising above marshes, spreading orchards, and small patches of intense cultivation that luxuriate in their emerald green brilliance between the scorched ochre of arid cliffs and rocks. The Segura, like a lethargic snake, crawls through whitewashed villages, above one of which a neo-Moorish dovecot stands like a mosque, furthering the African mirage around us.

Parting briefly from the river, we climb up to Ricote, an unpicturesque village of anaesthetized whiteness but with a history that suggests that the African look of the surrounding landscape may not be entirely coincidental: Ricote was the last place in Spain from which the moriscos were expelled.

Mariela promises to expand on this curious historical footnote once we have sat down for lunch in Ricote's competing and more popular attraction, the Venta del Sordo, a restaurant to which businessmen drive all the way from Murcia for their midday break. *En el corazón de la tierra del pijo* runs the bizarre and suggestive motto printed above a list of dishes so long and exotic that the history of Ricote has to wait until Mariela and I have made our way through the entire menu and agonized over whether to chose 'grilled frogs in a pepper sauce' or 'gypsy stew with pears'.

With my decision finally made, we turn back to the no less complex and idiosyncratic subject of the moriscos of Ricote, who, she says, were descended from a line of distinguished Moors. Among these was Mohammad Ibn Abubeqer al-Ricoti, a man so learned in the alliterative fields of mathematics, music and medicine that Alfonso the Wise, on conquering Murcia in 1245, granted to him his own school, or *madrasa*. Above all, there was the brilliant, Moroccan-trained soldier Ibn Hud al-Yudami, who, from his base at Ricote, rose up in 1228 against the Almohads, and fashioned for himself a large, wealthy and short-lived kingdom out of the disintegrating Almohad state.

Ricote's moments of glory and independence under Ibn Hud might well have been nostalgically recalled in 1614, when the village's predominant morisco population heard about the expulsion order issued by Philip III. Their immediate response was a desperate appeal to the king in which, through hypocritical invocations to the Virgin, Christ and the Catholic saints venerated in their valley, they managed to sway the king's heart. Alone of the Spanish moriscos, those of Ricote were allowed to stay on in Spain. They did so for seven more years.

'When they eventually had to go from the valley,' Mariela continues, 'the impact of their departure was tremendous. There was virtually no-one left, something like 83 people, I think.'

I try to pour out some more of Ricote's strong and famous late-season young white wine, *mosto,* into Mariela's glass. She protests, she has to drive, she gives in. She is soon straying from history, revealing more and more of the vulnerability underlying her quietly professional façade. She mentions a Lonely Hearts Circle founded by her and her friends.

'I'm its only remaining member,' she mumbles, slipping her spoon into my *tomates acojonantes,* a Moorish tomato jam.

Thoughts about her son, about being late to collect him from school, bring her back to her professional senses, make her ask for the bill. If we leave now, she says, we'll just have time to continue along the Segura right up to the 'ruined medina' at Cieza.

We return to the river, follow it through a narrow gorge to where the Segura's vega widens and loses some of its enchantment. The district, disastrously depopulated and impoverished after the moriscos left, has experienced since the 1960's a resurgence of wealth that has changed some of its villages into miniature cities whose inhabitants, Mariela acknowledges, have preferred to pull down their old houses and move into blocks that, for her at least, are grey and inhuman.

But the old has not been obliterated entirely, as we find when we deviate from the road after Abarán and drive through reeds and fields of high crops down to a noria that at last is functioning as it is supposed to do, its wheel making the groaning sound to which the Arab word *nura* refers, the water spluttering and churning and conveying images of freshness, vitality, and the uncanny persistence of the Moorish tradition.

And finally to Cieza, whose modern town, as ugly as Abarán, has a small museum showing exquisite pots and other assembled shards from the ruins of Moorish Siyasa, our day's ultimate destination.

Medina Siyasa is a few kilometres away from the modern town, isolated and unsignposted high up on a barren peak.

'The authorities like to discourage tourists from coming here,' Mariela explains once we ourselves have lost our way and are forced to ask directions from a family of hippies mysteriously picnicking in the late afternoon. We eventually approach the site in the most difficult way possible, scrambling through bracken down a crumbling slope. A group of men digging at the site are surprised to see us; one of them puts down his shovel to take us on a tour of the ruins.

The walls of Cieza look from above like an intricate stonework maze suspended on a ledge above a mountainous panorama. Inside, the maze begins to make sense as our guide verbally reconstructs what the place was once like, talking all the time as if he himself had lived there during its heyday in the twelfth and early thirteenth centuries. The ruins have for him the eloquence of those of Pompeii, and are likewise testimony to a town suddenly abandoned at the height of its prosperity – in this case with its incorporation into the kingdom of Castile in 1243.

The whole site is a network of alleyways separating dwelling-houses of varying affluence, all with kitchens, latrines, wells, stables, cisterns, living and reception rooms, and an interior courtyard in which traces of ornamentation have been found, some revealing the artistic influence of Umayyad Cordova, others in a highly refined style uglily defined by archaeologists as 'proto-Nasrid'.

From a latrine protruding over a sheer drop at the north-eastern extremity of the former walled town, we look back at the mountain on which the site is built.

'The whole of that slope you clambered down,' our guide tells us, 'is also part of Siyasa, the mosque is somewhere over there. So far we've only had the funds to uncover a tiny fraction of the medina. It's the largest ruined one in Spain.'

He is not an archaeologist, he confesses, just a labourer with a great enthusiasm for history. Mariela says that she's learnt more about Siyasa from him than from any specialist.

As we continue to stare over the site, I tell them that when I get to Morocco next week I shall think back on the layout of Cieza when I'm wandering through the medinas of Fez, Tangiers, Rabat, Marrakesh.

He's never been to Morocco, he admits, and probably never will. But he doesn't feel the need to see those places I mention to be able to fill the empty alleys of Cieza with the sights, sounds and smells of its past – the laden donkeys, the crack of their owners' whips, the shopkeepers crouched behind the dark portals, the shouts of the pedlars, the draped women swerving to avoid the running boys, the sipping of tea in shaded patios, the mingled odours of spices, fetid drains, sizzling kebabs, horse shit, perfumes from Damascus...

The reddening light of the late afternoon sun complements his unexpected poetic outburst.

'We're in Morocco now,' he smiles.

The last of Spain's moriscos set sail to Africa from Cartagena, a town their present-day descendants perceive in the same mythical light Westerners reserve for Timbuktu. 'Kartajanah!' they exclaim, using its Moorish name, whenever they and their fellow African Muslims want to invoke a place of fabled remoteness.

Mariela, a native of Cartagena, offers to drop me off there on a visit to her parents' home. We take the motorway, and pause for coffee at a service station named after the Virgin. Already we have crossed the frontier dividing the land of the Belmonte from the land of the Asiático, a drink of identical ingredients but served with a sprinkling of cinnamon in a conically-shaped glass fashioned only in Cartagena. Famed for being a popular cure for yellow or Asiatic fever, and successful only when made with the worst coffee and the cheapest cognac, this concoction encapsulates the qualities that go into the making of Cartagena's richly idiosyncratic character – tackiness, pungency, a surreal exoticism.

On arrival at Cartagena, I go on a final walk with Mariela, up into the park that has been created out of the citadel. The highest point is the round fourteenth-century keep, from the top of which we survey the town and its beautiful natural harbour, ringed by bare volcanic-like peaks defended by fortresses. Whereas Murcia has buried its past under a prosperous modern veneer, Cartagena has exposed it in a way recalling some battered and dusty plasterwork model sliced open to display a cross-section of different archaeological layers. The outer town of modern blocks encircles a legacy from the days of Cartagena's industrial fame, a sooty art nouveau crust, collapsing and with gaping holes revealing such fragments of an earlier past as a romanesque cathedral rising from rubble, Byzantine walls, and a Roman amphitheatre pushing up from below a bullring.

Beyond the Roman period, the traces of this town's long history – the longest perhaps of any Spanish town – thin out almost entirely, leaving only as a spectral presence the years of the great Carthaginian empire.

'And what about the Moorish occupation?' I ask Mariela, who replies by pointing to a round tower below us, apparently a lighthouse from Kartajanah.

Then, turning around, and directing my attention beyond the fishermen's district of Santa Lucia, she makes me look at some outlying slum dwellings that straggle an untidy, thistle-strewn slope fringed by a ragged profile of masonry.

'A Moorish castle,' she says, 'but we can't go there. It's behind the gypsy district, a no-man's land which even the police won't visit.'

She gives the reason, using a slang term with suitably Moorish overtones.

'It's where the "camels" hang out.'

'I think I'll wait for Africa before meeting them,' I respond, but the double meaning is either lost on her, or else she is politely ignoring it; we're on a different wavelength.

Time is preventing our separate worlds from ever getting closer, her parents are waiting for her, she has to go, we say goodbye – a quick embrace, mutual hopes that we'll see each other again, the knowledge that the traveller's life is a series of meetings without consequence, of friendships intensely lived for a few days, replaced by other friendships, other worlds.

She leaves me at the office of a good friend of mine, Antonio, who will soon lead me into a different world to hers, older in age but younger in behaviour, no less serious at heart, but more hedonistic, more outward-going, more able to shake off life's problems in the pursuit of superficial pleasures.

Antonio, a reluctant civic employee whose serious, stately demeanour is belied by childlike eyes and a ready laugh, is a socialist with a passion for food, its history, its preparation, its consumption. Over the years that I have been visiting Cartagena, Antonio has been making sure that I try out as many as possible of this district's curious dishes – and that I do so in an equal number of its even more curious eating establishments. He gives me details of today's planned lunch as we go off to a Santa Lucía bar to have a *reposo*, a mixture of cognac and wine also peculiar to Cartagena.

We shall be eating, he says, outside the town, in 'a totally decadent place' – a private home whose owner, Don Eusebio, cooks on commission for paying clients. Knowing of my present interests, Antonio has asked him to prepare as a last course 'the strangest and most Moorish of all Murcian dishes' – a *pastel de Cierva*.

Don Eusebio is a retired chef and restaurateur who worked for Spanish embassies all over the world before opening a celebrated but short-lived restaurant along the Valencian coast. He is still in jeans and shirt-sleeves when Antonio and I – the advance party of a large group of friends – arrive at his outwardly ordinary, flower-bedecked modern chalet. Steps lead up to the main entrance, which is fronted by a long terrace overlooking a garden ablaze with colourful exotic plants and flowers. We catch Don Eusebio on the narrow street in between his house and a hut that he uses as the kitchen of his improvised restaurant. Spruce, slight in build, and with neatly cut white hair and moustache, he is a youthful-looking seventy-year old who greets us like a charming but slightly flustered host. Smiling camply, and in a voice that wavers into a high-pitched tone, he asks us to excuse him, he absolutely must get ready, there is still such an awful lot to do. He walks up to the terrace, where he gesticulates briskly to a younger and portlier man, who has a red face and a wave of dyed black hair. A boyfriend perhaps?

The rest of our group turn up in a convoy of cars that bring an unexpected animation to this quiet village lying under the shadow of the barren hills that separate Cartagena's fertile huerta from the sea. The 'boyfriend' has by now had a change of clothes, and is dressed like the headwaiter of an elegant restaurant – jacket, bow-tie, starched white shirt, and shining black shoes that click smartly to attention as we ascend up to the terrace to take our places on a long table that has been laid out with the finest white cloth, silver candelabra, bouquets of flowers, and napkins that have been contorted into baroque twists.

An aperitif is served, then canapés, tapas, wine, a large salad, each stage of the lunch being followed by an increasingly long gap as the 'headwaiter' puffs and sweats and gets ever redder in the face while carrying everything over from the distant kitchen. Don Eusebio finally makes a showy appearance complete with chef's hat, an immaculate apron, a blue and white necktie, and a gigantic paella dish filled with a saffron-coloured caldero that draws a round of applause as he holds it at an angle in front of us. He serves it himself then disappears, leaving his friend to continue walking up and down the steps between the kitchen and the terrace, bringing more bread, more wine, and even the fish whose stock has flavoured the succulent rice. The friend now seems to be drinking on his every visit into the kitchen, his shirt is becoming more and more stained by wine and sweat, his tie comes askew, his hair hangs lank like that of a toupee, his breath takes ever longer to recover after climbing the steps, he starts to tell us jokes, he sings us a song, he pours half the wine onto the table.

Our stomachs are full, our livers over-abused, the prospect of the culminating pastel de Cierva is no longer an appealing one. Don Eusebio, re-emerging on to the terrace to receive another eulogy, proposes a pause of at least an hour. In the meantime he takes three of us on a tour of his chalet, whose modern makeshift-looking walls shield an interior decorated to the hilt in 'Murcian taste' – gilt-framed painted angels against a vinyl background, a Lladró porcelain of a boy and swan, leather chairs in a Castillian Renaissance style, a velvet-covered 'Book of Honour' crowded with the signatures of marquises, ambassadors, film stars and other distinguished figures who have been Don Eusebio's clients during his years of greatness. In the bedroom, lying on top of a tasselled four-poster that he urges us to sit on, is a life-sized statuette of the baby Jesus resting in a cradle of plastic straw.

The headwaiter, whom we have caught half-asleep on my chair on our return to the terrace, later almost collapses under the weight of the pastel de Cierva – the gastronomic equivalent of the interior we have just seen.

Antonio lists for me its basic ingredients – chicken, hard-boiled eggs, and a sweet pastry made with lemons and two kilos each of sugar and lard.

'It's exactly like the Moroccan *pastilla*, except that this is a pudding and it has chicken instead of dove.'

The origins of this are disputed by others at the table. One person asks why a Moorish dish should be named after the Murcian inventor of the helicopter, the Marquis of Cierva. Another replies that the Marquis had paid a visit to Hungary after the First World War and had been so impressed by a rich sweet he had eaten there that he had later asked his Murcian cook to reproduce it on the basis of his rather vague description.

Antonio has little patience with all this.

'There's no getting away from the fact that the dish is completely North African in character. In any case it's far more Moorish than many of the dishes listed in a book I bought the other day on 'The Food of al-Andalus'. On the first page I turned to there was a recipe for 'avocado soup' – avocadoes didn't even get to Europe until at least the sixteenth century!'

I propose that the Hungarian dish that had reputedly inspired the Marquis could have been one of the many in Hungary reflecting the period of Turkish occupation.

'It's a Moorish dish that travelled to Hungary by way of Turkey, and from there came back again to Murcia.'

'Let's just call it Murcian,' says Antonio, putting to an end an argument which threatens to last until sunset, fuelled by whisky and that other metaphor of Murcian strangeness – the Asiático.

Thoughts of Ibn Arabi, that had accompanied my entry into Murcia, recede somewhat as my stay here, and in Spain itself, draws to an end. Antonio and his intimate circle of childhood friends are gathering for an extended weekend party that hardly concords with the spiritual precepts of the Murcian Sufi. The need for such a party has become acute among all of us, if for different reasons: I am trying to get over the loss of the Moorish Queen, others the loss of their youths.

Five of the group have just reached the age of forty – the nominal excuse for our planned celebrations in a house we have hired in the heart of the Murcian interior. Some of us are driving there from Cartagena, others from Murcia itself, several people are coming down from Madrid, and there is even a couple flying in from Mallorca. The ties of childhood and adolescence are bringing together a disparate if incestuous group ranging from a lawyer to a nurse, a bookseller to a paediatrician, an historian to an estate agent, a fisherman to an ecologist, a psychiatrist to an economist, a Quique known as 'El loco' to a Quique known as 'El profundo'. By midnight on Friday we have all assembled at a remote and isolated farm enigmatically marked on the map as 'the House of the Moroccan'.

The woollen clothes we resort to on the pitch-black night of our arrival are put away the next morning and replaced by summer T-shirts. A warm and brilliant sunshine brings to life the aromatic slopes behind us and lights up to the south a view of a mountainous parkland which was planted with pines early this century by the Marquis of Espuña.

The weather and the landscape encourage a modicum of healthy, outdoor activities. Several times, led by the aptly named 'Quique the Mad', we scour the rough slopes behind the farm in a hunt for the elusive *nisculo* mushroom. Others in the group, with childhood memories of holiday camps in the Sierra de Espuña, encourage instead a quest which could be summarized as the chapter heading of some novel of magical realism – 'In Search of the Ice Wells'.

We discover the 'ice wells' near the top of the Sierra, commanding a vista that seems to include the whole, mountainous northern half of Murcia. They are ringed by a bright green meadow where Antonio's quieter brother Perico, suffering now from the break-up of a marriage, remembers romantic moments in a tent. The wells are like gigantic stone eggs half-buried in the ground and with small entrances that lure the unsuspecting visitor to the edge of the abyss in which the ice was stored. The ice was transported from here to the city of Murcia until at least the 1950's, Perico informs me, but neither he nor anyone else in our group has any idea about when the wells were built. They have the venerable look of Mayan ruins that have been hidden for centuries in the jungle. 'They are many centuries old,' says Antonio. 'They're Moorish, I'm sure.'

But history, like the outdoor life, is not a dominant concern of our four-day-long weekend, which seems mainly taken up with endlessly protracted breakfasts, followed by equally extended preparations for lunches that last well into night, climaxing always in dancing sessions in which 'Quique the Profound', not so profound after all, recreates our youths by putting on all his favourite tunes from the sixties and seventies. The exotic, long-haired Patricia, of French Algerian descent, seems more than ever like a clone from that period, as she swings and twists in her mini-skirt and knee-length boots – an over-enthusiastic participant at an orgiastic rite.

The past returns, the festivities are relentless, the sole and brief hiatus comes when we wake up one morning to discover that a dead squirrel, with a trickle of blood in its mouth, has been hung over an outside window. Is this a curse, or a gesture of good will? We try not to think of it, we go back to our eating and drinking and dancing, but the image of the squirrel persists until eventually, on our last night, we resort to the ultimate of pleasurable oblivions. We visit the Baths of Mula.

I have been to the baths several times by day, they haunt me more than almost any other place in southern Spain. They lie a few

IN THE GLOW OF THE PHANTOM PALACE

kilometres beyond the town of Mula, whose dusty core of forgotten palaces is pressed against rocky slopes that lift the ruins of a crenellated Renaissance castle high into the air. Between the town and the baths, the orchards cease and the desert begins, Moorish ruins succeed Christian ones, and a glimpse is had of the purple-domed Sultana – a neo-Moorish villa with a crowning crescent moon.

The baths, with their decrepit ochre buildings, are camouflaged inside a shallow gorge whose water has been reduced to a narrow, foul-smelling stream like that of an exposed sewer. The recent attempt to dignify the spa's promenade with a row of Isabelline-style lamps has failed to halt the spread of terminal decay. The lantern of one of them has already rusted away at its neck, and now dangles like the head of a hanged man at the spa's entrance – a grim but suitable welcome to a place as seedy and disreputable as Archena is smart and wealthy.

The lingering ill fame of the baths of Mula is such that as we drive there at night from the House of the Moroccan, a talkative divorcee feels it necessary to tell me about it. How shocked she had been as a teenager, she says, when she and a girl-friend had hitched a lift from a man who had offered to take them there. The place was a brothel, she adds, no, not a brothel, but an enclave of 'alternative morality' in the middle of Franco's Spain. Businessmen from Murcia had been been taking their mistresses there since the nineteenth century, the Romans and the Moors had probably done the same. She's convinced that there's a magic component in its waters which stimulates desires and fertility, cements relationships, brings strangers together – and she's got a story to prove this. The story is of a foreign woman living in Murcia and expecting a visit from her American boyfriend. 'What shall I show him?' the woman had asked her, to which she'd replied, 'Los Baños de Mula'. The woman took her advice, married the friend two weeks later, and conceived their first child in the baths.

There's certainly magic in the air if not in the water, as the cars of our group pull up single file behind a psychedelically-painted customized caravan daubed with the English words KOSSOFF'S CIRCUS, MOSCOW, WORLD TOUR, 1994-1995. The performers have

138

disappeared, the promenade is empty, there's no sign of a fair or a circus, the only noise is made by the seventeen of us, pulling ourselves up the steep metal steps that ascend alongside the cascading water from the hot thermal spring. In the bar at the top, there's just the man with the keys to the baths, a sullen old man whose face mirrors a lifetime of keeping secrets. He gives a key, asks no questions, makes no judgements.

'Bathing costumes to be worn at all times,' reads the sign outside a dimly-lit, barrel-vaulted Roman bath where we are soon taking off all our clothes and jumping naked into the steaming water.

Some of the men end up arranged against the sides of the pool like satiated emperors, while the women become nymphs who glide gracefully up and down as if in a constant search for Hylas. Bottles of whisky have been brought out, the conditions for drinking are ideal, the steam sweats out the alcohol, the effluent pipe gets rid of the rest – contamination of the body goes hand in hand with its purification.

Drinking provokes singing, songs echo in the vaulted chamber, echoes inspire strange shouts and cries, the cacophony increases, the volume gets louder. A woman lifts her arms above her head, her breasts rise above the water, she sways her body, she's Liberty leading the people, we fall in line behind her, the Conga begins. Figures of eight are drawn in the water by our chanting procession, then the geometry is shattered, there's a chaos of nakedness, an overall languor and exhaustion, a vision of the last days of an empire.

The holiday is over, I take the Almería bus from Murcia, my ferry is leaving the next day. There's time for a short stop at Cuevas de Almanzora.

Wearily I drag my luggage and my body to the top of this small town on the eastern, cave-pocked edge of Almería. I'm here to find out more about the place's ties with Timbuktu – ties that the present mayor is currently trying to strengthen.

Entering the town hall, I'm told that the mayor is away on business, but I'm given in his stead a book the town council has recently published on Yuder Pacha – the Cuevas-born morisco at the head of the Moroccan troops who conquered the Songhai empire in the late sixteenth century. The author is the elusive Mahmud Zakari from Granada.

'You've missed him by a few days,' says the town's archivist. 'He was here last week. He's a good friend of the mayor. They were in Timbuktu together at the beginning of the year.'

Just below the town hall is a small square named after Yuder Pacha. I sit down here to read the book, on a stone bench placed directly in front of a house encrusted all over with a kaleidoscopic explosion of Moorish-patterned mosaics. I try not to look at the house. I'm feeling delicate this morning.

Mahmud's book is a scholarly attempt to rehabilitate a man who had virtually disappeared from history, and whose remarkable life had hitherto only inspired a recent work of fiction – *Las Españas perdidas* by Manolo Villar Raso, a Granadine professor whose novel on ETA had included the memorable line, 'the asphalt was having an orgasm on the streets of Bilbao'.

Mahmud, dismissing Manolo's fictional speculations, looks only to the facts of Yuder's life; but, sadly, the facts relating to his early life are virtually non-existent. A discussion of Yuder's strange name takes up much of the book's first chapter. Was it possible that a morisco could have been baptised with a name that must be a corruption of Jawdah? Mahmud, I notice with relief, entirely discounts the theory that Yuder is a derivative of *joder*, the Spanish word for 'fuck' – an ironic possibility given that one of the few well-established facts about the man is that he was a eunuch.

Tiring of the bench, I go off to see the castle, hoping that this sole survival from the days of Yuder Pacha will help flesh out the vague picture I have formed of his years at Cuevas.

The Bloomsbury theorist and painter Roger Fry had studied the monument from the selective point of view of someone extracting 'significant form'. I try instead to invest its almost too perfect geometry with the romantic, Moorish associations that Fry would certainly have despised. Luckily it's market day, and there are crowded stalls and bars facing the Islamic keep and bringing the whole monument alive – making me imagine for a moment the bustling morisco community whose memory is likely to have haunted Yuder Pacha during his half-crazed march across the African desert.

My impatience for Morocco is growing and I eagerly resume my journey to Almería, arriving there at nightfall. I do not stay in the town, but choose instead to spend my last night in Spain at the spa of Sierra Alhamilla.

The taxi drives me towards an isolated scattering of lights halfway up an otherwise black range at the northern limits of the flat, untidy area of palms, small industries and erosion that spreads east of Almería. The lights are those of an austerely detailed spa hotel, which appears at night-time like the classical shell of a Fascist railway station. Inside, the atmosphere is more that of a half-abandoned convent, symmetrically arranged around two scantily-lit courtyards with di Chirico-like arcading. The few guests who are staying are mainly German.

The manager gives me a tour of the building once I've been allotted a numberless room. The late eighteenth-century structure, which had fallen into terrible disrepair, has been recently refurbished, with parts of the neo-classical vaulting being stuccoed in a neo-Moorish style 'in keeping with the building's history'.

A dark and grand stone staircase takes us down into the 'Moorish Baths', where more stucco of this type decorates the corners of two long, echoing rooms. But the baths themselves – sunk, rectangular pools lined with marble – are unmistakeably Roman. 'We call them Moorish,' says the manager, 'because the Moors appropriated the original Roman structure.'

He leaves me on my own to try one of them out. I sink naked and vulnerable into lukewarm water, thinking how distant Mula now seems. I had planned on a quiet reflective night at Almería, but the solitude and gloom of the spa recall the perils of too much silence and thought. The thirteenth-century author al-Quizini wrote that ill people always got over their ailments after taking the much praised waters of this spa; on me, however, they seem to be having an exactly contrary effect.

Upstairs in my room I telephone Miguel, a Sevillian friend who has been settled in Almería for the past year. It's ages since I've seen him, he offers immediately to come and collect me, he doesn't listen to my protests, he's dying to show me his new apartment.

We go first of all to a cafe. He's brought with him a young and handsome Moroccan who's studying marine biology at Almería University. When I talk about my current Islamic interests, and my forthcoming trip to Morocco, Miguel's deep-set eyes register astonishment and delight. 'Its amazing,' he comments. 'I always knew we had much in common.'

'Much has happened since you last saw me,' continues Miguel, a man with gypsy-like hair and waistcoat whom I have known up till now mainly in the context of festivals, dancing Sevillanas. 'I've been going to Morocco whenever I can. I've got so many friends there; it's my favourite country.'

A love of Morocco has encouraged him to reassess the whole Islamic heritage of his native Andalucía, a subject on which he begins questioning me with a naïve earnestness. He wonders what books he should read, and makes me write them all down on a piece of paper. One day, he insists we'll have to go together to Granada, 'a dream of a town'. 'But now let's go to my apartment,' he adds. 'I think you're going to love what I've done.'

In the car the young Moroccan, Aziz, breaks his silence to talk about his country, and asks me whom I'm intending to see once I get there. I mention a controversial writer called Mohammed Choukri.

'He's an enemy of the Moroccan people,' he responds with an unexpectedly hostile tone. 'He writes what Westerners expect to hear about our country. He's got nothing positive to say about it.'

Miguel continues driving with his habitual beatific smile, oblivious to the cultural divide that has grown up between myself and Aziz, unwilling to confront an Islamic world that impinges on his sentimental, harmonious fantasies of the Orient.

He parks the car in the garage of a newly-built estate on the outskirts. We take the lift to the fourth floor while he starts telling me about his meeting at the Seville EXPO with the chief artisan responsible for the Moroccan pavilion – a man who had also worked on the massive new mosque at Casablanca.

The modern, yellow-painted door of his bachelor apartment opens onto a small sitting-room whose low ceiling has been coated with elaborate Moorish stuccowork out of harmony and all proportion with the space it decorates.

'This is also his work,' he says. 'I got him to come here after he'd finished his job at the EXPO. There are few people in Europe capable of such refined and skilful craftsmanship.'

Aziz nods his head approvingly, as Miguel fills me in with his plans for the rest of his half-completed apartment.

'I'll have tapestries on the walls and seating arranged below them stacked high with cushions... all the doors will be those lovely wooden ones you can buy at Fez... the tiles in the bathroom will be from Marrakesh... there's a person in the Alpujarra who makes these wonderful gilded bronze lanterns... perhaps I might have a musical corner with some rebec or other instrument lying around on a stool... what do you think of my idea of turning this place into some Islamic cultural centre where musicians and poets can come and perform, or scholars such as yourself have a discussion?'

We continue talking in a kitchen where the dreams of the East dissolve into the formica, laminated plastic reality of a modern housing estate. Out of the near empty fridge he finds three bottles of beer.

The Melilla boat is due to leave at midday. I fit in a morning's appointment in the old heart of Almería.

The surroundings of Almería's fortress-like cathedral still have the outward squalor and decay that Brenan, with his genteel upbringing, had found so exotic and seductive. But the architect's office I enter has a designer elegance and modernity.

This is the practice of Ramón de Torres, a good-natured and unpretentious young architect whom I see as a particularly appropriate person to go and visit immediately prior to the crossing from Spain to Morocco: his intellectual and professional interests make him a bridge figure between Spain and the Islamic world.

In Almería he belongs to exactly the sort of intellectual circle that my friend Miguel envisages for his new apartment. A central figure in his circle is the elderly, Galician-born poet José Ángel Valente, whose works are obsessed with death, deprivation and exile. Valente and Ramón share a fascination with Morocco, which partly accounts for their friendship with Juan Goytisolo, a frequent visitor to Almería ever since the days of his two controversial travel books on the region – *La Chanca* and *Campos de Níjar*.

'Are you thinking of seeing Goytisolo in Marrakesh?' enquires Ramón, who disputes my view of Goytisolo's writings as being as fundamentally romantic towards the Islamic world as those of the Orientalists whom he so brilliantly criticizes in works such as *Crónicas Sarracinas*.

'He is one of the few Europeans who has truly assimilated Islamic culture,' according to Ramón, who urges me to go and see him while also warning me of the man's reserved and timid character.

Turning now to Ramón's own work, I mention that the last time I visited Almería's Alcazaba there was a camel posing for tourists at the entrance and a huge Arab tent where you were served Moroccan tea. Ramón laughs at the remembrance of this, and stresses that he hates the ersatz culture of today, and that his own attitude towards the restoration of ruined monuments combines a healthy respect for history with a belief in applying appropriate modern solutions.

His current, most cherished project is the rehabilitation of the medina at Tetuan in Morocco – a project which is being partly financed by the Junta de Andalucía and other Spanish organizations. There are, he elaborates, very close historical ties between Tetuan and his own town: he talks about the many Almerians who settled in Tetuan, and about the the great influence they had on the local architecture. With the aid of a map, he guides me through the medina's fast decaying streets, revealing to me the smallness of what he's already achieved, the enormity of the task ahead of him, the probability of funds running out. In the circumstances, he's remarkably positive and optimistic. He believes passionately in the coming together of European and Islamic cultures, and sees the inhabitants of Tetuan as unfailingly supportive of what he is doing.

I leave him to his theoretical Morocco and rush down to the port.

Edmondo de Amicis' house in Fez

CHAPTER SIX

EXILES IN THE ORIENT

The scenes of departure can easily be imagined. They are echoed in the tired images of modern journalism – the emptying of ghettoes, bags crammed with a lifetime's belongings, entreaties at airports, over-laden boats, roads packed with fleeing convoys, the desperate distribution of food, the chaos of refugee camps.

The ethnic cleansing that was initiated in Spain in 1492 climaxed here over a century later in a final solution involving the expulsion of at least one third of a million moriscos from a country numbering at most nine million inhabitants.

Earth tremors, high waters, celestial and other portents reputedly speeded up the signing of this last order of expulsion, which was carried out to the accompaniment of the incessant sound of church bells proclaiming what one monk defined as God's love of Spain's Catholics and his desire to punish 'the infidelity of these barbarians'.

They travelled to the ports on foot or in hired carts, their only permitted belongings being those they could carry on their persons. There were elderly men who could hardly walk, invalids dragged from their death beds, poverty-stricken people with threadbare clothes and sandals that were falling apart. They travelled together in sweaty, dusty, tearful convoys that made such an impression on a certain Father Áznar Cardona that he was compelled vividly to record all that he saw: he perceived the refugees as 'tired, in pain, lost, exhausted, sad, confused, ashamed, angry, crestfallen, irritated, bored, thirsty and hungry'.

Not everyone was so unhappy: there were those who thought that Allah had come to their need, not only in allowing them freely to rejoin their fellow Muslims, but also in making the Christians offer to pay for their sea crossing. But the patience of even the most stoical and accepting of the moriscos must have been tested beyond endurance on arrival at the ports.

Now came the implementation of one of the cruellest clauses in the expulsion order: children under the age of seven were not allowed to travel directly from Spain to Muslim lands, thus obliging their parents to continue on to France – a dangerous undertaking – or else abandon their young children to Christian orphanages, the preferred if also most painful of the options.

Then there was the discovery that ships freighted by the Crown had begun to charge for the passage, whereupon many of the moriscos began haggling for cheaper fares with other captains, some of whom would leave them where they did not want to go to, or else rob them of the little they possessed, or even kill them.

And on top of all the hysterical confusion, physical debilitation, conflicting emotions, anguished decisions, and bureacratic formalities that must have reached nightmare proportions on reaching the ports, there was the constant and ever growing uncertainty of what future lay in store for the moriscos in Africa. An Africa from which they had been cut off for centuries.

The port is quiet on this early December morning, only a handful of people at the ticket-office, no sign of those over-filled gift-laden vans that set off from all over Europe in a kamikaze rush to take Moroccan emigrants home for their holidays.

I buy my ticket, and, as I wait patiently to board, recall the moment in Amin Maalouf's *Leo the African* when the hero's father is joined at the port at the last minute by his slave mistress from whom he is so loath to part.

I'm secretly hoping for a sudden appearance by the Moorish Queen. I give her a ring in Granada, whereupon this ridiculous hope finally dies. She talks cheerily to me as if nothing has happened between us, she's gone back to work at her old office, she's reconciled with the Usurper, she tells me to look after myself and to send her a card. I put down the phone, remember a line from Ibn 'Arabi, and wish I too could resolve like to him to have a clearer sense of my life's direction.

'When, in Andalucía, I arrived at the Mediterranean sea,' he wrote to a pupil, describing his feelings prior to sailing for Africa, 'I resolved not to make the crossing until I had been allowed to see all the internal and external states that God had destined for me until the time of my death.'

The loudspeakers announce the imminence of departure, and I climb the gangway on to a large ship that seems to have been left untouched and uncleaned since its plastic-coated, orange-carpeted heyday in the early 1970's.

The boat leaves, a view of the coast unfolds all the way east to the Cabo de Gata, an amber jewel flickering in the sharp sunlight before vanishing in the ever widening sea. A young Moroccan places a beach-bag beside the empty pool on the first-class deck. He takes out a towel and lays it down on the worn astro-turf. He kneels down. He prays towards Mecca.

In crossing from Spain to Morocco, I am not only retracing the fate of the Spanish Moors and moriscos, I am also following the example of those many romantic travellers whose oriental yearnings had been awakened in the Alhambra and who now wished to perpetuate these yearnings with a visit to what they thought of as the Orient itself.

The cultural shock that awaited them on the other side of the Mediterranean was beyond what even the Alhambra had prepared them for. For Sir Arthur de Capell Brooke, author of *Sketches in Spain and Morocco*, the change between Spain and Morocco was so striking that 'you almost imagine yourself to have been transported at once to Timbuctoo'. 'I find myself in a new world,' exclaimed the painter David Roberts. 'I thought Spain different, but this excels all I have seen.' If Africa began in Spain – as Victor Hugo reminded readers in *Les Orientales* – then Asia began in Africa.

An ocean not a sea separated Spain from Africa, wrote the irre-pressibly romantic de Amicis. And the immensity of this divide was one that must also have been felt by Spain's moriscos, who were exchanging a country in which they had come to be treated as strangers for an alien world to which they would adapt with far greater difficulty than Spanish Moors had done in earlier centuries.

They had forgotten Arabic, they dressed in European costume, they had known a different form of Islam to the one practised here, as well as different customs. Their foreign status was such that they would sometimes be called 'Christians of Castile', and some would even suffer martyrdom on account of this. Many remained Christian by culture if not in practice, as an admittedly biased observer – an English agent called Harrison – emphasized in a letter written from Tetuan in 1625: 'I've had dealings with the moriscos or Andalucían exiles from Spain, many of whom have confessed and declared to me that they were Christians at heart. They complained bitterly about their cruel destiny... desiring as they did to be back once more under a Christian government.'

Dusk turns to night as the boat approaches the Spanish enclave of Melilla – another world lost between two cultures. Boabdil had landed here on fleeing from Adra in 1493. But the town was captured four years later by the Spaniards, who, in response to their fears of a Moroccan invasion of Spain, established here a Spanish garrison that survives today as a town divided equally between Muslims and Catholics.

The boat moors beside the sturdy sixteenth-century ramparts that for many centuries had comprised the whole of this Spanish Gibral-tar. I take a taxi into the New Town, which is in itself an enclave – an enclave of Francoist Spain encased in a dusty, seedily evocative art nouveau framework echoing that of Cartagena.

The taxi, one of a fleet of old and discontinued Mercedes, drops me at a pension situated at one of the livelier corners of a regular grid of streets proclaiming the now tarnished glories of the army and the fatherland. It brings back memories of my earliest days of Spanish travel – a dingy stairwell taken up by a cast-iron lift, bare, lime-green walls, a reception area in plastic wood with a heavy-breasted woman who hands over my bedroom key from a large board with crudely stencilled numbers. The woman is talking in an indeterminate guttural language to a younger female companion who flashes me a smile with pink-ochre lips. The words are in Spanish, Arabic, perhaps even Berber.

I go back on foot to the walled medina, where I hope to have my first encounter with the oriental picturesque in the mysterious streets beyond the spotlit gateway with its sculpted crest of Charles V. But the whole of this dimly lit quarter is under restoration, its buildings hidden by scaffolding, its streets pulled up and emptied of all but a couple of bored soldiers, a group of playing Moroccan children, and the odd robed figure appearing out of the shadows.

The place is a sepulchre from which I return eagerly to the New Town to look for somewhere to have a drink among its crammed, ramshackle rows of art nouveau offices and duty-free shops. I settle for a bar that adjoins a synagogue and appears in the half light to bear the name of a famous brand of rum. On closer inspection I find it's called the Bar Sefardi.

'What has become of the Andalusian Moor?' asked Sir Arthur de Capell Brooke, 'Where is the Spaniard of former ages? Both races have passed away, and in their descendents scarcely a trace remains of a once powerful, generous, high-minded people. The Jew alone remains unaltered…'

With the Jewish waiters of the Bar Sefardi I make my first contact with a people descended from the refugees of 1492, and have instant evidence of a hybrid culture – the tapas include 'Sephardic tortilla' and 'kosher chorizo' made from beef. 'We're a sizeable but diminishing community,' the waiter tells me. 'There are so few jobs here. But at least there isn't the threat of fundamentalism. Almost nothing's left of the great Jewish communities of Morocco – everyone's leaving for Israel.'

The cultural anomalies of Melilla, together with an element of sexual ambiguity, colour the late-night bar I visit afterwards to drink a cocktail shaken by a Moroccan waiter with a piercing high-pitched voice. He feels himself to be Spanish, but talks only Moroccan to his family. He has never been across the sea to Spain, nor has he ever entered Morocco. I have a final drink, but the bar remains empty. I'm in a red velvet void, in an indeterminate country.

The next morning I'm made further aware of the isolation of Melilla when I ask about buses from the frontier to Fez. No one can tell me. Morocco is a world away, little seems known about it, apart from the black-market rate of the dirham, which is sold in the streets by persistent groups of men whom I try hard to avoid before eventually being referred to them by an employee at a bank.

With my dihrams acquired I feel ready to leave, and have a farewell breakfast in a shady bar whose fat, mean-looking owner coughs up phlegm and jokes about Moroccans. On the palm-lined Plaza de España I catch a town bus to the Spanish side of the frontier. Art nouveau dreams fade away, Melilla peters out into a single road with sun-scorched blocks and industrial warehouses. The Spaniards all get out, Moroccans begin appearing as if from out of the wasteland, they fill the bus, crowd the sides of the road, and finally spill over into the dusty road itself after the bus has reached its last stop, a hundred metres or so from the Spanish frontier post. I become a solitary European sweating with my luggage among a flowing, pungent, murmuring stream that sweeps along robes, veils, cloths, pots, ghetto blasters, spices. Africa has arrived with the exhilarating, disconcerting suddenness that had taken so many romantic travellers off their guard.

Chaos and colours were exactly what these travellers were expecting of the Orient, but the thronging masses that suddenly confronted them on reaching Morocco induced also the fear of imminent robbery, deception, exploitation, pestering and haggling – aspects of an African journey that would lead the travellers to hate the very people in whom they saw reflected their oriental dreams. Even such an empassioned Orientalist as de Amicis would end up believing that the Moroccans were 'false, pusillanimous, cringing to the powerful, insolent to the weak, governed by avarice, devoured by egotism, and burning with the basest passions of which the human heart is capable'.

The confusion at the border conveys to me the prospect of hours of waiting, arguments with border guards, missing my bus to Fez, another night at Melilla. I'm determined not to lose either my patience or my temper, I shall adopt a Sufi-like detachment, I'm now in Africa, time has less meaning than ever. I'm also strangely excited: difficult border crossings are what travel is really about, they add to the remoteness of a place, they no longer exist in western Europe. I remember the exotic lure of Irun during the Franco days.

The first hurdle is easily passed. A Spanish guard waves me past a long and paralysed queue of lorries and Moroccans. He says there's no need to have my passport stamped. I walk with cheerful confidence the 300 more metres to the Moroccan frontier post where once again I'm told to avoid the queue. There's a special window reserved for foreigners, I'm the first European of the morning, I'm given forms to fill, I hand in my passport.

A plump guard stares at my travel-worn passport, damages it further by pulling off its protective case, and leafs through the entire document, breaking back its spine with every turn of the soiled pages. He shakes his head, tells me to wait. A tall young man is sitting behind him, reading a newspaper, uninterested by the passport he has just been given by his colleague. He takes his time, folds his newspaper, finally rises to his feet, looks at me as if I were a criminal.

'You need a new passport,' he says.

'Why?' I ask, trying to force a smile.

'This one is dirty and torn.'

'I use it a lot.'

He shrugs and remains unconcerned when I tell him that the nearest British consulate is in Seville.

'The passport is not valid,' he repeats.

'But it says there valid until August 1997.'

'All British people today have the new European Community passports. These old black ones aren't valid.'

The hopes of reaching Fez by nightfall recede, my dreams of the Orient are being curtailed. Remaining as calm as I can possibly be I make an exaggerated case for the importance of my mission – a government-sponsored mission that will make a vital contribution to the strengthening of Spanish-Moroccan relations.

'You need the passport stamped by the Spanish authorities before we can talk any more,' he retorts, shutting his window.

My luggage weighs more than ever, and the heat is greater still as I trundle back to the Spanish border post. A soldier shouts at me to stop, his face is friendly and apologetic.

'Don't worry about what that man told you. You don't really need a stamp in your passport, but if I were you I'd have it done just to keep him happy.'

I keep on walking.

The chief Spanish officer with the necessary stamp is unavailable, he'll be back in about half an hour, there's a group of Moroccans waiting in front of me, they recommend patience and calm, 'otherwise you'll never enjoy your holiday.'

The officer returns and stamps my passport with a bewildered shake of the head. 'The Moroccans,' he sighs.

I feel I've become a puppet dragged backwards and forwards in a no-man's land between two countries. There is a further argument with the Moroccan guard, he wants to know how much money I've got on me, he shakes his head again, now he wants proof of how long I'll be staying in Morocco, if ever I get there that is. Then he gives up, he's become bored with this whole game, or perhaps he's concluded that he's not going to be offered a bribe after all, and that I'm too naïve to realize that this is all he wants. 'This is the last time you'll be allowed in with this passport,' he says curtly. I thank him profusely, I don't know why, and he goes back to his newspaper, hiding his pleasure at having exercised his modicum of power.

I'm finally through, and have put my watch back an hour – I've reached the proverbially exotic Orient and am back on English time.

'M'sieur, M'sieur!' the shouts have already begun. 'M'sieur, Msieur!' Boys and young men are surrounding me on all sides. 'Come to my taxi! Don't go to his!' 'His taxi is dirty!' 'I have limousine for you!' 'His car's dangerous!' 'You change money? Change money?' 'Over here, my friend! Over here!'

Fate directs me into a sordid back street, where a car that must once have seemed opulent is parked like an old actor awaiting his come-back. The driver is told to take me to the bus-stop at Nador, though the man who has guided me here decides to come as well. 'You'll need a hand in buying your ticket.'

Rats prowl in the field of putrid rubbish where women are standing next to a trickle of water, washing clothes. The car joins an empty, scarred dual carriageway that runs between the sea and a bare mountain slope ringed on its upper level by an apparently infinite row of crenellations, like a modern wall of China.

'That's the largest and most recent of the king's palaces,' my self-appointed guide tells me. 'He comes here about once a year for a few days.'

At Nador my luggage is tied on top of the bus, together with crates of live chickens and wickerwork baskets packed with textiles and vegetables. My guide leaves me, extorting beforehand a large tip and warning me 'as a friend' to look out for pickpockets and 'bad men'. I take him seriously, remembering stories of marauding bandits who found easy targets in the newly-arrived moriscos journeying from the coast to Fez.

The landscape we pass through is like a yet more desolate version of that of Almería, mesmerizing in its dimensions, devoid of any comforting corners. Our jolting progress is continually interrupted by police blocks – at least two of them at the entrance and exit of every town and major village, others in the middle of nowhere. Sometimes all the luggage is taken off the roof, usually there's a policeman entering the bus, slowly scrutinizing the passengers, asking me for my passport. Not even when travelling through Communist Europe have I been so conscious of being in a police state. Contraband from the coast explains the tightness of the security measures, I am told. But there are other factors – the proximity of Algeria, the recent gunning down of Spanish tourists at a hotel in Marrakesh, the present tensions and uncertainties in a Morocco kept together by a king who is now ill with cancer.

The sky has turned a sinister bronze, and drops of rain – the first I've seen in weeks – have striated the dust-obscured windows of the bus. We make a twilight entrance into a city the French had dubbed 'la mystérieuse'.

❧

The shops and offices are closing, it is the hour of the café, the hour between work and evening prayers, the hour when the men have emulated the roost of the starlings and the egret, and flocked together in dense, dark masses. They have gathered in their grey suits and robes at the cafés of the New Town, and are swarming around the serried rows of chairs and tables, observing new arrivals, watching a distant television, gesticulating in animated groups, shouting to friends across grey smoky spaces, sipping tea from murky glasses choked with sugar and sprigs of mint.

Inside the Café Zanzibar I shelter from the rain while awaiting my meeting with Elena.

Elena, a sister of a Murcian friend, has been living in Fez for nearly a year, teaching Spanish at the Instituto Cervantes. As a student of Arabic in Madrid, she had once spent a whole night talking with me in the bars of that city, after which I had received in the post an unexpected parcel filled with books about Sufism, one of which was inscribed 'Enjoy them if you're still in the mood'. I had not met her before, nor seen her since, but an image had remained with me of some latterday Carmen – an image largely created by the gossip of others, but partially sustained by my memories of her dark looks and husky voice.

Stories of her love life abound, of the hearts she has broken, of the colourful range of men whose attraction to her has been turned to obsession by her independent nature and unwillingness to commit herself to long-term relationships. But I've heard she's changed greatly ever since coming to Fez. She's living quietly on her own, she enjoys teaching, and has neglected her study of Islamic culture to absorb herself in Spanish philology. She loves the life of Morocco and is apparently happy within those limitations that an Islamic land invariably imposes on even the most open-minded of Westerners, especially single women.

I have brought with me a recent Spanish novel to give to her – *Mimoun* by Rafael Chirbes. I had been drawn to it in a bookshop in Almería because it dealt with a Spaniard tiring of Madrid and escaping to Morocco to teach Spanish at Fez. I now begin to look at it more closely, and am soon engrossed in a powerful short tale based on elements common to some of the greatest Western fictions about North Africa, such as Paul Bowles' *The Sheltering Sky* – a fascination with the exotic that ends in a nightmare, and passes through a stage of alienation from both Western and Islamic cultures. 'I had the sensation,' writes the book's hero, 'that I had abandoned one continent, and that I was never going to reach the other. I was adrift.'

I go off to meet Elena at the end of her day at the Instituto Cervantes. She even looks different from the person I'd known four years before. Her curly locks have been clipped short, and she wears round, gold-rimmed glasses that magnify the boss-eyed expression she develops when breaking into one of her frequent deep laughs.

'So your interest in Sufism has led you to Fez,' she smiles, recalling the time when I had investigated the recent spread of the Sufis in Granada – a community led by the mysterious Sheik Abdalquadir, alias Ian Dallas, former producer of the Beatles.

We eat in a restaurant serving French food and a red burgundy wine from nearby Meknes, the only wine-growing area of Morocco. She tells me she's tired of Fez, a place whose beauty never ceases to impress her but which at the same time is closed, conservative and gossip-ridden. She has made no close friends here.

'This is the only thing that keeps me in Fez,' she reveals at the end of the evening, when we drive up to a smart, modern colony at the edge of the town. An old, sleeping man wakes up to salute us and open the barrier to a colony apparently occupied almost entirely by university teachers. Elena's house is a white cube of a villa exuding a modernist luxuriousness I find difficult to associate with the Elena I remember from Spain – a person of spartan tastes who travelled everywhere like a gypsy.

The interior, calm and light, is tastefully decorated with ceramics from Marrakesh, 'imperial' carpets from Rabat, cedarwork carvings from Fez. Aided by whisky, I slip off into a deep sleep on top of a sweet-smelling divan swathed in oriental silks and rugs. I wake up disorientated, bathed in a sunlight dappled by the exotic plants and flowers of a lush, overgrown garden. A beautiful negress in a red cotton dress carries in breakfast on a wooden tray. I rub my eyes, and shake off strange dreams.

The Orient is a world that Westerners have shrouded in dreams – dreams of hell and of sensual reverie, dreams brought on by troubled nights and the smoking of kif, dreams that are metaphors of a world that entices but is not understood. Whole books on Morocco have been written as if under the spell of a dream that is disturbed occasionally by the impinging of a reality so intense and vivid that this itself takes on the character of another dream, a nightmarish dream. De Amicis, following on from his oriental ramblings in Spain, brought the genre to perfection in a work on Morocco that has a chapter on Fez in which the waking dreams induced by the singular sights and ocurrences he witnesses and experiences here give him at night 'such strangely intricate dreams of severed heads, and deserts, of harems, prisons, Timbuktu, and Turin, that when I wake in the mornings, it takes me some minutes to find out what world I am in'.

Elena is wandering around like a phantom in a white flannelled dressing-gown. The maid has taken away the breakfast tray, and I'm lying half-awake on the terrace, unable to accept the reality of this state of oriental indolence, or indeed of being in a town whose old quarter has so often been described as an intact survival from the Middle Ages.

Fez is a labyrinth, and Elena has offered to guide me through it. The arrival at night has entirely confused me, and it is only in the course of a great loop made in Elena's car that I begin to appreciate the town's sprawling layout, swung between fortified hills below the cedar-covered Atlas mountains.

The New Town, created by the French under General Lyautey, is tactfully separated by a kilometre or two from the rest of Fez, which forms what de Amicis called 'a monstrous figure of eight' divided between the walled townships of Fez Djid (New Fez) and Fez el Bali (Old Fez).

We drive towards the former garrison town of Fez Djid, in which the Marinid rulers of Morocco once kept an army for the main purpose of continuing the campaign against Spain. Inside, we pass the royal palace with its enormous forecourt, skirt the Marinid-protected Jewish quarter of the Mallah, then leave by another gate, and make a baffling circle that deposits us on the northern side of Fez el Bali, which only now comes fully into view, stifling inside its Almohad walls, a frayed honeycomb of cubes and minarets that owes much of its medieval completeness to the economic and political decline consolidated early this century by the decision of the French to transfer the Moroccan capital from Fez to Rabat.

Elena, with her fluent command of Arabic and street-wise toughness, extricates us from the young guides and street sellers who pin us down the moment she parks her car outside the Bab el Guissa gate, from whence we descend into the dark depths of a warren in which even those who have lived all their lives in Fez continue to get lost. 'Chi mi dara la voce e le parole!' de Amicis had wanted to exclaim inside this indescribable labyrinth, which is said to be best explored by wandering freely, following the urges of the subconscious, inhaling the drug-like pleasures of alleys whose only discernible logic is as threads in a web of crafts guilds centred around the exotic spider of the Kairaouan Mosque, behind whose walls, closed to Westerners, lie the further mysteries of a fabled library that had managed for centuries to hide the memoirs of the last of Granada's Ziri kings.

My interest in the Andalucían legacy fails to give much focus to our wanderings, for this legacy is diffused throughout the town – a town whose ninth-century rise to become one of the spiritual capitals of Islam coincided with the beginnings of an influx of refugees from al-Andalus that would gather momentum with the Christian reconquest of Spain.

The leather-backed wooden chairs, the showily-coloured kaftans, the gold-threaded slippers, the basket-like patterns of the local cedar-workers, the wealth of decoration that the Marinids lavished on their palaces and madrasas – these and other traces of al-Andalus mark our slow progress towards the area of the old town officially designated as that of the Andalucíans.

Beyond the district of the tanners, where sprigs of mint protect tourists' noses from the viler odours of the Orient, is the insignificant stream which splits Fez el Bali into quarters associated respectively with refugees from Kairouan in Tunisia and refugees from Andalucía. A wall had once further separated these two quarrelling factions, but even after this had been pulled down by the Almoravids and a bridge built, rivalries and differences between the two had remained. The thirteenth-century chronicler of Fez, Ibn Abi-Zar-el-Fasi, had said that while the Kairaouanis had most of the money, the Andalucíans boasted the bravest soldiers, the best cultivators of the soil, and the prettiest women.

Stepping today into the quarter where nearly all of the town's leading Andalucían scholars and craftsmen had lived, the sensation is of entering the most neglected part of old Fez. Even Elena, who has explored so many corners of Fez el Bali, confesses that this is unknown territory to her. We are almost tempted to hire a guide, but for once no one bothers to approach us – tourists are no longer in evidence, the monuments are few and mainly modest, the atmosphere is provincial and almost rural, the streets are quieter, more widely spaced, more residential, and with a life that revolves less around crafts than the daily necessities of life. We are returning slowly to a more normal world.

The days pass, the exotic and the romantic are tempered by repeated exposure to everyday life, but not enough to control my persistent sentimental urges to hunt down the tombs of the great Andalucíans who have died in Fez.

Elena is amused by this 'English obsession', but she dutifully drives me to the cemetery where the great Loja-born scholar, Ibn al-Khatib, is supposedly buried. However, I'm left on my own to try and imagine the final resting-place of Boabdil, of whose last days in Morocco contradictory tales are told. Ironically, the most glamorous version is by a Spanish chronicler, Diego de Torres, who has Boabdil dying at the age of eighty while fighting for the king of Fez at the battle of Abu 'Aqba of 1536: 'In this battle [Boabdil] died, which made a mockery of Fortune, for death struck him as he was defending the kingdom of somebody else when he had not dared to defend his own.' I prefer to believe the Islamic scholar al-Maqqari, who visited Fez in 1627 and met descendants of Boabdil who were drawing charitable relief. According to their story he died in Fez itself, either in 1518 or 1533, and was buried near the Bab Mahrouk Gate, above what has become, I find, a busy ring road.

I have followed Boabdil's footsteps to a point where I can go no further. Now I've only one remaining wish in Fez – to see for myself one of the lavish palace interiors that are said to hide behind the dark, crammed alleys of the old town.

The wish is granted with a quick phone call made by Elena. A young man in an open red Mercedes turns up at her house an hour later, he compliments Elena on her beauty, he urges her to come with us, it's not often he opens up his palace. She declines politely, she's too busy.

She's already warned me about Hassan. He's a kind man, a good friend, but he's a playboy, he's on a different planet from her. The number of times he's wanted to show her his palace! But she's not interested, she can't really explain why. 'I'm just not impressed by those things.'

'A beautiful girl, Elena,' Hassan winks to me as he drives me off towards Fez el Djedid. He speaks with an American accent, he's studied at UCLA Berkeley, he's a trained agriculturalist who looks after his family estate near Fez. He talks with a broad smile, asks me what I think of his 'beautiful city'; the question must be rhetorical, for he's not really interested in my answer. 'And the women of our city!' he adds, putting on a tape of 'California Girls'.

He parks his car in a private compound near the entrance to the Mallah. 'A couple of American friends should be waiting for us here; they've just flown in from the States.'

The five of us walk single file along the narrowest of alleys, as Hassan shouts back at us, 'This is what I love about our city – the unexpected.' Women on the way from the market, running children, turbaned old men, cripples on crutches, artisans carrying their tools, all squeeze past our little procession headed by a Hassan who is soon holding a mobile phone against his ear and mumbling what appear to be instructions.

A meek-faced man is waiting a few hundred metres further on, below the lintel of a humble door. He bows to each of us in turn as we pass through the door and into a sombre corridor that emerges into a vast, glazed courtyard.

'Wow!!' exclaims a newly-married Californian woman visiting Morocco for the first time. 'This is what the East is all about.'

I'm wondering instead about the suitability of applying the word 'neo-Moorish' to a Moroccan palace built in the 1920's by Hassan's grandparents. The Marinid palaces contemporary with the Alhambra have all disappeared, to be replaced by buildings such as these, where the distinction between the continuation of a tradition and the revival of one have become blurred.

The furniture is all covered and the palace hasn't been lived in for years. 'We use it every six months or so for receptions,' says Hassan, his mobile phone constantly in his hand. He poses with a waving hand as I photograph him in an alcove with blue silk curtains that frame as in a royal portrait this new sultan in his Californian jeans. He answers his ringing phone. 'We can now all go upstairs,' he tells us.

We climb up into the open air, and have a view over rooftops towards the distant Marinid tombs, now casting long shadows over their gaunt orange-red hill. Fez, seen from the top of one of its buildings, takes on a different aspect, as Hassan points out palace after palace, some as unused as his, some with roofs that can be opened and closed with hydraulic gadgetry, all of them taking up such a large area of central Fez that I begin to think that the Orient is just as so many Westerners have imagined it – a playboy's toy, a playboy's dream.

I escape with Elena by moonlight. We're like a fleeing couple, our enemies have been shaken off, and we breathe the smell of cedars as we climb into the Atlas and head south to Marrakesh.

A sudden impulse on a Friday night has set us off on this nocturnal rush – Elena's time is limited, and I have to resort to the pleasures of the imagination to compensate for not being able to see the beautiful mountain landscapes that Elena describes to me as they glide past us in the silvery darkness.

Dawn begins to break only after we have descended from the forested mountains and entered the flat desert-like plateau in which Marrakesh extends, in its oasis of palms. We drive down wide, empty streets to the famous large square of Djemaa el Fna, which is slowly rising out of its brief moments of somnolence with the arrival of the first orange vendors, their wares shining brilliantly in the early morning sun.

The porter is dozing in the dingy lobby of the Hotel CNP, on the southern side of the square. Elena had intended at first to stay in the outlying and rather more respectable Hotel Moussafir, a place belonging to a chain of establishments she said were 'modern, reliable, reasonably priced and completely indistinguishable from each other' but, thanks to exhaustion and an amused tolerance of my foibles, she's given in to my desire for a hotel 'with character' overlooking the square whose every sound and activity has been chronicled by writers ranging from Goytisolo to Canetti. 'This brings back my early days of travelling in Morocco,' she smiles, collapsing onto the dirty sheets of an airless, courtyard-facing room with blistered, dark-green walls.

I have my breakfast on the roof terrace, surrounded by back-packing tourists immersed in their guide-books. The luminous pink expanse of Marrakesh, with its palms and minarets, dissolves under the cloudless sky into an apparent mirage of mountains, snow-capped to the south.

The writer and historian Khalid Kamal, recently returned from Granada, is standing waiting for me in the lobby, a diminutive figure with a goatee beard, a puckish smile, and a wave of grey-streaked black hair like that of an ageing flamenco musician. His voice, exuding a delight and fascination with the world, develops a high squeak in its more excited moments.

'They tell me,' he says, 'that you've hidden a beautiful and mysterious Spanish woman in your room. And she's a driver as well? You're a lucky man.'

There's no time to disillusion him about the nature of my

friendship with Elena, for he's already launched into an erotic anecdote about the Alcalá poet Ibn Sa'id. He has phrases and stories for every occasion, they issue from his fertile, encyclopaedic mind like the musings of a humorous Islamic sage.

'"You love wine, you love women, Vous êtes sur le bon chemin", Ibn Sa'id told his Jewish friend.'

He chuckles as he concludes the story, then wonders if Elena will be coming with us on our morning's walk.

'She won't?' he exclaims surprised, 'She'll be sleeping all morning? You must be an exhausting man!'

Abruptly he turns to face the wide expanse of the Djemaa el Fna, which is losing its pink mellowness in the ever fiercer morning light.

'Then we must go,' he says. 'We have little time.'

He sets off across the square, dispersing with his sprightly step the hustlers who pounce on tourists the moment they leave their hotels.

'And how is our mutual patron in Granada?' he asks, allowing me a few moments to outline some of the political problems that the Sultan has recently faced, and the classically eloquent letter he wrote in his defence to a local newspaper.

'He's a great man, a noble man,' Khalid comments. 'He's too intelligent, that's why he has enemies, the mediocre envy him. History never changes, the same happened to Ibn al-Khatib of Loja.'

'You must tell him,' he adds, 'that my researches are continuing into his renegade ancestors. They probably ended up in Tetuan; there are many people there with his surname. Will you be going back soon to Granada?'

'Granada!' he sighs, as we exchange the heat and blinding light of the square for the cool, dark labyrinth of souks that opens up on its northern side. 'If you're feeling nostalgic for that city like I am, you'll appreciate my telling you how similar its Islamic market must have been to the place we shall now visit.'

Sunlight filters through the canework canopies of the vast covered area we pass through on our way to the town's oldest mosque, which I am told stands among market stalls like the mosque that is now the cathedral of Granada. Nearing the centre of the labyrinth we walk below wooden beamed ceilings

('Andalucían in style') that span a group of long narrow halls displaying leatherware, textiles, shoes and other wares of distant Andalucían origin. Briefly we emerge into a small, dazzling square where spices have always been sold, laid out in neat piles along the ground, 'just as they are in that hippy's stall outside the cathedral door in Granada.' Some of the spices are aphrodisiac, he adds. 'You might need some for your friend.'

We reach the mosque, an Almoravid foundation at the historic heart of the city. The Almoravids, a nomadic desert tribe originating from the same part of the Sahara now occupied by the Tuaregs, had emerged by the mid eleventh century as a puritanical reforming movement dedicated to divesting Islam of the decadent ways that some say had been the legacy to Morocco of the wealthy Muslims of al-Andalus. Their greatest leader was Youssef ben Tachine, who was the very personification of the ideals of simplicity advocated by his people.

'He was a man of about my build,' Khalid tells me, as he begins to summarize in his lively style the early history of Marrakesh. 'His eyes were the deepest black, but his voice was soft and his face as smooth as that of a woman. He clothed himself always in the coarsest woollen garments, and lived on an exclusive diet of the meat and milk of a camel. It's difficult to imagine him adapting to such a sybaritic place as Andalucía.'

In 1085, long after founding Marrakesh and bringing Morocco under his dominion, Youssef made his first visit to al-Andalus, invited by a group of Muslims anxious about the future of their country after the loss of Toledo to the Christians. He returned five years later to help further restore Muslim control and to annexe the place to the Almoravid empire. Unwilling to relinquish Marrakesh as the capital of this empire, he stayed briefly in his newly-acquired Spanish territory, which he left in the hands of governors whose puritan ideals were soon exposed to the political corruption and moral laxity that Youssef had seen as endemic in al-Andalus.

Ali ben Youssef, Youssef's son and successor, was no less pious than his father, but the ceaseless military threat to his empire forced him to lay aside his religious principles and employ Christian mercenaries to help him maintain power. The fact also that Ali had spent many of his formative years studying in Andalucía rather than experiencing, like his father, the rigours of desert life, encouraged the eventual infiltration into Marrakesh of such decadent Andalucían ways as the drinking of alcohol and the rejection of the veil. More immediately, and less controversially, Ali's leanings towards Andalucía led to the participation of Andalucían architects and craftsmen in the great building boom that was then initiated in the city.

Ali's 33-year reign saw the construction of much of the city's existing adobe defensive walls, as well as that of the underground channels, or *khettara* that helped to transform the few skimpy palms on the city's outskirts into the lush palmery and gardens of today. It was also during this period that there were founded the mosque to which I had been led by Khalid, and the adjoining teaching school, or *madrasa*, that likewise bears the name of Ali ben Youssef.

The present mosque is a wholly nineteenth-century structure, and Khalid rushes me round its exterior to take me to a hidden monument on its southern side – a monument which, for all the modesty in its size and function, he describes as the most important survival of the Almoravid period. Known as the *koubba*, this small kiosk originally covering an ablutions pool, was itself covered over for many centuries and only excavated in 1952. Here the Andalucían impact can be truly felt, as it must once have been in the actual mosque – here are decorative motifs new to Morocco such as pine cones, palms and acanthus, as well as complex ribbing and octagonal vaulting of the kind developed in tenth-century Córdoba. In this humble, Andalucían-inspired structure, Islamic historians have even managed to find the embryo from which all subsequent Moroccan architecture would evolve.

But Khalid's real passion is for the neighbouring madrasa, where he is soon guiding me upstairs into some bare and tiny rooms.

'This is where the students lived and studied. Do you remember the fictitious one I included in my book on the madrasa?' he asks, stopping in one of the rooms to recreate again this particular student's life.

We have skipped several centuries, past the apogee of Marrakesh under the Almoravids' successors, the Almohads, and past too the long period of the city's dramatic decline following the transfer of Morocco's capital to Fez by the country's new rulers, the Marinids. We have reached the late sixteenth century, when the Saadians have come to power, reinstated Marrakesh, and made it the capital of a Morocco now extending as far south as Timbuktu.

'Let's imagine this student as the son of refugees from al-Andalus. His parents have lost most of what they had possessed, but fortunately the boy does not have to pay anything for his education: the madrasa itself was financed out of public funds, while each of the students was supported by the pious foundations known as the Habous. The boy has to work hard in return; he has to take on an extraordinary range of subjects – astronomy, Islamic law, theology, Arabic literature, and so on. He is required to commit everything to memory, to spend his free hours learning huge texts by heart.'

Khalid moves over to the window as if to escape from the ascetic austerity of the study.

'Can't you imagine the dreams the boy must have had every time he looked out into the courtyard?'

Within the courtyard decoration blooms as in the most luscious of gardens: a flower bed of mosaic tiles bursts into an arbour of stucco arches, trellises of carved stone panels, a cedar lintel festooned with pine cones and Kufic script, and a honeysuckle of arabesques entangling the horse-shoe-arched mihrab. There is a reassuring familiarity in all this.

'The Alhambra,' says a smiling Khalid, who goes on to talk of the Granadine craftsmen who must certainly have worked in Marrakesh for the Saadians, not only on the madrasa but also on the Saadian tombs in the southern half of the old town.

'We should be going,' says Khalid, interrupting his historical discourse. 'The morning is nearly over, your friend will be getting impatient, we don't want to find her looking for another lover. The Spaniards are impetuous, I believe.' Once we have left the building, however, he stops abruptly as if an idea has suddenly occurred to him.

'She'll have to wait a bit longer,' he announces, leading me off into another corner of the great labyrinth of souks.

From the courtyard resonant of the Alhambra I am drawn once more into the Orient of the Western imagination. Soon we are back in the Middle Ages, squatting on low stools in a tiny workshop in the iron-clanging heart of the metal-workers' district. The elderly head of the guild, an old friend of Khalid, has welcomed us in, and is preparing to serve us mint tea from a silver kettle warmed on a charcoal brazier. Serenely featured, and with a turban perched on his prominent forehead, he squats on the ground in front of us, pushing aside a metal lantern he has tooled from implements of medieval aspect. He talks in a kind and gentle voice, and though Khalid translates his words, there seems in the way the old man looks at me an understanding that transcends the language barrier. When we all stand up to say farewell, he acts like a patriarch in an old romance, placing his hands on my shoulders as in a gesture of paternal blessing. He holds them there for a few moments, then kisses me on the cheek.

We finally collect Elena from the hotel, and she shields her sleepy eyes from the brutal midday light as we walk off towards the most famous of the town's Almohad structures – the Koutoubia Mosque.

'Don't you feel at home?' Khalid asks her when we stop in front of its minaret, one of several Almohad towers of the late twelfth century based on that of the Mezquita at Córdoba. 'I'm from Murcia not Andalucía,' she corrects him as we continue looking at this sturdily geometrical structure to which a certain Andalucían grace has been given by some elaborate blind arcading, an upper band of blue ceramic inlay, and three crowning golden spheres said to have been presented by a sultan's queen as a penance for missing three hours of fast during Ramadan.

'But I was once here with a Sevillian friend,' she adds, making us anticipate a tale of sentimental rapture. 'He couldn't hide his disappointment when he first saw the tower. He said it looked like a poor man's Giralda.'

'But that was built by the Almohads a few years later,' Khalid responds, 'when their tastes had evolved with greater exposure to the sophisticated delights of Seville. If such an otherworldly and refined Spanish Muslim as your Murcian compatriot Ibn 'Arabi could succumb to Seville's temptations, just imagine the effect of the city on a tribe of fundamentalist Berbers brought up in the desert.'

Continuing to walk, he points to a car he has parked on the other side of the mosque. 'Now it's our turn for some worldly temptations.'

We drive from the thirteenth century into what seems like the twenty-first – a spacious, palm-lined new town with wide straight avenues forming a modernist grid like that of an American town which has grown up in the desert. Parking the car near a sign marked 'Restaurant Le Jardin', we proceed into a cool shaded oasis where smart groups of people are seated at tables around a central fountain.

Over beers and wine, Elena and I are spirited away from the modern town and charmed once more into Khalid's world of oriental tales – tales of Ibn Sa'id, Ibn al-Khatib, Ibn 'Arabi, and all the other great figures of al-Andalus whose presence, like the Alhambra, echoes in this land of their exile. And in the telling of these tales, fragments of Khalid Kamal's own life make their brief appearance, confirming something about him I had guessed at from his books and from our short acquaintance in Granada – an inability to function within a university context, despite, or perhaps because of, the depth and enthusiastic breadth of his learning.

Intentions to resume our sightseeing in the afternoon are forgotten as lunch leads on to an invitation for coffee in his home – a modern apartment block that Khalid thinks will appeal to my specialist 'baroque' tastes. The place is indeed just as he describes it, a Cecil B. de Mille confection with swollen, Egyptian-style columns that spread from the façade into the luxury interior, where Khalid's wife and other female members of the household are waiting for us in a palatial sitting-room ringed with cushioned benches as if in expectation of a hundred guests. In this room, and in the many others of its kind throughout Morocco, modern urban life assimilates the habits of the desert, where space is limitless and hospitality legendary. We sink into the cushions and only raise ourselves from them when Khalid proposes, in the remaining hour of daylight, to show us a part of Marrakesh where traditional images of the Orient attain their post-modern apotheosis.

The Marrakesh I had always imagined had been the town of the Medina and the Djemaa el Fna – the town some travellers might think of as the 'real Morocco', and which has as its antithesis the prosperous, American-style and ultimately no less 'real' Marrakesh that has grown up around it. But Khalid is now taking us to a Marrakesh that extends further out still, a Marrakesh in which the old and the new are joined together in an outer ring of fabled gardens and villas.

We circle the whole town, which begins now to seem like a succession of walled gardens – gardens laid out with orchards, olive groves, raised walkways, summer pavilions, and huge basins that famously reflect the distant snows of the High Atlas; gardens of medieval origin that have inspired the horticultural creations of Western residents purveying a look of neo-Moroccan chic; gardens in which it is possible to imagine glamorous models posing besides pools for features in *Vogue* and *Marie-Claire*.

'The garden of the Impressionist painter Jacques Majorelle belongs today to Yves Saint-Laurent,' Khalid tells me as we eventually drive north into the vast palmery that Almoravid irrigation schemes had unwittingly created for the eventual delectation of Western millionaires. The sun is setting as we loop around this secretive residential expanse, where the luxury dreams of Westerners retreat behind palms and security cameras, finally to disappear altogether in the falling night. 'That property has just been acquired by Hermès, the one beyond is owned by a notorious homosexual admiral, over there you see...' Khalid keeps up a constant commentary even when there is nothing left to be seen.

He leaves us where our day began, in the Djemaa el Fna. With his departure, we become isolated Europeans let loose in a now dark and crowded square of magic and nightmare. The hypnotic hum of drums, plucked strings and oboe-like wails becomes progressively louder as we are pulled into the chaos, obeying a trance-like instinct which guides us past clouds of smoking fat, lanterns, fires, performing snakes, fortune-tellers, story-tellers, dancers, acrobats, healers. Impressions to be scribbled later in my notebook are forming, but then my notebook is symbolically stolen as I pause for a few moments to watch a large audience captivated by the power of the spoken word. And as we press on in our obscure, distracted way, we are made ever more conscious that we are not just observers but are ourselves being observed, our every movement being mysteriously, uncannily registered in the square's collective memory. 'Don't you remember me?' a young boy says to an incredulous Elena. 'You were here a couple of years ago with your parents, your hair was longer, and you had a blue skirt.'

In a café on the square's north-eastern corner a bespectacled Spanish writer sits among Moroccans watching the whole spectacle, his glasses streaked red by the glint from the fires. He is always here at this hour, every day during the six months of the year when he exchanges the literary environment of the Parisian *rive gauche* for a home with a terrace overlooking the Djemaa el Fna. He is the great exile of Spanish letters, the great outsider, a man appreciated more abroad than in his native Spain, a country he criticizes with the venom of an Unamuno. I walk with Elena towards him, towards Juan Goytisolo.

I think of the forces that have led him here, to this seat in a Marrakesh café, and remember the taste for low life he had acquired as a young man, when he had rebelled against his bourgeois Catalan upbringing. He had prowled the seedy bars of Barcelona, where he met Almerían immigrants, who encouraged him to go to Almería, where he became obsessed with the African-looking landscape and the ruins of the Moorish past. That he should have moved on afterwards from Andalucía to Morocco seems an entirely logical progression, wholly in line with the path taken by his romantic predecessors, whose sentimental attitude towards the Orient he has none the less repudiated. He is a great admirer of Edward Said.

The strength of his own romanticism may be open to question, but there is no doubting the depth of his immersion in Islamic culture, and the originality with which he uses this culture in his writings. Nowhere is this more apparent than in his short novel *Makbara*, an extended prose poem set between Paris, Pittsburg and Marrakesh, but without unity of time, place or character, emulating the speech patterns of the Moroccan story-teller, borrowing from Arabic sources, but also weaving in threads of authors such as Genet, Sade, Joyce and Fuentes. In its cultural schizophrenia it echoes the mudéjar art of medieval Spain; in its chaotic complexity it mirrors the great square which inspired it, the square where he is now sitting, waiting for my arrival.

I have only met him once in Europe and in the company of his French wife, but now that he's in Marrakesh, he's with his Moroccan boyfriend: conflict in his cultural affiliations is perfectly matched by his sexual ambiguity. He lifts himself a few inches from his chair, mumbles a few introductions, then resumes his previous position, his arms resting on the table, his eyes staring not at me but to the square beyond. Since our first meeting, age seems suddenly to have shrivelled and weakened him, and made his bald head resemble that of an alopecic squirrel. He makes no attempt to open the conversation, and neither do his robed companions, who appear only to speak Moroccan. His thickset, moustachioed boyfriend, whom I recognize from photographs, eyes me at first in an almost aggressive way, but soon loses interest, and turns his look towards the strolling crowds.

I mention my Granadine sultan, into whose web of patronage Goytisolo himself has been drawn.

'I call him "el hombre relámpago" ["the lightning man"],' he mutters, finding him clearly as much of an enigma as I do. 'He suddenly turns up here, spends five minutes or so with me, then moves on elsewhere. But he makes things work, I don't know how. And he helps people in need.'

He talks about the Algerian writer whom I had met in the Sultan's cave and about the way the Sultan had brought the man from Algeria to Granada, thus saving him from a likely death at the hands of fundamentalists.

'They tried to shoot him as he drove his children to school. His crime was to be an intellectual; he had glasses.'

The subject of Algeria, and its recent disintegration into a state of terrorist turmoil, is very much on Goytisolo's mind, and he goes on to talk to me about his last visit to the country, and the fear and sense of isolation of being a European there.

Like an engine trying to ignite, the hesitant conversation promises briefly to take off but then loses its impetus as Goytisolo's reflections on Algeria give way to brooding pauses.

I'm interested in how the upsurge of Islamic fundamentalism has affected Goytisolo's position as a Western liberal in the Islamic world; and I am also curious to find out how someone of his liberal position could defend, as he has recently done, the present Moroccan king – a man who has done an enormous amount to westernize Morocco while imposing an autocratic, almost medieval style of government. Inevitably, I cannot help wondering what will happen to Morocco after the king's death, and whether the country will go the same way as Algeria.

But I fail to articulate what I want to say, the time is not right, Goytisolo's shy, quiet manner exaggerates my own, I become nervous and incoherent. The conversation splutters and stalls, and almost dies out completely. Our eyes never meet, our soft exchange of phrases is made inaudible by the noise of the square, on which Goytisolo's glance soon becomes permanently fixed. We switch from Spanish to French, then back again to silence. The occasional passer-by stops to greet our table, bringing smiles to Goytisolo's companions but not to Goytisolo, whose features flicker for a moment but not enough to rid them of their melancholic stillness. He retreats into his own strange world, a no-man's land between Europe and Africa where no voices appear to reach him. Not even the pauses in a Beckett play are as long as the ones now separating me from him. Behind his off-hand manner, I can sense a fundamental kindness and absence of intellectual arrogance, but I cannot rise above my feelings of idiocy and humiliation to express anything that might arouse him from his distractedness. The pauses encourage a futile search for profundity: for a while I struggle to find in my failure to engage with him a metaphor for my own, anchorless wanderings between cultures.

Elena looks at me sympathetically, anxious to relieve my discomfort but unable to do so. In a last, desperate conversational gambit I break the silence by referring to our brief visit to the Palmery, and to my surprise on finding there a Western colony of a size I had never suspected.

'I've been told about a French society hostess who lives there,' Goytisolo responds with his usual obliqueness. 'She's always complaining that no one ever sees me when I'm in Marrakesh, that

IN THE GLOW OF THE PHANTOM PALACE

I never socialize, that I never go to the Palmery. "Il est invisible,"
she says.'

His lips contort into his nearest approximation to a smile.

'Isn't that extraordinary?' he comments. 'I who spend every
evening seated here in the sight of thousands of Moroccans, ready
to speak to anyone who approaches me. It is they, the ones who live
in the Palmery, it is they who are the invisibles.'

The boyfriend mutters a few impatient words to him, he rises
to leave, I am left with the frustration of what has not been said and
the relief of no longer having to try and say it. He shuffles off with
his light grey donkey jacket to blend in anonymously with the
parading crowd. The suddenly emptied table prompts in me a
momentary confusion. Perhaps the society hostess had been right.

Elena and I set off in silence across the Djemaa el Fna but soon
brush aside the accumulated tensions with a mutual fit of giggles.
We are agreed that the Jacobs-Goytisolo encounter is unlikely to be
recorded in the history of meetings between great minds. Our
arms briefly entwine as if in response to a need for touch after my
failure to connect with Goytisolo. Leaving the square we walk to
the only hotel in the Medina to serve alcohol.

The place would probably not appeal to Goytisolo, and even less
to the residents of the Palmery. It seems favoured instead by slightly
down-market tour groups, whose clients are relaxing around a
lounge and reception area that mock the great works of Islamic architecture in a ghoulish, dirty decoration of fibre-glass horse-shoe
arches, gilded plastic lanterns, and dripping plaster. The seating is
comfortable and the beer is cool. We begin to relax.

'The boyfriend was different to how I'd imagined him,' says
Elena. 'Somehow I was expecting someone more open, more charming, or, at the very least, incredibly handsome. It makes you
speculate about their relationship. I wonder what on earth they have
to talk about.'

'It's strange,' she reflects further, 'a pair of Moroccan homosex-
uals wouldn't be able to live openly together like that; such
relationships would only be possible if one of them was a European.
And yet I've never been to a country – except Spain, of course! –
which has so many sexually ambivalent men. Perhaps that's another

of Spain's legacies to Morocco.'

There's not much ambivalence in the sexuality that is slowly tainting the atmosphere around us, prompting us to exchange confidences about our own recent disappointments, but finally making us voyeurs within the hotel itself. The guide-book-carrying package tourists have gone to bed, and the hotel is filling up with beer-drinking Moroccans, prostitutes, pimps, gigolos. A long-haired, middle-aged blonde allows her generously exposed legs to be stroked by a local toy-boy; a couple of German men joke and share whisky with two robed and bored Moroccan girls, less than half their age. The blonde disappears kissing behind the cushions, while the Germans make a pretence of saying goodbye to the girls, then walk upstairs. The girls burst out laughing, talk excitedly, and, after an appropriate delay, start climbing up the staircase after the men. Halfway up one of them pauses for an instant to turn round to look at us, suddenly conscious that we have been observing them and that we are aware of the whole intrigue. She throws us a smile and a wink.

An *amour de boue*, a love of low life, is about the only type of love likely to be fuelled by the sight of the double-bed that awaits us in our stifling room off the Djemaa el Fna. As we prepare to lie down on its dirty sheets Elena says she has an embarrassing confession to make. It's not the sheets, she says, nor the heat, nor the smell, nor the bedsprings that lacerate the flesh. It's the cockroaches, she says, she's just spotted several of them, they're all over the place, she's tried to forget them but she can't, they'll give her nightmares. 'I'm getting old and spoilt,' she sighs.

At two o'clock in the morning we pack our belongings and drive away from the Djemaa el Fna. Entering the new town, we relinquish the oriental picturesque for the regulated comfort of the Hotel Moussafir.

'You must get up at dawn,' Khalid had insisted when I'd told him of my wish to see the tomb of al-Mutamid, the poet king of Seville.

Elena was smiling and shaking her head at the prospect of another sentimental pilgrimage, but Khalid had rushed to my defence. 'The mausoleum is modern, nothing special. But the setting, oh the setting, it's ravishing, you've never seen such colours, such wonderful vegetation, such a beautiful dawn light... No, I completely understand you, Michael, the place must be visited, and you must get there early, have breakfast there, breathe in the atmosphere.' Then, as his parting words, he looked at me straight in the eyes and said, 'The two of us have much in common, you'll sit down near al-Mutamid's mausoleum and write some beautiful lines, I'm sure you will, we're like brothers.' We laughed.

It's now six in the morning, and the prospect of a dawn visit to the tomb of a Sevillian king seems ever less enticing as we lie in our comfortable beds trying to ignore the alarm clock after our three hours of sleep. But when we finally get to our feet and walk outside into the silence and clarity of another beautiful dawn, a sentimental tremor, as if from Andalucía, shakes me out of my somnolence and into daydreams.

I'm driving south with the Moorish Queen, heading across an orange-pink plain towards the snows of the High Atlas. The narrow side road extends in an endless straight line past scatterings of palms, the odd pair of camels, cultivated patches of emerald green, and adobe hamlets walled like small fortresses. The rising sun brings back her memory, paints the surrounding flatness with the colour of her presence, illuminates the road on which our futures are once again united.

'The night of your absence is long; may our amorous embrace be like the dawn.' The landscape near Agmat merges into the poetry of the man who is buried there – a man whose exile in the Maghreb is like a poetic distillation of the whole experience of exile, of the whole fate of al-Andalus. Son of the cruel al-Motatid of the flower-pot-skulls and bricked-up baths, al-Mutamid had a life that reads like the worst and most romantic of historical fiction. There is his hedonistic youth in what is now the Portuguese town of Silves, where he discovered the consoling powers of wine ('when I don't drink worry eats at my entrails'), indulged in the pleasures and pains of love ('Oh you who reject me, I don't deserve this abandonment and rejection'), and came to realize that 'impotence is terrible' ('don't speak of it'). There is his friendship with his fellow poet Ibn Ammar, which blossomed in Silves, and survived his accession to the throne of Seville only to die dramatically in a tale of political enmity whose bloody outcome was Ibn Ammar's execution by an axe-wielding al-Mutamid. There is the story of his love for the slave girl I'tamid, whom he eventually made his queen, and from whom even the briefest of separations was enough to make him write of being 'inebriated with the wine of my longing for you, crazed with the desire to be with you, to sip your lips and embrace you'. But, above all, there is the loss of his throne to the Almoravids, and his days languishing as a prisoner in what has been described as the obscure hamlet of Agmat.

'A Berber hamlet in the mountains, in between cacti and palms. In the courtyard of a miserable dwelling, al-Mutamid, bedraggled and with his feet in fetters, is writing...'

With these glib, clipped phrases, intentionally cinematic in their effect, a last sigh issues from the pages of *Ben Ammar de Sevilla*, an historical novel whose author Claudio Sánchez-Albornoz has incurred the wrath of Goytisolo for consolidating a clichéd and fundamentally European approach towards Islamic Spain. Sánchez-Albornoz, a lofty eminence among Spanish medieval historians, had devoted himself to fact and not fiction before undertaking this novel during a summer holiday when the rain had not stopped and the spirit had been in need of diversion. Was it not significant that he had turned to the subject of a Sevillian exile when he was one himself – one of the many Spanish intellectuals who had taken refuge in Argentina after the Civil War? And was it this or the beauty of his sub-Andean surroundings that made a sober, fact-obsessed historian pen a sentimental fiction in which Agmat is referred to as a mountain hamlet and not as the major town that it had been during al-Mutamid's liftime, when Marrakesh had barely been founded?

Even today, as I now find out, Agmat is not a hamlet but a prosperous village, lifted from Sánchez-Albornoz's mountain heights and dropped among orchards and flat fields at the foot of the High Atlas. We avoid its centre and diverge onto a track skirting a high adobe wall that restrains a jungle of sugar cane. The track gives out in a wide dusty enclosure, where a large domed structure, garish pink in the sun, stares across orchards towards distant snows. Boys surround us from out of nowhere, then scatter as a young man appears carrying a key. 'You must be from Seville,' he says.

We take off our shoes and enter the mausoleum of the poet king. 'Our visitors are almost all from Seville,' he continues, taking out a book of signatures that confirm this. I encounter the name of a Sevillian writer friend, Diego Carrasco. The book is almost more engrossing than the building, whose unexciting exterior shields a no less plain interior centred on a simple slab of a tomb, 'crafted in the 1960's', we are told. On one of the white walls, a long inscription records in Arabic a famous poem of al-Mutamid in which he imagines his tomb. Elena provides a halting translation.

'Tomb of a stranger, let you be watered by the evening and dawn drizzle... Reason, science and generosity lie within you... Yes, it is true, the celestial decree has arrived, and with this, my death... Even the tears of the dew cry for you... The blessings of God over your tomb never end...'

Other poems of his exile, more poetically translated, take up a small anthology of his verse that I have brought with me from Spain. They correspond more to the mood of pathos, regret and nostalgia that draws romantic visitors to his tomb. As with the autobiographical musings of his contemporary and fellow exile Abd 'Allah, last of Granada's Ziri kings, they look back on his past life, on the wealth, and happiness, and power he had known, and compare all this with his present state, reduced to 'a stranger, a captive in the Maghreb'. There are tears of self-pity, but also a sad resignation to his fate, an admission of the mystery of divine will. He cannot challenge God, and asks of him only one thing – 'Let God decree that I should die in Seville!'

I ignore Khalid's plea just as God had ignored al-Mutamid's. I do not linger at Agmat to take in the setting and compose lines of my own. We've no longer time to dwell on the fate of al-Andalus, there's been a change of plan, we're not going back yet, we're continuing south. Elena has agreed to drive me up into the mountains, but no further, she insists, the weekend is nearly over, reality is looming in the spectre of Monday. We drive away.

I study the map as we climb with the sun into the High Atlas. My attention strays from the route we are taking, and for a moment scans with excitement the ever emptier spaces that fill up the section of the map beyond where we are going. Absorbed in the sparse network of roads and tracks that trail off into the sands of the Sahara, I think of ways of persuading Elena to keep on driving, never to return. But daydreams soon become real dreams, as tiredness, the winding motion of the car, and the glare of the sun all conspire to send me asleep, against my wishes.

'You're like a child,' smiles Elena an hour or so later when the bumps in the road jolt me awake in the middle of a barren mountain valley. 'Every time you get in a car your eyes begin to close. I can't understand how you can write travel books, you must go round the world half-asleep.'

'That might be an advantage,' I reply, wanting to quote to her what the Portuguese café-philosopher Fernando Pessoa had said – that travel books are worth only as much as the imagination of the one who writes them, and that if the writer has imagination he can enchant the reader with the detailed, photographic description of landscapes he's imagined just as well as with the necessarily less detailed description of the landscapes he thought he saw.

At present I think I'm seeing a wilder, distorted version of the Alpujarras, with a torrent of a river, a streak of snow above immense, scorched slopes, and cowering honeycomb clusters of flat-roofed mud dwellings that lack only the balconies and whitewash to be those of an Alpujarran hamlet. Abandoned, hilltop castles dating only from the present century stand on top of rocky mounds to remind the visitor of the medieval, feudal world that has persisted in this remote valley into modern times. Only one monument disturbs the medieval illusion – it is the monument we have come to see.

We have left the road, and are forcing the car over stones and pot-holes towards what looks like a redbrick industrial building covered in scaffolding. 'This must be it,' I say with a still lingering uncertainty as we struggle the last few metres up to the twelfth-century mosque of Tinmel, cradle of the Almohads.

It was here, in this site marked today by a mosque undergoing an apparently drastic restoration, that Ibn Toumert, a native of these mountains, preached to the Berber tribes who would form the Almohad or Unitarian movement. Ibn Toumert, known to his followers as the Mahdi or 'Chosen One', found the ruling Almoravids guilty of the same failings that the Almoravids had criticized in others – a love of wine, music and other decadent luxuries, and a tolerance of women mixing freely in male society. Eventually he and his group went to Marrakesh to taunt more directly the pious and tolerant Ali ben Youssef, who only banished the movement after his sister had been thrown off her horse for going out in public without a veil. The Mahdi and his followers retreated to their mountain stronghold at Tinmel, and planned from there the overthrow of the Almoravids. After the death of Ibn Toumert in the 1130's, this plan was carried out by his successor Abd el Moumen, who took Fez in 1145, and Marrakesh four years later. Soon afterwards, as if in celebration of these victories, the great mosque at Tinmel was erected and given a heavily fortified aspect in keeping with the town's new status as keeper of the Almohad state treasury. When, nearly eighty years later, the Marinids arrived at Tinmel to finish off an empire now tainted itself by the luxuries of al-Andalus, only this mosque was allowed to remain standing. Over the centuries, the mosque fell into ruins alongside the crude hamlet that came to replace the fortified stronghold. But the site has never ceased to be venerated – a testimony to the continuing respect felt by the Berbers for their former spiritual leader, the 'Chosen One'.

Khalid, an adviser in the present restoration campaign, had warned me that I might be disappointed should I ever make it as far as Tinmel. 'You're going to have a shock,' he said. 'We've used authentic materials as far as possible, but I can see you're one of those romantic people who only like their ruins when they're overgrown and collapsing. In many ways I'm like that myself, but I'm also an historian.'

We leave the car in between the unchanged Morocco of a mud-brick hamlet and a mosque that resounds to the noises of hammering, sawing and the whirling of concrete mixers. As we walk towards a tall young man we identify as the foreman, I try not to think of how beautiful the site must have been as a huge fading ruin in this wild, mountainous landscape.

The foreman wonders if we have any cigarettes to give to the workers; he seems to regard this as just recompense for wandering around the site. Elena hands over a couple of packets, and we are allowed through into the mosque, where the piers have largely been rebuilt, and the walls resurfaced. The place is still exposed to the sky, but roofing has already begun, with a view to reconstruct the mosque exactly as it had been during the twelfth-century. 'When that's finished,' the foreman explains, 'Westerners like yourselves will no longer be able to stand where you are now.'

In its present state, the mosque is the only old one in Morocco that tourists can visit. I try to make the most of this now threatened opportunity, and study the building's T-shaped plan, which, like that of the Koutoubia Mosque in Marrakesh, has as its model the Mezquita of Córdoba. The fragments of stalactite decoration, the intricacy of the arches, and other elements of the decoration have echoes of Córdoba, as does the emphasis on the mihrab, the prayer niche, as the central focus of the building – a development in Islamic architecture that reaches here its apogee with the placing of the minaret directly above the mihrab.

We walk up to the top of the stunted and eccentrically positioned minaret. The foreman, though only in his late twenties, talks to us about his six children, who live in the hamlet, and are in need of new clothes. Do we have children, he asks? Are we married? Are we lovers? He does not believe our answers, then demands some money for his 'historical explanations'.

We have reached a point in Morocco where we can go no further south in our search for the legacy of al-Andalus. I long to cross the Sahara and take up the story of this legacy in the Mali town of Timbuktu, but for the moment reason intervenes to curtail these growing longings. There's certainly no way of persuading Elena to keep on driving, not even to the nearby pass of Tiz-n-Test, from where, the foreman assures me, the desert can be seen on clear days like today. I look towards the pass, but Elena firmly shakes her head, reminding me that it's well past midday, and that there are friends of hers waiting for us for supper in the north. 'In any case,' she laughs, as we walk back to the car, 'you'll be asleep.'

I wake up after nightfall in Casablanca. The main road north of Marrakesh is as quick as any motorway, and renders painless and unexotic the journey to this town whose name is almost as fabled as that of Timbuktu. Humphrey Bogart's Casablanca, like Rita Hayworth's Buenos Aires, is a town of displaced foreigners living in the cultural vaccuum that moriscos must have experienced on their arrival in Africa. The real Casablanca, in contrast, is said to be a disappointingly ordinary town that denies through its Western-style modernity the picturesque qualities that tourists have come to Morocco to find. Yet in the darkness it retains for me some of the exotic glamour of the film. We drive to docklands worthy of some film noir, and eat there with Spanish friends of Elena in an isolated smart restaurant packed with other foreign residents, attended by bow-tied waiters who could be from some Parisian restaurant of the 1950's. Outside a mist is descending, and a Russian tanker is leaving, sounding its horn as it turns back to St Petersburg.

Tinmel and Marrakesh are a world away, but the day is no longer over. After supper we keep on driving, ending up well past midnight in a 1920's flat in Rabat, the Moroccan capital.

This is where Elena always stays, she tells me as we climb the dark stairwell. The flat belongs to a former colleague of hers, Encarni, who lives here with her Moroccan boyfriend, Lamin.

A dazed Encarni, in a hastily put-on kimono, opens the door, gasps with surprise, and warmly welcomes us inside. She is small and friendly, with mouse-coloured hair and a homely, slightly naïve look.

'You better come and talk to us in the bedroom,' she tells us.

When we go in, a young, pale-skinned black man sits up naked in the bed, bending over with a smile to kiss Elena and to extend a hand to me. He is one of the most beautiful men I have ever seen.

Elena returns to Fez early on the Monday morning, leaving me in Rabat with Encarni and Lamin, an oddly matched couple whose relationship seems in keeping with this town where the West and the East sit uneasily together.

Encarni has little interest in the past, and none of my fascination with ruins. Unromantic, down-to-earth and unable even to speak Moroccan, she is as unashamedly European as Rabat's gothic-style cathedral – the centrepiece of a New Town built by the French over a large area of land that the Almohads had begun to develop more than seven centuries earlier.

She is clearly unimpressed as we walk across the principal survival of the Almohads' ambitious but thwarted urban plans: a vast stone platform supporting the foundations and truncated minaret of a mosque conceived as an even bigger version of that of Córdoba. I cannot convince her that this largely empty space is eloquent both of the spectacular collapse of the Almohads and of the heights they had scaled with their victories in Spain.

We go on to the walled medina, which surroundly confronts the New Town across a narrow, busy road. The French had wanted to pull this whole area down, but had been prevented from doing so by General Lyautey, who had first tried out in Rabat his ideas for integrating the West with the East. The wall that separates these two worlds is known aptly as that of the Andalucíans.

These 'Andalucíans' were the morisco refugees who, from the sixteenth century onwards, brought new life to a Rabat whose population had dwindled to a mere 300 families. They cultivated the surrounding lands with such skill and hard work that – according to one contemporary – they 'turned these into marvels that made them forget their homeland and what they had lost there'. But, of course, they could not really forget this homeland. They had retained their European features, their fairer skins, and sometimes even their Spanish names. And they harboured such strong desires to reconquer the land of their forefathers that they took the advice of the Saadian rulers of Morocco and formed the 'Army of al-Andalus'. In the end they had to satisfy their longings for revenge by creating out of Rabat and its twin town of Salé an effective pirate republic whose corsairs would terrorize European vessels right up to the nineteenth century.

We stroll among the market stalls of the medina before reaching the 'Kasbah des Ouidas', the kernel of old Rabat. This is where the town successfully creates an illusion of Southern Spain; and this is where Encarni begins finally to enjoy the past – a past made clean and sparkling for the benefit of tourists. After absorbing the fragrant smells of an 'Andalucían Garden' laid out by the French in the 1920's, we clamber up through an Andalucían-looking district of stepped alleys and freshly whitewashed houses until we come out on to a terrace overlooking an estuary that could almost be that of the Guadalquivir.

But as I look across the waters to the cheerful white cubes of Salé, the illusion of being in Spain is disturbed by morbid thoughts. The massed forms on the sandy banks opposite turn out not to be sunbathers but tombs, many of which I imagine to be those of the thousands of moriscos whose remains were exhumed in Spain to be reburied in the land of exile of their families. 'What a wonderful beach that would have made,' comments Encarni.

After nightfall we're back again in the New Town, where Lamin joins us in a narrow and crowded Jewish restaurant where the beer flows and the only food served is offal. Steaming intestines are slammed down in front of us as we listen to old Sephardic sounds played on a guitar and a zither. Then a bald and rounded middle-aged man, emerging from the smoke and chaos, raises himself up on to a table to the applause of everyone around him.

'That's Zerda himself, the restaurant's owner,' Lamin shouts to me above the mounting noise. 'I've known him since I was a child. I grew up like him in the Jewish district of the Mellah, the poorest part of the medina. He's now incredibly rich, a self-made man who has risen from nothing.'

Lamin starts talking to me about his childhood haunts, and says he'll take me tomorrow evening to some Moorish baths that always fill him with nostalgia. His words fade away as Zerda begins to sing.

The lively, euphoric rhythms of the background accompaniment seem to contradict the snatches of lyrics that Lamin translates for me – '... my heart has been left on the other side of a sea of emptiness... memories of my homeland are like roses in winter...

death has become a familiar friend, welcoming me at the end of my journey...' The zither is being plucked with a tachycardiac beat, the guitarist is almost jumping in his chair as he strums the chords, and Zerda's perpetual smile is opening into a groan of ecstasy, bringing to a climax a combination of sounds and words that makes me finally recall something half-heard in my half-Jewish past – the Sephardic song of rapturous joy at the approach of death in the concentration camps.

But when the instruments are suddenly silent, and only the voice of Zerda is left, by now slow and plaintive, another memory struggles to return. The voice turns from plaintive to visceral, the half-formed memory sharpens into focus: I can almost hear the Sultan reciting in his Sacromonte cave.

I am thinking back again to Spain on my final evening in Rabat. Steamy memories of Los Baños de Mula, Alhama de Granada, Zújar, the body of the Moorish Queen, are drifting through my consciousness as the androgynously sensual Lamin steers me in the half-light of the Mellah towards the vaporous world of the Moorish bath.

Nervous anticipation is contending with my nostalgia.

Am I about to experience the drab reality behind the ultimate romantic dream of the Orient? Or will I retain something of my original vision? For the moment I continue to picture a strange, yellowish light, clouds of steam, a confusion of shadowy nudity below horse-shoe arches green from centuries of damp.

But the building that we eventually reach is a 1950's block just outside the old town, with a large swing-door leading into a crowded changing-room that, for all the fezes, exotic robes and elderly people present, awakens in me the most depressing school memories – my horror of changing for sports, dislike of naked male cama-raderie, complexes about exposing my own body. A resurgence of inhibitions comes over me as I sit on a long bench undressing next to Lamin, whose physical confidence exaggerates my lack of it.

We hand over our clothes to a man who places them in a locker and gives us in return a bucket each and a bar of soap as hard as a stone. Pushing a heavy glass door protected by drapery, we enter Moorish baths that contain neither baths nor any Moorish feature. There are just three small and nondescript rooms, progressively hotter and steamier but otherwise identical – simple, brightly lit boxes covered from floor to ceiling in plain and greying tiles. The only mystery is what exactly to do with your bucket and your body. Lamin explains this to me once we have reached the innermost room.

He fills his bucket from a tap of hot water and then throws the water over the part of the floor where he wants to sit. I follow his example and pull in my stomach as I stretch out awkwardly on the hard tiles, wondering if anything more exciting is going to happen.

'Naked we are all equal,' Lamin says, reminding me of the famous Islamic proverb, which does not ring so true when spoken by someone whose body stands out Adonis-like among the surrounding examples of flab and decrepitude. Neither is anyone wholly naked, for modesty prevails among Islamic men, all of whom are wearing underwear of varying degrees of bagginess. Even the favouring blur caused by the steam and the removal of my spectacles fails to instil any sensuality in the scene around us, a scene of such matter-of-fact ordinariness that only a twisted Westerner such as myself, unaccustomed to Eastern ways, could detect a homoerotic element in the sight of men taking it in turns both to massage each other and to rub the stone-like soap vigorously up and down the whole, outstretched length of their companion's body.

My timidity and self-consciousness make me grateful to Lamin for not assisting me in the cleansing process. We have lain so long in the steam that when I press the soap against my skin a mucus-like stream oozes out of my pores. Lamin, after finishing soaping himself, refills his bucket, and tips the water over his head. I do the same but manage to throw water over a couple of men behind me. There are cries of protest.

We move on to a cooler room, we clean the floor again, this time I spend longer in finding a comfortable position for my now aching limbs. And just as I think I am getting used to the whole ritual of the baths, Lamin poses to me a disconcerting question.

'Shall we begin?' he asks.

I've no idea what he means, I seem almost to be responding out of shock, as he pulls me to my feet, places his hands on my waist to turn my body around, lifts my arms into the air, then raises me high off the ground on his back before landing me again on the tiles and pushing my feet towards my head until my whole body seems on the point of breaking.

'You're very tense,' he comments, 'and heavy.' Then he disappears into a tiny, adjoining space that I've only just noticed. I imagine he's having a shower, I go there later myself, eager to cool off after the heat and the exertion. I search frantically for the taps before realizing my mistake. I am standing barefoot in the middle of a urinal.

'You must now be feeling wonderfully clean and pure,' Lamin tells me after we've dressed and left the baths. In one sense he's right. I feel like I did as a child after going to the confessional box – a feeling of inner cleanliness not entirely unconnected with the sense of relief in having got the ordeal over with.

Encarni comes to collect us in the basement of a smoky bar, where a few glasses of beer with Lamin help to rid my body of any acquired sense of purity. There is further indulgence to come, for Lamin and Encarni have promised Elena that they will take me on my last night to an extravagant place she was sure would enchant me. Lamin is not so keen on this venue. 'Only wealthy foreigners go there, it's a Westerners' dream of the Orient, it's totally over the top.' I tell him I don't mind missing it out, but he insists on keeping to his promise. 'Your senses are in for a treat, and your wallet for a shock. And you'll be able to visit the medina at night.'

A short time later, we're walking along an empty street towards a small opening in the medina's northern walls. We approach an elderly, white-robed man who's carrying a lantern, he nods his head, he'll lead us to his master, he could almost be saying, we must stick closely behind him, his lantern will guide us into the dark labyrinth. There are few other lights.

We weave in and out of the medieval alleys, I've no idea where we are, I've even doubts about where we're going, it doesn't matter, I've entered an oriental tale. We stop in front of an ancient wooden door, the old man raps hard with his hands and lets out a high-pitched cry. A pair of dark eyes observe us suspiciously from a tentative slit in the door. The pale light behind it turns into a flood of colour as the door finally opens wide enough to let us in. Plucked oriental music vibrates from a distant room; the eyes become a beautiful female apparition in silk pantaloons, her waist and breasts swathed in a light and diaphanous gold-threaded cotton.

Other such women, like the pampered slaves in an Orientalist painting, drift in and out of the fabulous patio into which we are led. Turbanned musicians squat on a row of dazzlingly coloured cushions, playing to a handful of men seated by a low-lying table of exquisitely carved cedar. One of the slaves shows me into a bathroom fit for a sultan: the toilet is raised like a throne, the ceiling is hung with drapes, there's a profusion of perfume bottles, and an aphrodisiac smell of sandalwood and musk. I return to the patio to take my place beside Lamin and Encarni, among cushions and hookahs.

Mint tea is poured out for us from a great height; the dark-olive navel of a slave-girl is exposed as she raises the silver kettle into the air. A gasp of astonishment would have been appropriate as a gilded tray is later brought in, borne by two black boys. On the tray is the greatest of Moroccan delicacies – one with which all travellers are welcomed into homes, its exact number of layers of pastry corresponding to the importance of the guest, the munificence of the host. The pastilla.

I've already tasted its hybrid Murcian relative, the pastel de Cierva, in distant Cartagena. But here is the real article, the authentic flavour of the Orient – millefeuilles and doves. There are many layers.

And as the banquet continues, with tajine, and couscous, and sweetbreads and pastries, and as my senses are gradually satiated, over-satiated, I take a closer and more critical look at my surroundings – the surroundings of Rabat's most pretentious restaurant. The handful of fellow diners are suited businessmen with mobile phones; the traditional wood-inlay cabinet hides a computer for accounts and table reservations; the patio is roofed with high-tech beams resembling the mechanical workings of a stage-set.

The old man with the lantern is waiting for us to lead us back. He is employed by the restaurant to do so. Perhaps his robes are on loan as well, for he too is just another actor – another actor in the theatre of the Orient.

They leave me on the night train. I make another nocturnal escape, this time alone, lying on a couchette in a deserted compartment. I'm travelling north, towards a Morocco more Andalucían still, towards the most Spanish of Moroccan towns. I have an appointment early the next morning in Tetuan. Tetuan's relationship with Spain is gloriously contradictory. As capital of the Spanish Protectorate, the town was the base from which Franco embarked on his nationalist conquest of Spain, cynically recruiting in the process an army of Moroccan mercenaries prepared to emulate the Moorish invasion of 711 in the interests of a fatherland that wasn't theirs. Had these Moroccans any qualms about assisting a traditional enemy who, as early as 1400, had swept across the Straits of Gibraltar to destroy entirely the original Tetuan (a Marinid foundation that had grown up on the site of an ancient Berber settlement)? Or did they consider themselves Spaniards in the sense of being descendants of the thousands of refugees from al-Andalus who had flooded into Tetuan after 1492, when the Granadan-born general Sidi-Mandri, usually known as al-Mandri, refounded the town and populated it with Moors from Ronda, Baza and Motril?

The morning of my arrival from Rabat has so far been a blur – a dawn arrival at Tangier, a rush from the train to the bus station, a journey to Tetuan in a grand taxi which is now depositing me, together with the other six survivors of our cramped, dangerously fast ride, in the modern heart of a town where foreigners have immediately to confront the most notoriously tireless and sinister of all of Morocco's hustlers.

Luckily one of my fellow passengers, a native of Tetuan, offers to escort me through the formal grid of streets laid out by the

Spaniards early this century in a belated art nouveau style. I haven't been in Tetuan for many years, I tell him, and he retorts with a critical account of the recent transformation of the square where he is now taking me. Cautiously at first, but with increasing boldness, he attacks the present Moroccan king, whom he claims has entirely ruined the square named after him at the entrance to the medina.

I see what he means when we get there. 'This used to be the social heart of Tetuan, and look at it now,' he says, reminding me of the cafés that once stood here, the Moorish-style Spanish consulate, and the central formal gardens that had reinforced the overall Andalucían character of the whole. All this has now gone, to be replaced by a square coldly paved with Islamic motifs, guarded at the corners by minaret-style floodlights, and presided over by a brand new royal palace, 'where the king spends about two weeks a year'. 'And to add insult to injury,' my companion continues, 'you can't even walk now across the square; it's part of the palace.'

Most of the square is roped off, leaving only a narrow and congested passageway for those making their way to the medina. My companion says goodbye to me at the entrance to this funnel, after giving me his concise opinion of the face-lift the medina is currently undergoing. 'Another disaster,' he says, reflecting on this collaborative venture between the Municipality of Tetuan and the Junta de Andalucía. 'You could almost call it Spain's revenge for the eradication of Spanish motifs from the square. But I'd better not say more, I'll leave it to you to decide.'

My appointment is with a quiet and serious young man called Najr Probi – one of the local architects working on the 'rehabilitation' of the medina together with the Almerían architect Ramon de Torres. With him is a short and bespectacled colleague whom I'm told has done much research on the architecture of Tetuan in the seventeenth and eighteenth centuries.

We meet up at the entrance to the medina, alongside a stretch of the defensive walls built for al-Mandri by Portuguese captives who were housed at night in the city's grim *mazamorras* – a labyrinth of underground dungeons that were notoriously airless, without light, stiflingly hot, and unbearably rank. When Nasr asks me if there's anything in particular I want to see in the medina, I mention the mazamorras, but he tells me that their entrance has been sealed again following recent archaeological work. He can show me instead another hidden side to old Tetuan – the Granadine-style interiors of the many palaces in the medina now earmarked for restoration.

But first of all, on passing through the medina's gate, we have to inspect the one part of the 'rehabilitation programme' so far completed – a narrow main street I half-remember as a confusion of market-stalls crammed below raffia matting half-eaten by rats. Now the street has become a shining example of the architects' desire to preserve the past in a way which does not simply pastiche it. Tradition is respected, Nasr explains, while incorporating the latest in modern materials and design. I make ambiguous murmuring sounds while strolling in between rebuilt stalls of identical size regularly laid out below a designer canopy straight from 1990's Barcelona.

Then the conversation switches from the restoration of the past to the past itself as the post-modern shopping arcade we are walking down emerges all of a sudden into the old, unchanged medina that Nasr says is in danger of total collapse unless 'rehabilitation' work is continued soon. Nasr's bespectacled colleague provides the historical background to the palaces I am about to see.

He talks about a Tetuan whose inhabitants of Spanish origin continued to speak Spanish well into the eighteenth century, some of them even retaining the titular documents to homes the Christians had wronged them of in Granada. As embittered refugees from a Spain now under the yoke of an intolerant Christianity, they frequently made a living in Tetuan from subjugating others. Tetuan's slave population, composed in part of Christians captured in the Straits, grew by Leo the African's day to a reputed 3,000, and supplied much of the money enabling the construction of the town's palaces.

Deviating from a narrowing whitewashed street, we pass through one of the hundreds of arches that enhance the secretiveness and Spanishness of Tetuan's medina. In a sad cul-de-sac, under a sky turned grey, we enter the courtyard of what had been the palace of the eighteenth-century governors of Tetuan.

A few drops of rain begin to fall as we stand in a tall, arcaded courtyard not unlike one of the larger ones in Granada's Albaicín.

Architectural detailing has been obscured by successive layers of blistered, damp-stained whitewash that wrap the arches like a tattered shroud. A bent-over woman is mopping up the dirt from a ceramic floor of loose and missing tiles.

'This is one of the palaces that the Junta de Andalucía would particularly like to restore. But where do you begin?' asks Nasr, his face becoming ever more sullen as he surveys the damage, the rubbish, and the signs of a once grand structure being gradually transformed into a slum dwelling.

Our tour continues, the sky goes greyer, the palaces multiply. One of the buildings is an old people's home; another, covered inside in dust-sheets, is hired out for occasional banquets; a third one is an infant's school, while a fourth is a weaver's cooperative, whose female members sit behind crafted doors of Granadine inspiration. 'And now for a Jewish palace,' says the bespectacled didact. 'There were many important Jewish families in Tetuan, who integrated well with the Islamic population, just as they had done in Granada. This particular family was called Paez. The name seems familiar to you?'

The palace of the familiar name has a no less familiar Granadine-style courtyard of superimposed arcades, just like the others we have seen. But its atmosphere is peculiar, with peeling, dark-grey paint, and a solitary old blind man sitting in the tomb-like silence.

'This is a foundation for blind children,' Najr says, introducing me to the young but rather lugubrious director who comes out to greet us in a tie and frayed jacket.

'We're a fund-starved institution,' apologizes the director, gesturing towards the parts of the structure desperately in need of repair. 'You must write about us when you return to Spain. You must draw attention to our plight,' he says, smiling like a sinister, Dickensian headmaster as he begins showing us round a place as sparse and austere as Dickens' Dotheboys Hall.

There are tiny, barely equipped classrooms, and windowless dormitories stifled with campbeds like those from some improvised refugee camp. There is a disconcerting and unexplained emptiness.

We walk out on to a roof terrace, where, under a slow drizzle, we survey a view ringed by gaunt mountains. The medina spreads around us like the last stages of a skin disease, as putrefying as the smell of the tanners' district that comes unexpectedly into view at the back of the palace. 'Al-Mandri's tomb,' murmurs Najr, looking towards a large mausoleum rising above the damp graves that extend in between the tanners' vats and an upper row of fortifications as dark as the mountain slopes behind. The sombre scene is suddenly interrupted by the sound of giggles.

Two young girls, their hands entwined, their eyes hollow, march laughing around the terrace. 'New arrivals,' says the director. 'They've only been here a few weeks, they're from different villages, but they're now completely inseparable.' He places himself in between them and rests his arms on their shoulders. 'The tragedy is that their blindness was preventable; infections that could have been cured with the most basic medicines. They were in a terrible state when they arrived, but look how happy they are now.'

They smile and run away down the stairs, we turn back again towards the view, where a large break in the clouds has now appeared to the south, over the mountains where the small town of Chefchaouen lies hidden. The sun is shining in the distance, and I long to be there.

Ali Raisuni, Ali Raisuni, everyone tells me that I should go and see him, the great sage of Chefchaouen, its holy man, its imam. The mountains close in around me as I ascend by bus into his lofty domain. Climbing into the late afternoon sunlight, I near the rocky peaks of the high Riff that give Chefchaouen both its name and its reputation as an impregnable stronghold.

When Spanish troops undertook this same dramatic journey in 1921 to try and oust the Berber rebel leader Abd el Krim from his mountain lair, they did so in the knowledge that only three Christians had been to this town before in modern times. The most recent of these was an American who came and was killed here in 1892, nearly ten years after a strange and earnest Frenchman, Charles de

Foucauld, had passed through the place on his pioneering tour of Morocco disguised as a Jew. The third visitor was the eccentric and famously witty *Times* correspondent in Tangier, Walter Harris, who claimed that he was almost killed here in 1889, giving as his main reason for coming here in the first place 'the very fact that there existed within thirty hours' ride of Tangier a city in which it was considered an utter impossibility for a Christian to enter'.

Harris was a man wholly unable to distinguish between fantasy and reality, but a sense of the meaninglessness of such a distinction must also have been felt by those Spaniards who reached Chefchaouen in 1920, and found themselves, as if by magic, in an enclave of Moorish Spain. Here truly was an Andalucían mountain town, with stepped alleys, Ajimez paired windows, wrought-iron grilles, and cheerful houses washed in white and a luminous pale blue; but here also were mosques and minarets and a Jewish population that still spoke a medieval Spanish.

Spanish voices still resound in the Chefchaouen of today – the voices of the growing number of Spanish tourists who think of the town as a weekend retreat, and reveal a possible affinity with their Hispano-Moorish predecessors in their characteristically Spanish obsession with the acquisition of knick-knacks. There are few tourists around on the afternoon of my arrival, but the signs of tourism have greatly increased since my last visit to the town – a mushrooming of restaurants, crafts-shops and pensions, and the construction high above the houses of an isolated luxury hotel block reeking of the package trade. I find a room in the 'parador', and begin my search for Ali Raisuni.

Everyone has heard of him, everyone seems to know everything about his whereabouts, he is treated like one of the saints or *marabouts* who have always frequented this most holy of districts – a district whose aura of sanctity and traditional hostility towards 'Christian dogs' is due to the presence of the tomb of Moulay Abdessalam ben Mchich, one of the 'four poles of Islam'.

Ali Raisuni is not at home, the parador's receptionist tells me. He has been sighted on his way down to the town hall, where there's an important meeting this afternoon. I walk hurriedly through the showpiece alleys of the medina and descend into the fast-spreading new town. I beat Ali Raisuni to the town hall, where I am greeted by the friendly vice-president of the town council, who behaves as if he has almost been expecting me.

'Ali Raisuni won't be long, we hope you'll join us at the meeting, you'll find it interesting.' He opens the door into a neo-classical, grey-painted functions room redolent of the days of colonial Morocco. An elderly, jacketed delegation of history professors from Rabat University is seated at a long round table, and the four of them get up to shake my hand. 'We're reaching an accord about a conference we want to organize about Chefchaouen's history,' the Vice-President explains. The conversation resumes in Moroccan, mint tea is brought in, I try and shield my utter perplexity behind smiles and noddings of the head.

'The Andalucían legacy will of course be central to our conference,' the Vice-President tells me in an attempt to bring me into the discussion. All eyes fall on me as I ask about the number of the town's inhabitants who can claim direct descent from the Andalucían refugees who swelled the town's population shortly after its foundation in 1471. 'Here's one of these descendants,' smiles the Vice-President as a dark, thick-set councillor enters the room. 'His name is Laze, which must certainly be a derivative of Lazaro.'

But Laze's moment in the limelight is soon eclipsed by the arrival of Ali Raisuni, who brings an unworldly element into the municipal surroundings, not simply because he is the only Moroccan present not to wear European dress. Ageless and agile, he sweeps into the room in a white cotton robe, from which protrudes a sensually rounded face with large, inquisitive brown eyes and a close-cropped head and beard simultaneously suggesting a medieval prophet and a Milanese fashion designer. He quickly takes his seat, mutters a few words, uses his left hand to support a face apparently capable of only the slightest of smiles. Within twenty minutes or so of his arrival a general agreement seems to have been reached. A typed document is handed to the head of the Rabat delegates, who searches in his pocket for the crumpled brown envelope containing the seal of the university. The seal is stamped down on the document, everyone shakes hands to ratify the deal, the Vice-President insists I do so as well. I've absolutely no idea of what I've so enthusiastically endorsed.

Ali Raisuni walks next to me as our pensive, puffing group climbs up to the café-lined main square of the medina to attend an evening lecture in the kasbah. 'We still call that the Andalucían mosque,' Ali Raisuni tells me, as his expressive head directs my glance beyond the town and towards an isolated and now dusk-shrouded minaret. Within moments of his gesture, floodlights are switched on, turning the minaret into a glowing candle in the imminent night.

The luminous robe of Ali Raisuni becomes a sacred apparition as it crosses the darkened square, impelling the few passers-by to bow their heads on their way to the upper, kif-smoking rooms of the surrounding cafés. We enter the ruined kasbah, which had been the stronghold of Abd el Krim before becoming his prison after his defeat by Spanish troops in 1926. Under a crescent moon, we cross an 'Andalucían garden' and head into a tower that has recently been made a 'Centre of Andalucían Studies'. Its young director shakes hands with all those who have come to attend the evening lecture.

My bafflement increases in the course of listening to a talk in a language I do not understand. The diminutive, white-haired speaker is described to me as a 'nationally known local poet and Sufi much influenced by the works of your T. S. Eliot'. He appears to be explaining the meaning of the universe; he refers frequently to the Murcian mystic Ibn 'Arabi. Halfway through the talk a man moves round the room distributing glasses of mint tea from a large silver tray.

When the audience disperses afterwards in the square, Ali Raisuni gestures to me to follow him. We walk down an alley behind the kasbah and enter a large old residence. Beyond an enclosed courtyard is a small room largely bare except for the cushions arranged on seating around the sides. Ali Raisuni reclines on these like an oriental potentate, his head resting on a wall. He claps his hands.

'I've been longing to do this all day,' he says. 'I've spent far too much time on my feet. I hardly slept last night; those niggling worries that keep you awake. I was up at three o'clock to say my prayers. I'm stiff and getting old.'

A tall black boy, no more than fifteen, answers his summons, silently obeys his orders. He holds his master's feet in his hands and begins to knead them. Ali Raisuni slumps completely on the cushions, and continues to talk to me as the massage takes place.

'You're in the oldest room in the oldest house in Chefchaouen – the house of the town's founder, my ancestor.'

He relates to me something of the town's history, then looks at me with quizzical eyes.

'Are there any questions you want to ask?'

The boy releases the feet, and lies down himself, his own feet facing those of his master.

I try to coax from Ali Raisuni something about his famous ancestor, a follower of Moulay Abdessalam ben Mchich. He is careful with his use of words, limiting his account of the man only to the few known facts, and allowing himself no fanciful speculation. I move on to another subject.

Is it really true, I ask, that the medina is divided into 'Moroccan', Andalucían, Jewish and Berber sections, each one separated from the other by gates that were once locked?

'There is no truth in that at all. Where did you read that?'

'In the *Blue Guide to Morocco*, a detailed English cultural guide.'

'Travel writers are fantasists.'

I agree with him on this, and quote another passage from the same book in which the women of the 'Andalucían' section are referred to as dressing 'quite differently from the rest, enveloping themselves almost completely in white robes'.

He shakes his head, the comment is not even worth a spoken denial.

'And the Andalucíans who kept the keys to their houses in Granada?'

The boy's feet are now pressing hard against his master's, forcing them into the air, pushing them back. The massage continues.

'Nonsense, all nonsense, *disparates*.'

Ali Raisuni claps his hands again, the boy disappears. The weary potentate sighs, and sinks back into what romantics would have defined as an oriental languor. The scene in front of me is that of an orientalist vision, but the rigorous mind of the man who lies there is the negation of these fantasies. I leave the room and the palace and continue walking under the stars.

I return to Tangier, to finish my Moroccan journey in the 'city of the dream'.

This is where the story of Islamic Spain began, for it was from this ancient town of mythical foundation that Tarik's troops set out across the Straits on their legendary expedition of 707. And it was to here, on the collapse of Islamic Spain nearly seven years later, that there came the earliest of that country's Moorish and Jewish refugees.

But it was not just the Moors and the Jews who contributed to that culture of exile which has so moulded the character of Tangier. A Portuguese possession one moment, a Spanish one the next, Tangier was acquired by the British in the seventeenth century as part of the same dowry that laid the foundations of British India. The British did not stay long, suffering as they did from poor diet, lack of funding, insanitary conditions and continual raids from the Moroccan leader Moulay Ismael; but they would be back with renewed vigour after 1906, when Tangier's new status as an international port cut off the town once more from the rest of Morocco and made the place a magnet for an international community of spies, prostitutes, criminals, political refugees, smugglers, artists, writers, outcasts of all description.

Tangier became 'a dream congealed in stone', to use the words of a perpetually stoned William Burroughs. Painters came chasing dreams of colour; socialites lived out dreams of oriental lavishness; the Beat Generation plunged into a twilight zone of drugs and sordid alleys; everyone dreamt of a world beyond the bourgeois conventions of the West – an unrestrainedly hedonistic world fed on hallucinogenic *majoun* and visions of olive-skinned youths.

In 1956 Tangier became incorporated into a now independent Morocco. Brothels were banned, the most outrageous bars were closed, the international colony dwindled, and the town's reputation as a leading gay resort – the world's first – was tarnished.

Is there anything left today of the 'city of the dream'? I ask myself as I meander off on the morning of my arrival, carrying my luggage like some distracted refugee. The obvious answer is the now octagenarian writer Paul Bowles, a Bohemian relic whose house is still an almost obligatory port of call for intellectual visitors to Tangiers. But the image of Bowles's world has become confused today with memories of Bertolucci's film version of *The Sheltering Sky*. I have little desire to see Bowles himself, but find I can't enter any of the rambling cafés of the medina without discovering it to have been used as a setting in the Bertolucci film. Sitting down in one of these places, the Café Colon, I'm asking myself another question. Is Tangier a dream or – as Bertolucci himself has said – a giant film studio?

Sometimes the sets of different films seem to have been thrown confusingly together. Finishing my coffee I walk into the new town, aiming towards what would appear to be a corner of Tangier that is forever England – the Anglican Church of St Andrew. The tower, with its Union Jack flying from the flagpole, is a Home Counties apparition that later defies all expectations of Englishness by being decorated all over with Moorish motifs. Images of rural England appear again inside the church, brought back by the hesitant sounds of organ practice, and the musty smells of polished pews, but once more the incongruity of the Moorish detailing throws me into confusion. Is that really the Lord's Prayer written in Arabic above the chancel arch?

I am back outside in the shaded churchyard looking at the English tombs when a smiling Moroccan shouts out in English 'Sir! Sir!'. He hurriedly approaches me. He is not a hustler as I think at first, he is the church caretaker, or perhaps he is an actor. His English is a parody of Home Counties English tinged with a strong Moroccan accent:

'Good morning, how are you, you are well? Lovely day today, isn't it, nice weather we've been having lately. My name is Mustapha. Can I be of any help to you? Are you looking for Mr Harris?'

He takes me to see the tomb of Mr Harris, Mr Walter Harris, braggart, fantasist, practical joker, author of the brilliant but mistitled *Morocco That Was* – a book about a Morocco that never was except in the mind of Mr Harris, lover of boys and Morocco. The complexities and absurdities of Mr. Harris's life, his passion for adventure and mystery, accompanied him into death. Was it his weak heart or the French Secret Service that killed him off? As I stand in front of his tomb, I wonder if his spirit is smiling at the memory of his rumoured unnnatural death and of the strange circumstances of his burial – the burial of a nominal convert to Catholicism in an Anglican cemetery. The funeral service had to be conducted down by the port, the coffin was then draped with a Union Flag and carried in procession up to a grave which was said to have been secretly reconsecrated by Spanish Franciscans in the middle of the night. But the ultimate absurdity is the tomb itself, a miniature version of the church behind, a Moorish interpretation of a Christian symbol, with ceramic inlay, and a turreted headstone like some souvenir of the Alhambra.

'Lovely tomb, isn't it?' says a beaming Mustapha as I shake hands with him and go on my way. Taking my leave of Mr. Harris, I walk up into the district where other dreaming Westerners have left their mark – in French-style villas turned today into consulates, museums, a notorious police station; in a Grand Hotel saturated in memories of Matisse, but now boarded up and sadly waiting a taker like some old and unwanted prostitute. Then I pass the modern cathedral that could have been a literal dream in stone had the Catalan architect Antonio Gaudí been allowed to execute on this site the design he later used for Barcelona's Sagrada Familia – a design so ambitious that even Tangier's Catholic authorities feared it might offend Muslim sensibilities.

The wails of the late morning muezzin become louder: a large mosque appears, merely a street away from the Spanish Library I've come to visit.

I'm looking for Jaume Bover, I tell a surly-looking, white-coated librarian. 'What do you want?' he replies in a hushed, hurried tone that leaves me unsure as to whether he's shy, unsociable, or genuinely so busy that even the slightest of interruptions is a terrible imposition on him. I remain unsure even after he reacts to my bibliographical request with a burst of manic activity in the index cards. Soon a pile of books connected with the Andalucían legacy in Morocco begins to mount on the table where he makes me sit, surrounded by Moroccan schoolchildren noisily engaged in their Spanish homework. With every book he brings he makes a brief critical assessment, reserving his rare praise for any work that meets his exacting scholarly standards. Most of the works are curtly dismissed as 'slight', 'fantastical', 'lacking in all seriousness'.

There is an obsessive quality about Jaume that makes me understand a bit better how this passionate bibliophile trapped in the world of his books could be the same Jaume who is said to have walked all over Morocco in the footsteps of Walter Harris's French contemporary Charles de Foucauld. Eventually I ask him about these walks, but he shrugs off his own achievements as of no consequence and turns immediately to the subject of the Frenchman who inspired them.

'I could spend all day talking about Foucauld, but we've got no time. The library is about to close.'

He says something about Foucauld none the less – about his spoilt and dissolute youth, his subsequent repentance, his immersion in Arabic culture, his 4,000-kilometre walk across Africa, his conversion to Islam, and his espousal of Berber ways and costume while leading an ascetic existence in Paris.

'He remained obsessed with Islam even after his eventual return to the Catholic faith. His writings have been used as propaganda both by Catholic colonialists and Muslim anti-colonialists.'

A bell rings, the schoolchildren rush out of the room, Jaume straightens the papers on his desk, then switches off the lights. As he walks towards the door he compares Foucauld with the latter's great predecessor in the forbidden North African interior, René Caillié.

'Caillié was another enormously complex and much misunderstood person. When he claimed his reward from the British government for being the first European in modern times to reach Timbuktu, no one in Britain believed him. The place he described sounded too ordinary.'

'People only want to hear fantasies,' he adds cryptically, locking the library door, and curtly inclining his head as his way of saying goodbye.

'What did you make of Jaume?' I am asked half an hour later by Mariano, yet another of the Spanish teachers in Morocco who has offered to look after me.

I have barely time to reply before Mariano, with a shake of a greasy forelock, hurries me out of his house and on to the street. 'We better go now if we want to catch Choukri while he's sober. He's impossible when drunk.'

Mariano knows everyone in Tangier. He's been living here for over five years, and has picked up a colloquial Moroccan through trawling bars and mingling with all types. His curiosity in people is near limitless, his limits now being defined by the writer Mohammed Choukri.

'Everyone finds him interesting at first,' he tells me, as we walk into the business heart of the new town, 'but then he begins to pall on you. He's a great performer whose act is always the same. He's a phenomenal egoist who rarely listens to other people. But perhaps I'm just jaded. I'm fed up with Tangier generally. It's the only place in Morocco where I could live. It's more sophisticated and cosmopolitan than any other town in this country, but I've no longer got the energy for it. I've reached a plateau in my relationships with the people here, and I can't go any further, no Westerner can.'

We turn off the main street and walk towards a bar called the Negresco. 'And in any case, my heart's no longer here, it's in Granada,' he continues, alluding to a recent boyfriend with whom he's fallen in love. 'I'm spending most of my time now going back to Granada at weekends. I'm desperate for a job in Spain.'

As he pushes open the glass door of the Negresco, I ask him if he's sure that Choukri will be here. 'It's the one thing you can count on in Tangier,' he replies. 'If he's not here at this time, he'll either be dead or desperately ill.'

The Negresco promotes itself as an 'English Bar', though it looks much less like an English pub than it does a capacious Parisian café of the 1950's. In keeping with its hybrid, indeterminate status it serves Spanish tapas with the drinks. Mariano, whispering into my ear, insists that we stand for a while at the bar, surveying the limp tortillas gathering flies behind the counter.

'He's sitting at that table by the window, but we better not go and join him yet. I don't trust the person he's with.'

Choukri, with his back to us, is talking to a man with a thick moustache, a long raincoat, and an overall appearance that parodies the sort of person Mariano claims him to be, 'a police informer'.

I discuss Choukri with Mariano while waiting for an audience with him. My knowledge of the writer comes largely from the autobiography that brought him international fame in the 1960's but is still banned in Morocco – *For Bread Alone*. It's a sensational, picaresque and totally unsentimental story about what it was like to have grown up as an impoverished Moroccan in the same, internationally administered Tangier that had satisfied the frivolous, voluptuous dreams of Westerners. It's a tale of pus, excrement, malnutrition, tuberculosis, and worm-ridden corpses; of a crazed father who strangles one of his children, abuses Allah, and ends up in prison for desertion from the army; of a mother resigned to the continual beatings of a husband whose dominance over her is decreed by Islam; of a boy who survives by salvaging from gutters, stealing, giving blow jobs to old men at fifty pesetas a time, and discovering when only twelve the consolations of majoun, kif and alcohol.

How much of this story, I wonder, is due to Paul Bowles, who is often thought of in the West as a sort of amanuensis to a generation of Moroccan writers that includes not only Choukri but also Mohammed Mrabet, Abdesiam Boulaich, Larbi Layachi and Ahmed Yacoubi? It was Bowles who encouraged the literary talents of all these figures, and then presented these talents to the English-speaking world in his own pared-down, Hemingway-like translations.

Bowles's name brings a broad smile to Mariano's worn face.

'You mean that "robber of Moroccan tales" – that's what they call Bowles here. He gets illiterate Moroccans to tell him their stories, which he then retells rather than translates. To be fair on him, however, his relationship with Choukri was a very different one. Choukri was the only one of Bowles's protégés to overcome his illiteracy and write in a very elegant, classical Arabic. You know, of course, that Choukri has been a teacher of Arabic for most of his working life, first at a local primary school and then at Tangier's Ibn Battuta College? Now he lives purely from writing – I think he's the only Moroccan writer in this country to do so.'

Mariano pauses for a moment to cast a furtive glance towards the table where Choukri is sitting. Then he lowers his voice slightly.

'I've never been a great fan of Bowles, but I think he deserves some of the credit for Choukri's success. When Choukri was emerging from his dreadful childhood and adolescence, Bowles and his literary circle must have seemed very glamorous to him – a true incentive to pursue a literary career. This is what writing is all about, he must have thought – making money from getting perpetually pissed, stoned and laid. He says today he has no nostalgia for this period in Tangier's history. At the time, however, I'm sure he really enjoyed being lionized by Genet, Tennessee Williams, and all those other glittering figures in Bowles's world. But I better not say anything more about Bowles – I'm sure his name will crop up almost as soon as you start speaking to Choukri.'

The 'police informer' finally leaves the bar, we move over to take his place. Choukri, shaking our hands, says how sorry he is that we've just missed a fascinating friend of his – 'a lawyer who represents the poor'. Mariano winks at me as if to stress that nothing Choukri says should be fully believed.

Choukri, a man in his late fifties, sits nobly upright in his chair, proudly playing the role of some writer from a vanished generation. He has an orange, sleeveless cardigan shamelessly displaying its holes, and a hat that seems worn purely as a statement of Bohemianism and creativity. His self-conscious dignity is accentuated by a large forehead and a nose that is hooked like the beak of a parrot – an animal he is soon imitating in a parody of a Japanese tourist who had approached him earlier in the day. But it is to another bird that he compares himself when Mariano gently mocks him about the inevitability of his presence at the Negresco.

'I am like a stork,' he says. 'My homing instinct brings me back every day at the same time to the same table in the same bar.'

I notice that he has used a bottle of mineral water to lift up a small section of the net curtain that protects the drinkers from the stares of the more orthodox Muslims on the street.

'That's my little window onto the world,' he explains before returning to the subject of his daily routine. 'I do most of my writing in the morning, never more than about one and a half or two pages a day. From twelve to two I'm here in the Negresco, you could call this my office, the place where I receive visitors such as yourselves. Then I go back to my house, a few more drinks perhaps, a bit of writing, a fair amount of television – in recent weeks I've been glued to these nature programmes they've been showing. I rarely go out now in the evenings, and I allow only the most intimate friends to come to my home. Solitude is essential to me, and I strongly believe that marriage is incompatible with the writer's life.'

Mariano politely asks me how Choukri's writing schedule compares with mine, but Choukri intervenes with a query of his own, a rhetorical one.

'I suppose you've been to see Bowles? He's turned himself into Tangier's main tourist attraction. I wouldn't be surprised if he charged people for their visits, he's got such an obsession with money, and he's so selfish with it. I don't go near him anymore, I'm tired of going to see him and then finding myself in a room full of his sycophantic admirers. In the old days I used to go to his house a lot, and I was always alone.'

Then he tells us about his collaborative ventures with Bowles.

'Ours was a complex working relationship. As Bowles can't read a word of Arabic, I had to give an oral rendering in Maghrebi of what I had written. The finer details would then be debated in French or Spanish. This elaborate system worked rather well, at least until Bowles started claiming sole copyright on these stories.'

I stop the waiter to order another round of drinks. Given Choukri's reputation for unpleasant drunkenness, I'm slightly relieved if also surprised to see that the liquid at the bottom of his glass appears to be fruit juice. But when I check with him to see what he's having I find that he has not become a teetotaller after all.

'I'll have another Campari and Pastis,' he says.

'That's a strange mixture,' laughs Mariano.

'Well, as you say in Spanish, "Todo entra bien en el cuerpo".'

He finishes off with a smile the dregs in his old glass, and continues talking about Bowles. He talks about him not with bitterness but with an amused exasperation heightened by an obvious love of shocking his listeners. His conversation has the quality of a polished performance.

'I'm now writing a short book on Bowles in which I shall be serving him up, as it were, *a la plancha*. Mind you I shan't be doing so out of malice. I'm just curious to know why he's lived in this country for so long. I know he loves its landscapes and its culture, but he absolutely hates the Moroccans, he's got nothing but disdain for them.'

The Moroccan world, the Moroccan reality, is gradually imping-ing itself upon the strange European enclave in which our meeting is taking place. As Choukri talks, his eyes turn repeatedly to the small breach he has created in the bar's net curtains. He keeps a constant watch on the world outside, and warns us whenever intruders from this world are about to descend on us. At one stage he disappears outside to deliver a plastic bag to his housekeeper. The next moment he takes out a coin and a cigarette in preparation for the arrival at our table of a bedraggled woman he says has been coming to him for years. Other beggars, 'all regulars', follow in their turn, each being given a different sum of money depending on their needs. 'I've many clients, as you can see'.

The most pathetic of these is a tall young man with an enormous goitre on his neck, a deformity that Choukri says would have been easily treated in the West at no great cost.

'I am sometimes asked,' he says after the man has gone, 'why I bother to give money to someone like him who is just going to spend it all on drink. But why shouldn't they get drunk? I reply. What would you do if you woke up every morning unable to face the day because you've got no money, no future, and, on top of all that, you're ashamed of a repulsive deformity? Wouldn't you too get drunk?'

As more drinks arrive at our table, Choukri's conversation turns rapidly into an instoppable monologue.

'Some people say laziness is Morocco's problem, the root of its poverty, but laziness to me is a virtue, a sign of how sophisticated a nation really is. The Moroccans are like the Spaniards, or at least how the Spaniards were once perceived: they think in the past, they live in the present, they don't give a thought for the future. West-erners today are ridiculously obsessed with their careers and their futures, they're rushing around so much that they've even forgot-ten how to shit, they're half-shitters, then death gets to them, and they really haven't achieved anything, they haven't enjoyed all the money they've gained from all this rushing around. There was this

Catalan businessman I once knew who didn't even set aside enough time to sit down and eat properly, he was too rushed even to chew his food. And what of course happens? He dies. He chokes to death...'

A burly, elderly American is standing over our table with a battery of cameras in his hand, he wants to take Choukri's photograph, he's doing a series of portraits of Tangier's 'interesting personalities'. Choukri's posture becomes haughtier than ever, he grants the man permission with an imperial wave of the hand.

While the photographer shoots at Choukri from every conceivable angle, we all speculate about the other 'personalities' the man should be choosing. Tangier, even today, seems like an island of human misfits and curiosities.

I mention Jaume Bover.

'You mean the librarian?' asks Choukri. 'I've never got far with him, he's completely hermetic, he never seems to leave the library, he lives only for his books.'

I point out that Jaume has walked all over Morocco in the footsteps of Charles Foucauld.

'And what an absurd thing to do!' exclaims Choukri. 'Why bother to retrace the past, and why bother to follow in the footsteps of somebody else? You should always live in the present, and live for yourself.'

The cafés of the Place de la France, hub of the new town, balcony over the old, are filling up with men as the sky darkens and the evening sets in. I glance at my watch; they surely won't be long now. I continue waiting for them at the Café de Paris, the legendary meeting place with its chandeliered interior that once hummed to the conspiratorial murmurings of foreign agents.

Apologizing for his lateness, Mariano finally arrives, bringing with him the young friend whom he is keen for me to meet. He wants me to be aware of a Morocco that differs entirely from the foreign image of the country – a Morocco of fashion and modernity.

His friend is called Rachid, he is handsome and delicately featured, with stylish black clothes, and a smart, designer haircut. I've been told that he runs the only fashion shop in Tangier, but he exchanges smiles with Mariano when I ask him about this. 'We're having certain problems at present,' he comments.

Rachid's wealthy father-in-law has withdrawn his backing from the shop, Rachid's wife is in hospital, and Rachid himself has just come out of prison after being caught driving Mariano's dented old car without a permit. 'Are you up for a party?' Rachid asks me. I certainly am.

The party is being held in a cousin's house. We get into the same car that has caused Rachid a month's incarceration in a place that sounds like the mazamorras of Tetuan. The door is answered by a laughing, heavily-lipsticked young woman, the guests have yet to arrive, but there are the hypnotically monotonous sounds of Moroccan techno, *bacalao*, to put us in the party spirit as we drink whisky out of large tumblers. Our hostess sways her hips and clicks her fingers as she shimmies off to answer the door-bell.

A large, noisy group of women has arrived. I glimpse them all streaming into the vestibule dressed in the traditional robes and with their heads covered. But no sooner is the door closed than they are hastily removing their robes to reveal mini-skirts, boob tubes, black leather boots, navel-hugging tops, Fuck-Me shoes. They help themselves to spirits and cocktails, a dimmer switch turns down the lights, the women drag us out to dance, new arrivals keep coming in, ice cubes tinkle against glasses, the music gets louder.

I'm dazed and my head's turning, and I'm envisaging the vengeful fury of the Ayatollahs, the F.I.S., the Almohads. 'You weren't expecting this, were you?' a gyrating Rachid shouts over the music, 'But this is what Morocco is like: it's a huge façade, and Tangier especially. Do you know what Bertolucci called this town?'

I say I do, but he tells me all the same.

'Cinecittà.'

The party reaches a premature climax, a fast-forward button seems to have been pressed, the guests begin disappearing almost as quickly as they arrived, Rachid suggests we do the same, 'the party never really got going,' he concludes once we're outside, embark-

ing on the next stage of our nocturnal journey into the bowels of
'Sin City', as Rachid is soon calling it. 'That's a better name for where
we're eventually heading,' he says, leading Mariano and I down a
steep, pitch-black alley where we scuttle like rats over steps made
hazardous by the rubble of collapsed walls and the oily slipperiness
of decomposition. Only the flames are missing from this descent
into a hell from which we are briefly saved by a surprisingly smart
door opening off to our left. 'Let's have some stylish decadence before
going on to the disco,' suggests the devilish Rachid.

From the evil-smelling alley we are drawn into its sensory
opposite – a magical, perfumed chamber, suggestively lit, enveloped
by a canopy of green drapery that hangs from the ceiling like a ball-
room gown. And again, as so often in Tangier, there's a cultural
ambiguity about the place, an unmistakeable flavour of a Western
land as seen through the confused dreams of exiles. The Regency
elegance of the detailing, the framed photograph of an ex-
Household Cavalry trooper, and the ageing, neck-tied dandy sitting
behind the counter of the empty room, all help me locate my
surroundings more accurately in their mythical geography – we're
in some Brighton bar more extravagant and more camp than any
real bar I know in England.

The solitary barman addresses us in a deep and fruity English.
He brightens up when he hears I'm from his country, he starts telling
me about the history of his bar, a bar he has run for a quarter of a
century with his partner, the retired trooper, now retired to bed, it's
already a quarter to one, 'you should have come here earlier, that's
when the place gets lively,' a difficult-to-imagine concept at this silent
hour. 'Writers have always come here, there was that American chap,
what's his name, Burroughs was it? Wrote the *Naked Feast* when staying in our hotel, I've never managed to read the book myself, I could
never get through the first page, you look a writer type yourself, you
must be clever, you seem to speak foreign languages, I've never
mastered a single one, I wish sometimes I was back in England, no
more languages to worry about, people might understand me,
I've always loved Suffolk and the wool villages, I was brought up
there, so different to this shit-hole, no dirt, no rats, no bargaining,
no fucking thieves, excuse the French.' He pauses, he's fast slipping

back into his memories, his fantasies. 'Lavenham, Long Melford, I wonder what they're like now, I remember them as picture post-cards, so neat and tidy, the little ford, the duck pond, those wonderful half-timbered houses, the fireplaces in the wood-beamed pubs. "Time, gentlemen, please!"' We finish off our drinks, go outside, continue our descent.

Hell is a discothèque called Gospel. Red-eyed men, scarred and fierce, are blocking its gates when we approach. They recognize Rachid, they let us in, we go on down, down cold concrete steps reeking of sweat and urine, the earth is shaking far below, a scarlet-purple light is shining from the infernal womb. And, as we descend, I try and keep sane by considering the origins of the place's name. Was it intended as a misspelt homage to seventies musical or as a cruel slur on Christianity?

'Ten years ago this was Tangier's most fashionable discothèque,' Rachid enlightens me as I stand with him and Mariano on a balcony above the strobe-lit dance floor, 'Now look at it, no one is even bothering to dance.' Neither are there any women to dance with, just listless men with cans of beer, tapping out the rhythms of the distorted amplifications. 'The only women who would come to a place like this are prostitutes,' says Rachid, pointing to one who has just come in, dressed like a traditional belly dancer, her navel lost in a roll of fat.

'The show is about to begin,' grins Mariano, as a handful of men, following in the footsteps of the prostitute-dancer, assemble at the back of the cavernous room, amid a tangle of wires, drum-sets, and speakers. I expect the room to vibrate soon to the electronic sounds of Moroccan Rock, but instead the men squat on the ground and lift up instruments that Rachid describes to me as derbukas, kaman-jehs, rababs, tars and ouds.

'You know what they call this music?' Rachid asks me when the recorded heavy metal music of the speakers is abruptly replaced by sadder, slower sounds that seem to issue from the Moroccan past.

'Berber folk?' I suggest.

'Well, there's a bit of that, I admit, these aren't the purest of musicians. But essentially this is 'Andalous music' – they're playing a nawba, a classical form invented in Córdoba by the Baghdad musician Ziryab.'

I'm only half-taking in what I'm hearing. I'm distracted by the jostling men around us, the pin-pricked arms, the menacing drunkenness, the inability of the soothing music to calm the growing tempers. Only later, when the belly-dancer starts clumsily to move and the men begin whistling, does the full significance of Rachid's words come finally home to me – that even here, in these lowest of depths, plaintive chords are still echoing from the lost paradise of al-Andalus.

We rise up from hell, we walk back into the open air, the brightness of the starry night is lifting us out of the miasma of low life. 'Let's drive up to the Kasbah,' Rachid proposes. 'I know someone who lives there, he never sleeps. He loves people dropping in at all hours.'

We park the car at the top of Tangier and walk through the moonlit alleys entangling the citadel. 'His house is amazing, film stars always go there, David Bowie's a regular, the dope's great.' In one of the alleys I wonder if I'm already dreaming as I pause in front of a copper name-plate inscribed Count András Tekely – the name of one of the oldest Hungarian families attached to the humblest of doors. But Rachid and Mariano do not share my curiosity, I'm forced to rush to catch them up – the mystery of Count Tekely in the Kasbah remains unresolved. 'You can ask my friend about him,' says Rachid, when we finally reach the amazing house and knock hard against the door. But no one replies. 'He must be deep in sleep. How I envy him,' sighs Mariano.

Listlessly we stroll to the Kasbah's square to lean on the battlements and drift off into our separate worlds. Rachid takes out a cigarette, while Mariano, mumbling that he can 'almost touch the lights of Tarifa', quietly recalls the homesickness that the view from here had once aroused in him. As for me, I'm flying above the port, straining my eyes until finally I see it – the boat to take me on my distant voyage, the floating palace I had searched for in Málaga in a recent but now hazy-seeming past. 'The *Ibn Battuta* is here!' 'The *Ibn Battuta* is here!' I feel like shouting, happy to have found it at last, and to have found it here – in the town that gave birth to the great traveller.

It is a Monday morning in late December, and I am back in the Kasbah, searching for the tomb of Ibn Battuta.

'There's no evidence he died here. The tomb is almost certainly a fake,' says the young director of the Kasbah's Museum, where I begin my quest.

I'm sure he's right about the tomb, the facts are on his side. Ibn Battuta had little contact with his native town after graduating there as a law student at the age of twenty-one. On returning from his final travels, to Spain and Timbuktu, he settled at the sultan's court in Fez, where he is last heard of dictating his travel memoirs to the scholar he had met in Granada, Ibn Yuzayy.

But I'm happy to discount the truth and accept the more popular and satisfying version of Ibn Battuta's life as one long journey that ended where it had begun – in the Kasbah of Tangier. And, after all, isn't there a strong fictional element in the memoirs on which most of our knowledge of Ibn Battuta is based?

If Marco Polo never made it to China, as recent scholarship suggests, why should Ibn Battuta be believed? And whereas few people at the time doubted Marco Polo's exploits, scepticism was rife among Ibn Battuta's contemporaries at Fez. The famous Tunisian scholar Ibn Khaldun wrote of officials at the court who, on hearing stories told by a certain 'shaykh from Tangier', 'whispered to each other that he must be a liar'. 'Purely and simply a liar,' confirmed Abu l'Barakat al-Balafiqi, the Andalucían author of the earliest biographical notice of Ibn Battuta.

In recounting largely from memory the experiences of twenty-nine years of travelling, Ibn Battuta inevitably misremembered and distorted many of the details of these journeys, and indeed openly confessed at times to having forgotten certain names and dates. But the truth of his memoirs was further falsified by his scribe, Ibn Yuzayy, who, like most good travel writers, was obliged to create a cohesive narrative out of his subject's chaotic and imperfectly recollected wanderings. Ibn Yuzayy pretended that Ibn Battuta's routes never overlapped, and that the events described under a particular location took place on a single visit rather than on separate journeys, as was often the case. He also had to fill in the more important gaps caused either by lapses in Ibn Battuta's memory or omissions in the travels themselves. Just as Marco Polo is now said to have borrowed heavily from Ibn Battuta's memoirs, Ibn Yuzayy can be shown to have pillaged ruthlessly from the writings of earlier travellers, notably the descriptions of Mecca, Medina and Damascus by the twelfth-century Andalucían writer Ibn Jubayr. And, in the interests of including all lands to which Muslim influence had spread, Ibn Yuzayy related at least one trip that Ibn Battuta could not have made – his trip up the Volga to visit the Muslim community at Bulghar. Recent scholars have even cast doubts on the authenticity of his journeys to China and Byzantium, and to parts of Yemen, Anatolia, Kurushan and East Africa.

To what extent does all this matter? Hasn't the poetic construct that has been made out of Ibn Battuta's life a validity equal to the truth behind it? Isn't fact ultimately as inseparable from fiction as living is from dreaming?

The supposed tomb of Ibn Battuta seems in any case to bear no less relation to the real person than does the proposed tourist monument to the great traveller that the director of the Kasbah's Museum has begun describing to me.

'We've got permission to use an abandoned prison just outside the Kasbah… we want to present his life and times in an interesting way, we're trying to get away from the usual information panels and display cases… we're thinking of employing an opera designer… the idea will be to take the visitor on a journey through Ibn Battuta's life… there'll be music, sound effects, sand to walk through, dramatic lighting, clouds of dried ice, reconstructions of ships…'

He realizes I'm not taking all this in, I'm not taking the idea of an Ibn Battuta Museum seriously enough, I'm more interested in fantasy than in virtual reality. He returns to the subject of the tomb.

'The popular belief that Ibn Battuta is buried there is totally resistant to the facts; the local veneration the monument inspires is quite extraordinary. I can see I can't dissuade you from going to see it.'

I ask him for directions.

'You'll never find the place on your own,' he says. 'It's hidden in a back street, but you can ask any of the boys in the square, they'll guide you.'

Potential guides rush towards me once I'm in the square; I choose the most vociferous of them, abandoning my usual practice of going for the least aggressively demanding. I'm in a mysterious hurry to pay my last respects to Ibn Battuta.

My chosen guide is lanky and haggard, with a wispy, pointed beard that tries to cover up a pock-marked chin. He walks with even greater speed than I do, and I have difficulties keeping up with him as he rushes up and down a network of alleys that leads us below the Kasbah, ultimately convincing me that he's lost himself, and that he's got no idea of where he's going to. He worries me further by muttering something to a man in a doorway and then heading off up in the direction we seem to have come from. I begin to protest, he tells me to relax, the path to Ibn Battuta's tomb is long and circuitous.

We've arrived, or so he says. I still don't believe him. We're climbing the last yards up to a cubicle of a building, dwarfed among the tall houses, suspended at the corner of a vertiginous alley. The ceramic decoration above its door suggests a dating for the structure no earlier than the 1950's. The door is closed.

'The holy man isn't here,' says my incredulous guide. 'I don't understand, he's always here, he's meant to be guarding the shrine.' He thinks he knows where to look for him, he leaves me waiting outside, there are plenty of young children to keep me occupied, begging for their photos to be taken, pulling at my trouser pockets.

He reappears a good twenty minutes later, there's no sign of a holy man, just a disgruntled young woman carrying a key. 'You'll have to give her a little something,' my guide insists. 'Two hundred dirhams or so.' I try and haggle down the price, my words are translated for the woman, she refuses to go lower than one hundred, I make a final offer of fifty, she opens the door. I take off my shoes, I walk down a step, I've made it at last.

The oratory is tiny, entirely modern, and insipidly decorated with pale brown ceramics, paid for, I believe, by an American. The electric lighting is harsh and unmysterious, the atmosphere is one of banal domesticity. I pay undue attention to a portable fan, and a large radiator painted the same ugly colour as the ceramics.

Is this it? Is that really Ibn Battuta lying there under a black velvet shroud that the woman with the key is now impatiently shaking with a duster?

My guide attempts to translate the gold lettering embroidered on the velvet, but then halters and gives up. Instead he draws my attention to a box on the wall 'for further contributions'.

The woman is now anxious for me to leave, I've had my fifty dirhams worth. My guide wonders if I've any final request, then suggests one himself. I'm not sure if I've heard him correctly, I ask him to repeat the question.

'Do you want to kiss the tomb?'

I'm genuinely at a loss for what to say, I've been caught off my guard, my heart is battling with my scepticism, I'm almost persuading myself that by the very act of kissing the tomb I shall know that my journey has come to its end, that the imagination has triumphed over reality, that the person I call the Moorish Queen does indeed exist, that my love for her was not a fantasy, that the lost world of al-Andalus had been truly a paradise.

I stammer for a few moments. I shake my head.

Timbuktu

CHAPTER SEVEN

TO TIMBUKTU

Or is the rumour of thy Timbuctoo
A dream as frail as those of ancient time?
Alfred Tennyson, 'Timbuctoo'

This is the Granada where dreams end. The Alhambra has disappeared from sight, hidden behind the blight of grey blocks that has spread south to the vanished orchard of Lorca's last days. Winter is fading out without bringing any of the longed-for snow or rain, there are water restrictions unheard of in Granada for this time of year. On a wall of defaced posters, vandals have hacked away at the smile of Cecilio, mascot of skiing championships that have been postponed through lack of snow. Only Nassim, his turbaned boy companion, cartoon symbol of Spain's Islamic Heritage, has kept on smiling, oblivious of the swastika scrawled at the bottom of this dying poster in this part of Granada few tourists visit.

Life is hibernating on the night I set aside for 'El Rey Chico'. No one has either the money or the energy to go out, friends are resting at home with videos and newborn babies, others I know have mysteriously gone away from town, the Moorish Queen can only have been a figment of my imagination. The sole person left to accompany me on my nocturnal escapade is a Basque acquaintance who has come to Granada for a few days to gloat on the Christian town's misfortune and lend his support to the Moors, whom he thinks of as blood brothers, fellow victims of Spanish imperialism. He's excited at the idea of going to a place named after Granada's last king, in any case, he says, he's in the mood for 'meeting girls and getting pissed'.

In Tangier the Gospel is a discothèque; in Granada the nickname of Boabdil was once linked with a famous brothel. The 'Rey Chico' was no ordinary 'puti-club' or 'whiskería': it was a king among brothels that stood proudly in the Albaicín in a cheeky riposte to the Alhambra opposite. Ageing Granadine males, remembering perhaps the sexual initiations of their youth, have endowed this long deceased institution with an aura of myth and respectability, which is perhaps why its name has been taken over by the as yet unsung whiskería that the Basque and I are now entering in the bowels of the modern town.

I'm only following in the footsteps of Genet and Goytisolo, I tell myself once we're past the black security curtains and into a Granada that I'd never dreamt of. The Basque takes the place in his stride, he says there's a whole street of them in the business heart of Bilbao. But I'm not used to being in darkened bars with red leather walls and entirely naked women, mainly Brazilian I would guess from my hurried, nervous glances away from the long whisky and soda that is placed for me on the counter. There's something distinctly unsettling about having a chat with a friend at a bar while women, wearing nothing but a smile, are blowing you kisses, shouting compliments, pressing their breasts against you, pulling your arms, stroking the nape of your neck. I'm only here for the whisky part in the whiskería, I want to tell them, shaking off their limbs like a latter-day St Anthony as I pursue my researches into the ultimate degradations bestowed upon the name of Boabdil.

The Basque has a less theoretical interest in the place. He's soon won over by the sirens and wonders if I wouldn't mind waiting 'fifteen minutes or so' while he goes off with one of them into a back room reserved for more intimate encounters. I order another whisky, bury myself in a notebook, and look repeatedly at my watch. Soon, out of a corner of my eye, I begin to notice a slender and exceptionally tall black figure leaning against the wall to my side. I try not to look directly at her, but her beauty weakens me in my resolve. St Anthony might also have been tempted.

She has not even the smile to accompany her nudity, she alone of her naked companions makes no attempt to attract my attention, her Modigliani-like face is expressive instead of sadness and contempt. When she becomes aware of my glance, she responds with a reluctant, automatic voice, as if forced to show an interest in me by some hidden pimp.

'Where are you from?' she asks in a faltering, heavily accented

Spanish. 'You don't look from here.'

I put the same question to her, expecting her to say Brazil but in fact she mentions a country of which I know almost nothing – Mali.

In the arching of the eyebrows intended to convey my surprise, she seems to sense a genuine geographical curiosity, for there is a slight relaxing in her manner as she continues talking.

'I was brought up in a town on the Niger called Djenné. It's a very old and beautiful town like Granada. But that's not where I'm originally from.'

The Basque has by now completed his transaction and is returning to the bar, but the woman from Mali manages to finish what she is saying before he arrives.

'I'm from Timbuktu. You might have heard of the place from nursery rhymes.'

Is she having me on? Is this part of her rehearsed patter when approaching potential clients? I don't have the time to find out. The Basque is soon sitting beside me again, the woman is distracted, another man is going up to her, he favours a direct approach to seduction, his arm is soon around her waist, I look away.

I lose sight of her, others are now moving in around us, one of them asks if I want 'Foki-Foki', but all I want is to speak again to the woman from Mali, to continue where we had so frustratingly left off.

She's with yet another person when I finally see her again, on my way out of Boabdil's domain of sighs and groans. She's kissing in a dark corner, I'm too impatient to wait for her, I resolve to make do with a last glimpse of her face. She's not really kissing, her mouth is passively receiving the lips of someone else, the rest of the face seems disengaged from this activity, it registers my departure. She extricates her mouth for a moment, she gives me her first smile, a faint one.

'See you again,' she says.

'In Timbuktu,' I reply.

Truth is always naked, a female nude to be precise. The woman from Timbuktu was the fleshly proof of the reality of a town whose existence I had once doubted. Somehow she has brought me closer to a place promising something I had not found in Tangier – the ultimate conclusion to a journey in the shadow of al-Andalus.

Everything seems to be leading me to Timbuktu – the prostitute, Ibn Battuta, Leo the African, the paradox of ending up in a place of mythical reputation after a journey exploring the frontierland between fact and fiction. And now, after having consigned him to the chimeras that are haunting me, I try out a long forgotten telephone number and find myself talking to Mahmud Zakari.

I go and see him in his temporary residence in the Albaicín – an upstairs flat in an old house built around a shabby, whitewashed courtyard like those of the medina of Tetuan. The flat itself, in contrast, could be that of a Parisian intellectual, its walls papered with neatly arranged rows of severely bound paperbacks – works on philosophy, history, politics, literature. Whether or not these books belong to Mahmud or to the mysterious person in whose flat he is staying, their seriousness accords with the quiet, carefully considered tone of the young man who is now addressing me – a man whose height, ebony skin, and fineness of features lend further reality to the image I've begun to form of the inhabitants of Timbuktu.

What's he really doing in Granada? How does he make a living? Who is looking after him? Whose are the children in the framed photograph above the desk? These are some of the unaskable questions that come to me as he tells me of his researches into his country's Andalucían past, and of his embitterment at not finding anyone here in Granada to publish his remarkable findings – findings that would surely help the people of this town to understand more their own history.

He speaks about his studies as if they were the main driving force behind his life, as if little else mattered. His respect for scholarship is like that of Ali Raisuni or Jaume Bover – a respect that leaves no room for frivolity or fanciful speculation. He cannot even raise a smile when I tell him about local rumours that he has come from Timbuktu with the key to his ancestral home in Granada.

'People,' he says, 'are more interested in fantasies than in the historical truth.'

But the historical truth he goes on to recount is as fascinating and little-known as some mythical lost domain.

'Jews and Muslims of Andalucían origin were living in Timbuktu long before Yuder Pacha and his army of Andalucían renegades conquered the Songhai empire for the Saadian dynasty of Morocco. Timbuktu was not some obscure desert outpost but one of Africa's greatest centres of learning. A trio of outstanding Andalucían poets were active there in the fourteenth century. One of them was Sidi 'Ayah from Almería, another was Ibn Fazazi from Córdoba, whose poems have been recited every year in Timbuktu up to the present day. The third was al-Saheli, who is known today more as the architect of Timbuktu's main mosque than as a poet. This is unfair – al-Saheli's poetry was widely read throughout the Islamic world, Ibn Khaldun praised it, as did Ibn al-Khatib of Loja. It is saturated with longing for Granada and al-Andalus.'

When I ask Mahmud about the present-day Andalucían community in Timbuktu, he sketches out a rough map of the town, indicating what he calls the principal 'Andalucían quarter'. He is vague about his own ancestry, and does not respond at all when I allude to his reputation in Granada as the head of Timbuktu's community of renegade and morisco origin. But he talks about a 'historical centre we have founded recently to document our past'. And he refers to the wealth of important but virtually unstudied manuscripts on al-Andalus that can be found there.

And then he finally convinces me of the vital necessity of my undertaking a journey to Timbuktu.

'I want you to come to Timbuktu, you shall stay in my house, I shall show you a Timbuktu that no tourist or journalist sees. You will meet cobblers still making the shoes and boots that would have been worn in fifteenth-century Granada. You will find artisans crafting doors and furniture that Boabdil would have recognized. And I'll take you inside interiors that are certain to amaze you – interiors like those of Islamic Granada, interiors of unexpected richness.'

I'm soon agreeing to meet up with him in Timbuktu on his return there in a few weeks' time. I cannot believe that I'm so close to this fabled destination, and he tantalizes me further with the mysteries that await me there.

'Timbuktu is outwardly just like Caillié described it – a collection of impoverished mud-huts, terribly decayed, under constant threat from the moving desert sands. But as you begin to look deeper, you will realize the truth of what the French traveller Félix du Bois wrote. He called Timbuktu 'la mysterieuse', he discovered its mysteries, he found out that the external poverty was merely a façade. You too will make that discovery.'

He wishes me a happy journey to Timbuktu.

Back in the London greyness from which the Sultan's summons had rescued me nearly a year before, dreams of Timbuktu kindle the last embers of my vision of the Orient. But as these dreams persist so too does the desire to place this legendary town in a more sober historical and geographical context.

The books I turn to in the British Library confirm that Timbuktu has at least one factor in common with genuinely mythical places – that its reputation is based largely on gold and inaccessibility.

One of the oldest towns south of the Sahara, it lies at the southern end of a notoriously long and dangerous caravan route where survival had once been dependent on scarce and unreliable wells and water-holes separated sometimes by many days' march. Salt and slaves were two of the principal commodities from the days of Timbuktu's greatness as a trading centre, but it was above all the gold shipped along the Niger from Ghana that contributed to the lure and wealth of the land to which it belonged – the 'Beled-es-Sudan', or 'Land of the Black'.

It was in the fourteenth century, during the rule of Mansa Musa, that the world first began to perceive this land as bathed in the same glow that shone over Solomon's mines. Mansa Musa, the ruler of an empire that supplied an estimated two thirds of the West's reserves of gold, was shown enthroned with orb and sceptre in a fourteenth-century Catalan atlas that described him as 'lord of the Blacks of Guinea... the richest and most noble lord of all this region owing to the abundance of gold which is gathered in his land'.

The prodigal extent of Musa's riches became widely known after 1324, when he travelled to Mecca in a style more splendid and extravagant than that of any pilgrim before him. Bringing with him up to a hundred camel loads of gold, he liberally distributed gifts wherever he went until eventually, on his homeward journey, nothing of this gold was left. His immediate resources might have dwindled but his entourage had swollen though acquiring in Mecca the likes of the Granadine poet and architect al-Saheli, who was invited to Mali together with an accompanying team of Andalucían craftsmen.

Musa returned to a Mali that had itself greatly expanded during his absence thanks to the annexation by one of his generals of the vast riverain kingdom of the Songhai. Timbuktu, halfway between Musa's court at Walata and the Songhai capital of Goa, entered an age that was golden in more than the literal sense: while absorbing the trade of neighbouring caravan terminals, it also began drawing into its sandy embrace the intelligentsia of the desert.

But the material riches of Mali rather than its culture would have interested the first Islamic visitors from afar, all of whom displayed the traditional North African disdain towards black peoples. Ibn Battuta, who came to Timbuktu in 1352, was no exception, his descriptions of Mali revealing racist attitudes largely absent from the rest of his long *rihla*. He was critical of almost every aspect of the country, from the public nudity of its slaves to the way its women mixed far more freely with men than in other, less liberal Islamic lands. And he sneered at many of the court's curious traditions, even if in so doing he unwittingly enhanced the mystique of this country through describing a place where courtiers romped about in feathers and bird masks, royal attendants bore gilded staves, and visitors to the ruler threw dust and ashes into their eyes in a domed audience chamber in which an Andalucían poet sang.

Not until Leo Africanus, in the early sixteenth century, did a Muslim from the north travel without racial prejudices through the 'Land of the Black'. The great Renaissance geographer, observing aspects of the African interior that his racially biased predecessors did not think worth recording, went on to supply the West with the earliest detailed record of this interior. The irony is that such an objective-minded person was also the first traveller to portray Timbuktu in a glowing light worthy of the expectations raised by Mansa Musa's Mecca pilgrimage of 1324.

The vulnerably isolated empire that Mansa Musa had built up had barely survived into the fifteenth century, being eroded at its edges by rebellions and incursions, and weakened at its heart by dissent. But Timbuktu itself had come to thrive as never before under the Songhai leadership of Askia the Great. Architecturally, there may have been little to show for this. The town described by Leo Africanus featured 'huts of mud and straw' rather than the 'brilliant towers' that Westerners would later imagine (the only two buildings that Leo singled out were al-Saheli's large mosque and royal palace, which probably pleased him for being the works of 'an excellent master from Granada'). However, despite all this, the town's inhabitants were found by Leo to be so rich as to use gold nuggets for coinage, and so cheerful as to parade the nocturnal streets 'playing musical instruments and dancing'. These were people clearly affected by living alongside an exceptionally munificent court, which had attracted to Timbuktu an abundance 'of doctors, judges, priests and other learned men, who are bountifully maintained at the king's cost and charges'.

Pampered himself by this court, Leo is likely to have been misled about the extent of Timbuktu's wealth, which in any case rapidly diminished in later years. Already, by 1591, when Yuder Pacha and his renegades brought the Songhai kingdom under Moroccan control, the invaders found little of Leo's Timbuktu other than the 'huts of mud and straw'. Yuder, who ended up by being beheaded in Marrakesh in 1606, was inevitably disappointed by the land he had suffered the arduous Sahara crossing to conquer. But, under the rule of a negligent and distant Morocco, the decay could only get worse, leading to even greater disillusionment with Timbuktu among the many explorers who, from the late eighteenth century onwards, battled for the honour and financial reward of becoming the first Westerner in modern times to set eyes on what was now known to Christians as the 'unattainable city'.

When finally attained in the 1820's, Timbuktu proved to be, in Caillié's words, a 'mass of ill-looking houses built of earth'. Worsening poverty was exacerbated by hostilities with the Nomadic Tuaregs, whose raids on the town were ever more devastating in the years immediately prior to the French colonization of Western Sudan in 1893. The consequences of the period of Tuareg menace were vividly revealed in 1896 to Félix Dubois, who found Timbuktu to have a 'tumbled down and battered appearance'. That the enticing epithets of 'the golden' and 'the unattainable' could no longer be applied to Timbuktu was not the only reason that Dubois dubbed the town 'la mystérieuse'. The town had become mysterious, according to him, for entirely practical reasons: fear of Tuareg raids had forced the inhabitants to hide their remaining treasures behind the meanest and most unpromising façades.

What were the mysteries that Mahmud had promised? And would I really find in Timbuktu any tantalising traces of the town's Andalucían past? From my vantage-point in London, away from the Moorish haze that still clouds the judgement of visitors to Granada, my curiosity about Timbuktu is soon matched by a depressing awareness of the place's present-day reality as one of the poorest towns in the fifth poorest country in the world. There is also the practical problem of how I'm going to get there – the more I research this the more inaccessible the town still seems.

The vast size of Mali – over three times that of France – surprises me, but it is not the distance and desert wilderness of the terrain that soon dissuade me from my original intention of undertaking the traditional caravan route from Marrakesh to Timbuktu. I'm put off by tales of the civil war that has been raging in northern Mali over the last four years.

The tales are slightly confusing, as are the various predictions of the dangers I would face by going at all to Timbuktu at the present moment. From what I can gather in London the origins of the troubles lie in the renewal of hostilities between the Tuaregs and the country's dominant black population. Exceptionally severe drought in the early 1980's threatened the desert livelihood of the Tuaregs, compelling many of them to settle in Timbuktu. Others went to earn a living as mercenaries for Gadaffi before being curtly dismissed with the cessation of war between Libya and Chad. Penniless but now armed they began violently to enforce the dream of an independent Tuareg state, embracing the famous desert township that the Tuaregs themselves are said to have founded.

Tuareg raids on Timbuktu have begun again, government troops have retaliated by poisoning Tuareg wells. European aid workers and missionaries have all moved out of the town, a Swiss consular official has been killed fifty miles to the north. Travelling in the desert or to any of the outlying settlements should be avoided at all costs, but even in Timbuktu itself I should be wary about venturing out of doors after six o'clock in the evening, according to the Mali embassy in Brussels.

Lorry traffic to the town has ceased, all forms of road travel are ill-advised, and in any case there have never been any proper roads or buses that go all the way there. The journey by boat along the Niger from Mali's capital of Bamako is now also out of the question, irrespective of the current danger of Tuareg attacks. I shall be travelling in April, in the middle of the hot, dry season, when the ferryboats are all grounded and the covered canoes or pirogues are endlessly getting stuck in mud flats that have been made especially treacherous this year by drought.

The only possibility left is an internal flight on an airline company which might or might not be running following the recent crash of one of its two ancient planes. I can find out virtually nothing about this service from London, let alone book anything. I take a chance on the rumour that there is at least one flight a week from Bamako to Timbuktu.

Retired couples with golf clubs and sun hats – I could be going back again by charter to Málaga. But I'm on my way to Timbuktu, flying from London to Bamako with a midnight stop in Ghana, where the winter sun-seekers all stream out, emptying the plane of everyone save myself, a trio of young anthropologists, businessmen in gaudy suits, an adolescent deportee, a couple of large and noisy families with multi-coloured headgear, blaring walkmans, mounds of hand-luggage wrapped in white cloths.

Now it's the dawn – a clear, African dawn – and a smiling teenager in a dented yellow taxi is driving me at exhilarating speed across a flat landscape of shrubland, huts, ancient billboards. I'm returning to Bamako airport after a couple of hours' sleep in a hotel that seemed in the darkness to be in some jungle clearing. During the night I had been troubled by the sort of existential questions that Gauguin might have asked himself in Tahiti. Who am I? Where am I? What am I doing? Where am I going?

Optimism and a sense of purpose have returned with the dawn. The vagueness of the airport staff on the night of my arrival was unnecessarily alarming – of course there'll be an early morning flight to Timbuktu, and of course I'll be getting on to it.

I'm nonetheless incredulous after I've re-entered the airport and been handed over a ticket marked Timbuktu, which a friendly official has written out by hand. I can hardly believe that the unattainable seems now certain to be attained within little more than twenty-four hours of leaving London. I'm also slightly surprised by my fellow passengers, who stand with me on the runway, waiting to board a venerable-looking plane whose bolts are apparently being tightened in front of us.

A party of elderly Japanese tourists was not what I was expecting from a trip to Timbuktu, but 'the Japanese just love the African desert,' I'm told by a sweating, denim-jacketed American who looks like a disgruntled mercenary but talks like an effete New Yorker.

The heat is building up as we remain standing on the tarmac, and the American continues to enlighten me with his views on the Japanese race. He knows what the Japanese are like, he's been to Japan himself, in fact he's visited seventy-nine countries in his life, 'not counting San Marino and Liechtenstein'. He's nearing the end of a month's vacation in West Africa – six new countries for his list, and plenty of film to place with the travel videos he keeps in his bank vault. But to be perfectly honest with you, he's not really enjoying himself – too many disappointments, too few clean beds, too many 'rip-off merchants'.

Another person – the only other foreigner about to board the plane – distracts my attention from the droning American. He's white-haired but young-looking, with a bronzed bald forehead, khaki-coloured clothes, a warm, open smile, and a kindly manner of dealing with the growing stream of hawkers offering cassettes, luck charms, rugs, drums, a stuffed monkey's head. I manage to read the name on his boarding pass – Kapuściński.

Ryszard Kapuściński, I presume? The famous Polish foreign correspondent, author of such resonant works as *The Emperor*, *Shah of Shahs*, *Imperium*? He's surprised to be recognized; I blurt out that I've always been an enormous admirer of his writings. I truly mean what I say, I can think of few other journalists with such an eye for the quirky, human detail, and such poetic concision in the recording of what he experiences and observes. What other reporter would begin a book about Haile Selassie with an account of the man employed to wipe the urine from the shoes of dignitaries peed upon by the imperial dog Lulu?

He's the proverbial person who's been everywhere and done everything, but there's no hint of cynicism or world-weariness either in his books or in the traveller now before me – a cheerful person with an almost child-like enthusiasm who's telling me that he's never been to Timbuktu and who seems as excited by the prospect of going there as I am. His very company makes up for the anticlimactic presence of the Japanese tour party and the bored American. But I'm also slightly troubled by my knowledge of the sort of travelling destination he usually favours – the Ethiopia of the Communist terror, Persia in the last days of the Shah, Angola at the onset of independence, Liberia during the Civil War; anywhere in the Third World with a revolution; anywhere with a good chance of getting killed.

The pilot appears, we file into the plane, boiled sweets are sucked as we slowly rise like the sun above a bare panorama cleft by the glistening fracture of the Niger and its splinter tributaries. I'm sitting at a window seat behind Kapuściński, who turns to smile at me during the rare moments when his face is not pressed hard against the window. I almost expect him to jump up and down with excitement. I'm in a similar state of near euphoria, swept over by the metaphysical sensation of nearing a mythical goal.

We fly over isolated mud hut communities, Tuareg camps with igloo-like tents, clusters of statuesque baobab trees. At the approach of Timbuktu the plane swerves at a steep angle above the multi-coloured sands of the Sahara before turning back again towards the Niger and beginning its descent over cultivated fields hemmed in between sands and reeds. Stick-like pirogues are nearing the banks, tiny figures are running towards the giant of the airport.

Outside on the tarmac Kapuściński stretches out his arms as he tries to convey to me in his surprisingly haltering French the emotion he feels on arriving at Timbuktu – 'C'est... magnifique!' is all he can manage.

These are his last words to me, for now the confusion begins. The weekly arrival of the plane is a major event, and much of the male population of Timbuktu has covered the ten kilometres from the town to the airport to find out if family and friends have returned from the big city, if parcels have been brought, above all if tourists have come. In the now desperate hope of seeing tourists, competing boyguides struggle to peer over the barrier maintained by soldiers and customs officials. Headdressed Tuaregs, with their arms drooping with silverwear and painted leather, are waiting in the wings.

Kapuściński and the Japanese party are separated from me by the maelstrom of limbs; I see them for the last time disappearing into a mini-bus. 'They had no time to wait around,' says the official who has made me miss the bus by taking out every single item of my luggage. 'They're returning on the same plane to Bamako in three hours' time.'

Others are soon confirming the obvious – few tourists have been coming to Timbuktu since the troubles began, and hardly any of these stay for longer than it takes for their plane to make the loop to neighbouring Gao and back. Even Kapuściński is someone who has come to Timbuktu simply to say he has been there.

Beyond the customs barrier I'm pinned down by a crowd of boys, Tuaregs, taxi-drivers. Does anyone know Mahmud Zakari? Can anyone direct me to his house? One of the boys tells me that Mahmud is still in Spain, that his elder brother is also away, and that their father is very ill. But he'll none the less show me the family home, he'll introduce me to Mahmud's younger brother, Gamal. 'Gamal est mon frère,' he smiles.

The missionaries have left Timbuktu along with the aid workers. The Belgian-run pumping station feeding the rice project on the Ile de la Paix has also closed down. Only one other foreigner is going to be left with me in Timbuktu – the American tourist. He's waiting in the taxi outside, still wearing the denim jacket and disgruntled expression he had worn in Bamako.

'What a drag,' he says. 'You either spend three hours in this goddam place or a week; there's no plane in between. Well, what the hell, it'll give me a chance to relax, wash some clothes, do some reading, catch up with my postcards. There's bound to be a pool.'

The hotel where he's going to stay is on the outskirts of Timbuktu, exposed to the fast advancing sands. I don't want to depress him by repeating stories I've heard about the present condition of the place. All he knows is that the establishment had been built in the 1970's as Mali's only luxurious hotel outside the capital. He seems completely unaware of the recent troubles that have left the hotel almost permanently empty, with a non-functioning generator and a turned-off water pump. He's curious about why I'm not staying with him. I leave him to his fate as a solitary guest in a waterless hotel lit only by candles. I try not to be too smug; I might be ending up there myself.

The taxi continues into the sandy heart of Timbuktu, and I'm finally hit by the full force of a cultural shock greater than any I've ever experienced. Now that the American is no longer with me, I'm the sole anachronism in a town that looks as unchanged, as ancient, as 'Biblical' as any of the places that had figured in romantic dreams of the Orient. It might have appeared dustily disappointing to someone such as Caillié who had been hardened by months of the most horrific desert travel to get here, but to me, coming almost directly from London, it seems the conclusive proof that reality is equal to anything envisaged by the imagination.

Nothing in Morocco has prepared me for such an unsullied vision of the past. Even within the old quarters of places such as Fez and Marrakesh I was always conscious of these being medieval enclaves trapped by the modern world beyond. In Timbuktu the past seems constrained only by sand dunes. I can see little of the twentieth century other than the car I am in and the occasional electricity wires and scraps of corrugated iron. The rest is sandy streets, mud walls, camels, heads wrapped in indigo cloth, swathed women bearing terracotta pitchers as in some classical frieze.

The car stops at the entrance to a mud courtyard. My guide leads me across it, past playing children and women whose incessant pounding of millet is not even interrupted by the general astonishment caused by our arrival. Beyond is a second courtyard in which an old man is lying on a large, ironwork bed, a jug of water besides him. 'Mahmud's father,' my guide mutters.

The frail, smiling father struggles to extend his hand to someone whom he welcomes as a 'friend of my son'. His hoarse voice is barely audible, and his mouth fills up with saliva as he speaks.

A woman who introduces herself as his wife comes to join us, bringing out a stool for me to sit on. A young boy is sent off to fetch a charcoal burner on which tea is brewed. The tea, clogged with sugar, is poured out into a tiny glass, from which it is thrown back again into the kettle. The process is repeated several times until finally a frothy, sweet mouthful with an acrid after-taste is left. I hand the empty glass back to the boy, who passes it on to the father.

While the tea ritual takes place, Mahmud's father tells me that his son has had to stay on in Granada to receive a small delegation from Timbuktu consisting of the mayor and two friends of Mahmud of Andalucían descent. In circumstances more prosaic than my present ones I would scarcely have believed what they tell me next – that Granada is about to be twinned with Timbuktu.

I suggest that it is Mahmud's pioneering investigations into Timbuktu's Andalucían past that has brought about this strange betrothal of the two towns. Naturally I keep to myself Mahmud's sense of being totally neglected by Granada's officialdom. Instead I praise his book on Yuder Pacha and refer to a passage in which his father is acknowledged for having inspired in him a love of history.

The father responds with memories of working for a period in

Europe when he was young – a world impossibly distant from where I am now. The effort of talking begins to tire him out, his wife leads me away from him and into a plain darkened room where another woman, also a wife of his, is sitting spinning wool. More politenesses are exchanged, another stool is pulled out, an iced drink of ginger is prepared as a shrill, brightly coloured bird hovers over my head.

Someone has gone off to search for Mahmud's wife, and she arrives a short time later, with a couple of long tresses dangling from her otherwise short hair. She laughs as she explains that only today she decided to begin 'work on her hair': it was as if she had known that a guest would arrive.

Her height and sharply delineated beauty are striking, and are accompanied by a smile more mischievous than timid. There is a teasing tone to her voice, which takes the conversation beyond the level of mere civilities.

She shakes her head when she hears that I'm an historian like her husband.

'Historians have no sense of reality. Mahmud spends too much time with his books, he forgets his family. He went off to Spain last July for "a month or so". Now it's April, and he still hasn't returned.'

I recognize in her account of Mahmud aspects of my own behaviour. I tell her that I also have a strange conception of time, that I'm rarely at home in England, and that I've a tendency to get carried away with my researches.

'Of course,' she comments jestingly. 'You're also an historian.'

Her name is Hourria, and she's a nutritionist. She looks at my stomach and concludes that I'm in need of a more balanced diet. She hopes that this will be provided over the coming days, when I shall be a guest of the family.

I'm shown the part of the mud labyrinth which belongs to her and Mahmud. Their two children hide shyly behind the table where my balanced diet is going to be enjoyed. Four chairs and a thin mattress, on which I'm invited to lie, complete the furnishings of a small, bare-walled room that I cannot help comparing with the book-lined flat where I had met Mahmud in Granada.

The immensity of the Zakari household becomes ever more

apparent as more and more people come into the room to greet me, or, in the case of children, to have a glimpse inside and run away giggling. Rising up and down repeatedly from the mattress to my feet, I smile, shake hands, and desperately puzzle out the complex web of family relationships – wives, grandmothers, a galaxy of children of indeterminate parentage, brothers who might not be brothers, males indiscriminately referred to as frères, petit frères, grand frères, even Hourria jokes that she hasn't been able to work out who everyone is. 'It's impossible.'

Two of the less ephemeral visitors are Mahmud's genuine brother, Gamal, and a spiritual brother called Ahmad. The former is a cheerful eighteen-year-old, vividly robed in yellow, sparkily witty, obviously adored by the family, but with a latent cosmopolitanism that suggests a future far away from them. Ahmad, a man who looks older than his thirty-five years, is Gamal's exact opposite – sad, serious and solemn, with a shrunken head, large, bloodshot eyes, a dark mauve garment of ascetic dowdiness, and an overall air denoting an absence of worldly ambition.

Ahmad says he's been waiting for me for some time, he's heard about me from Mahmud, in whose absence he will act as my mentor in Timbuktu. He's told his friends that he won't be seeing them in the next week or so, it's his duty to look after me. His first task is to register me with the police.

We arrive at the police station just before the midday sun reduces the hushed, sandy streets to a desert-like silence. The policeman looks at my passport and visa with the careful scrutiny of an archivist scouring some close-written medieval document. He seems reluctant to stamp my passport with the official proof that I've reached Timbuktu. His particular doubt concerns my profession, which I've listed as 'historian' rather than 'writer' so as not to run the risk of being mistaken for some investigative journalist.

'Historian?' he says in a tone similar to that of Hourria on hearing this word. 'What sort of profession is that?' Then he laughs as he finally brings the stamp down on the page. 'You should get yourself a better job.'

Once we're back inside Hourria's hut, Ahmad closes the door to keep out the sun and to indicate that visits to the English guest are temporarily suspended. A lunch of sun-dried Niger fish has been prepared for the three of us, slightly rotting in flavour, and served with millet, which reappears for dessert in the form of a sweetened, porridge-like drink. I can now identify as millet the pervasive smell emanating from the outside latrine, where children had peered over the wall when I had first attempted some primitive ablutions. In my desire to rid my body of any after-taste of millet I abandon the traveller's usual precautions and help myself to the jug of cool well water placed on the table. Already I'm beginning to find some truth in Leo Africanus's fabulous-seeming description of Timbuktu – the water from the town's wells is indeed delicious.

Gamal rejoins Ahmad and I in the late afternoon, when the sun is sufficiently low for a thorough, guided tour of the town to begin. Stumbling, as if through snow, I am led through the sand-swept maze in which some 20,000 inhabitants are hidden.

Bleached mud cubes, walls like the remnants of sand-castles, and rounded nomadic tents made out of sticks and rush-matting are spread out over an enormous area of sand that threatens slowly to engulf the whole. The town's life and traditions are apparently impervious to the shifting terrain. Bread is still baked, as it was in Timbuktu's time, in conical-shaped street ovens; houses continue to be built according to the same technique introduced by al-Saheli in the fourteenth century – with bricks made by cutting up a large slab of mud that is left to dry in the sun. Other details lend further credibility to Mahmud's promise of a town in which the legacy of Islamic Spain has remained alive. The sparse decorative touches include lattice-work patterning, paired ajimez windows, and metal-embossed, Granadan-style wooden doors like the ones described by Dubois – sturdy doors 'armoured like any gentleman of Agincourt', resilient to the surrounding decay, supportive of the idea of interior mysteries.

I'm photographing the carved pattern on a humble lintel when a soldier approaches to protest at what I'm doing – I've no right, he tells Ahmad, to record aspects of Timbuktu of 'no touristic value', I'm accused of wanting to draw the outside world's attention to the town's poverty. Gamal defends me vociferously, I'm not a tourist, he insists, nor a journalist, I'm their 'grand frère', I can do what I like, I'm a guest. While Gamal stays behind to continue arguing, Ahmad takes me away, apologizing for the soldier's behaviour. 'He's not from Timbuktu,' he claims. 'No one from Timbuktu would behave like that to a foreign visitor.'

Gamal catches up with us to laugh off the whole incident before disappearing off with one of his many friends. Ahmad, as serious as ever, takes me on to see the town's few monuments of conventional 'touristic value'. There's the well named after a woman with an enormous navel – the well around which the original Tuareg settlement of Timbuktu was reputedly founded. Then there are the houses, now locked up, associated with the stays in Timbuktu of the first three Western explorers to have come here – the Scotsman Gordon Laing, who arrived in 1826 only to be killed immediately afterwards; René Caillié, who came two years later, and is sometimes accused today of seizing Laing's notes; and the German Heinrich Barth, humourless and unimaginative, and as such universally believed when he wrote about reaching Timbuktu in 1853.

The final 'sights' are the Sankore and Dyingereyber mosques, around which large communities of Andalucíans had settled. Either serendipity or else some benevolent spirit from al-Andalus has arranged for the sounds of music and dancing to welcome us into the Sankore district. A crowd of kaleidoscopic colour has gathered at the intersection of two streets to watch and participate in a wedding celebration. Some children are dangling from trees, while others have climbed up on to roofs and the tops of walls. Everybody else is packed into a circle, in the middle of which a dozen or so laughing men and women are dancing to the beat of drummers, to the mellow resonance of primitive oboes, to the discordantly expressive screech of stringed instruments that Ahmad claims are of Andalucían origin.

Ahmad leads me away, the music fades, but not its strange rhythms, which seem to echo around a Timbuktu waking up in the pellucid light before sunset. Under these poetically heightened conditions I have my first contact with the mud-brick mosques of the sub-Sahara.

This is an architecture which prefigures that of Gaudí – a cross between an anthropomorphic fantasy dreamt up by a Surrealist, and something that has been thrown together by a deranged child playing in the sand. Symbolic, decorative and practical concerns are united in structures in which ostrich eggs crown towers spiked with expressionistic wooden stakes that serve as scaffolding when the mud-bricks are annually replaced after the rainy season. And Islam is joined to indigenous Songhai beliefs in conical pillars that imbue these mosques with memories of the shrines encapsulating the Songhai cult of ancestors.

The Muslims of the Sub-Sahara are liberal and broad-minded. There are no objections when Ahmad asks a caretaker friend if I can see inside the town's oldest and largest mosque, the Dyingereyber or Grand Mosque. In the excitement of entering a practising mosque for the first time in my life, I forget for a moment that I'm also entering the main surviving work of al-Saheli. I'm not even conscious of being in a building; I'm reminded instead of a quarry as I walk around a shadow-moulded, undecorated interior whose multitude of arches are merely crude openings hacked out of the thick walls of earth. The caretaker explains what parts of the building are by al-Saheli himself, though I find it unlikely that anything of the original structure can remain after centuries of remodellings, expansions, and annual renewals after the rains.

A cracked stairway, like some abstract sculpture, joins the entrance courtyard to a roof-top not unlike that of Gaudí's Casa Mila in its wavy expanse of bizarre forms. A sunset view over an entirely flat Timbuktu fading out into orange-red sands is curtailed as Ahmad hurries me out of the mosque before the evening worshippers arrive.

The day's sightseeing is over, and Ahmad can now indulge in what he enjoys most – talking, discussing. He suggests that we sit down to do this in a place named after the organizer of the Paris-Dakkar rally, Thiérry Sabine. It's the only modern building I've so far been inside in Timbuktu. It was once a tiny 'supermarket' but is now a café-bar curtained off from the outside world and decorated with lanterns and hangings from Communist China. 'You can have beer if you like,' says Ahmad, adding that he himself does not drink alcohol but that many Muslims do, in the privacy of this café, away from the family and the glares of passers-by.

But the massive barman shakes his head, there's no beer left, and most of the soft drinks have also run out. The disruptions in road and river travel to Timbuktu are gradually leaving the town dry, though Ahmad is confident that it won't be long before the 'troubles' are over and the lorries are back. I'd almost forgotten that the leisurely, unhurried town I'm in is supposedly in the throes of a civil war.

Ahmad prefers not to say anything at first about the 'troubles', he's more interested in talking about Islam and other more permanent aspects of Timbuktu life. He paints an attractive picture of an unselfish society in which extreme poverty is balanced by the closeness of family ties and the fundamental importance given to charity. Family members are unfailingly supportive of each other, and the better-off families such as Mahmud's always help out the worse-off ones, often by taking into their care children from poorer backgrounds. The worst sin is for children to neglect their elderly parents, to do so is to become a pariah in society, old age is sacred. 'As a poet of ours once said,' Ahmad adds, directing his glance at the white hairs in my beard, '"when an old man dies a library burns."'

The Timbuktu I'm seeing, I'm hearing about, is becoming ever more compatible with the enchanting town described by Leo Africanus. Even when the 'troubles' are finally discussed, they are made to seem a momentary aberration completely out of spirit with the character of Timbuktu. The trouble-makers, the fanatics, are mainly from outside the town, the townspeople themselves are peace-loving at heart, they hardly know crime, they live in a racially mixed society too complex to be crudely divided into violently antagonistic sectors.

We make our way home. It's well past six o'clock, I should not be out in the streets at this time, I run the risk of instant transformation into a burned-out library. But I pay no more attention to the sensationalist warnings from Europe, I'm being borne along by a new-found serenity even as we deviate from the partially lit main street and into the pitch blackness of alleys where pot-holes lurk unseen, and invisible shrouded figures pass inches in front of me. The mutterings of the hidden presences have no hint of evil, the red glow from open doors is homely not infernal.

Mahmud's home, so different from anywhere I've ever known, seems now a place I've known all my life. I feel a homecoming contentment on re-entering the courtyards where the millet is still being ground, where the father remains sleeping, where a recumbent Hourria is still having her hair put in tresses, where children continue to play and women to converse, where Gamal greets me like a returning relative.

A moon of surprising brilliance has emerged, the extreme heat of the day has been replaced by the proverbial cool of a Saharan night. 'They are always like this,' says Ahmad. I sit outside between him and Gamal, finding out how people spend their nights in towns without either televisions or what Westerners would call nightlife. 'Talking,' mutters Ahmad. 'I'm always up talking with my friends, sometimes into the early hours of the morning. Then I rise just before dawn to say my prayers.'

'Music,' retorts Gamal, 'I love music.'

A Tuareg boy with a strong stammer has appeared, carrying one of the stringed instruments I'd seen at the wedding. 'Before the Andalucians came we only had flutes and drums,' Ahmad tells me as he instructs the boy to place in my hands this reputed predecessor of the Spanish guitar – the strings are of horse hair, the body is a gourd stretched with lizard skin. I return it to the boy, who begins to play with virtuoso ease, striking the strings with a resin-greased bow, plucking them with his fingers, beating out the rhythm by tapping on the gourd. The music attracts a growing audience, the boy breaks out in song. But then his playing is interrupted by the distant sounds of further music that soon have us all leaving the courtyard and walking into the streets, across a Timbuktu in which the sands and the walls have turned a glowing ivory white.

'I knew today would be a special day,' laughs Hourria as we reach the crowded open space from where the music is coming. 'No sooner do you arrive in Timbuktu than a peace treaty is signed. Everyone has come to celebrate it.'

'Those are ministers from Bamako,' says Ahmad, indicating a group of men and women seated in a row on a canopied podium like some imperial throne. The music is briefly halted for one of the ministers to address the crowd with words about peace and harmony, his speech inspiring a jubilant response, then the music returns and the dancing begins. The officials themselves are soon being pulled down from the podium by the hands of a buoyant crowd gripped by a celebratory fervour.

The dancing continues for hours; it has a hallucinatory effect. Songhais intertwine with Tuaregs, white and indigo robes sway in eerie slow motion through a speckled sea of flowers blossoming into exotic headresses. 'The inhabitants of Timbuktu,' whispers a ghost-like voice, 'are people of a gentle and cheerful disposition, and spend a great part of the night in singing and dancing through all the streets of the city.'

Leo Africanus, turbaned and bearded, mingles with the celebrants before vanishing with them as they disperse noiselessly into the spectral white landscape.

The lost paradise. Through investigating the fate of exiles who had looked back to an idealized Spain, I seem to have arrived at a paradise myself. I'm in danger of reaching the same sentimental conclusion that has ensnared so many travel writers in search of the exotic and the unspoilt – a conclusion in which the exaggerated spiritual virtues of my discovered 'unchanged' world throw into sharp relief the failings of the urban, capitalist West. A more worrying realization is that the picture I'm forming of Timbuktu is as saccharine as the romantic image of Islamic Spain perpetuated by so many of the writers I've criticized and made fun of.

I blame at first the shock of the truly exotic for blurring my critical faculties. But as the exotic wears off as I settle into the life of Timbuktu, I find that my perception of my surroundings is no less idyllic. I cannot explain either this or the ease with which I've adapted to social circumstances so utterly alien to the ones in which I've been brought up. The possibility of having known this world in some previous existence cannot entirely be discounted.

In any case I've have had few problems in slipping into a daily routine far healthier, more contemplative and leisurely than my normal one in Europe. After waking up early on a roof terrace that I share with some of the teenagers of the household, I'm met by Ahmad at the portal of Hourria's hut. While waiting for one of the children to brew the tea, I'm led by Ahmad on what had seemed the first time like some household tour of inspection. Dressed in my white shirt and trousers, I had felt like some British officer in India enquiring after the well-being of the native population. Now, as I daily shake hands with the household hierarchy, I'm more appreciative of the ritualistic importance of greetings in Mali society. A simple 'hello' or 'good morning' is not enough. A rhetorical 'Ça va?' has always to be followed by a 'Ça va bien?' and, sometimes, by a whole string of other polite questions lasting up to a minute or two but never requiring any answers. 'Ça va ton père?... Ça va ta mère?... Ça va tes grand-pères?... Ça va tes frères?... Ça va tes sœurs?... Ça va ton travail?...'

This duty accomplished, I can slouch into a chair in Hourria's welcoming hut, which I'm becoming increasingly reluctant and unable to leave. Sometimes there seems little need to go out, for an expanding cross-section of Timbuktu society is paying me visits – musicians bearing instruments, teachers coming to practise their English, vendors selling tapes, tailors fitting me with clothes, Tuaregs spreading out their silverware on the ground, friends of Gamal offering to find me a young and beautiful wife, women friends of Hourria sizing up my appearance before shyly lowering their eyes. And while all this is going on, Ahmad continues to talk to me while I continue to be absorbed in the apparently unending sight of Hourria's hair being pulled and twisted into ever more complex patterns. My growing acquisition of the Songhai language begins usefully to include the terms for every type of female tress.

I rarely allot myself more than one task a day. Life here is so unhurried that even the simplest task can take up a whole morning. A visit to a bank involves a trek into the desert to an isolated block where camels are tied to posts; inside I re-meet acquaintances, exchange greetings with a dozen or so employees, and wait around for much of the day while forms are written out by hand in triplicate. In the Timbuktu post-office the official in charge spends at least an hour searching for the stamp to frank my cards with the words 'Tombouctou la Mysterieuse'.

Lunchtime inspires a daily mixture of curiosity and trepidation. Though I'm thriving on my daily diet, I think this has less to do with its 'balanced' nature than with the absence of alcohol and the knowledge that my body has been able to withstand something akin to gastronomic torture. The food would probably have succeeded in tarnishing my Timbuktu idyll were it not for the pleasure of the company and my continuing fascination with all things culinary – a fascination which has prompted Hourria to prepare for me local specialities that are daily needing an ever greater effort of will to consume. The sauce made from the ground seeds of desert cucumbers had the virtue of mildness, but not the fakuhoy that is served the next day – sickeningly bitter leaves in a gelatinous black sauce the texture of bitumen. Everything is gritty with sand, which is as ubiquitous as the millet that I'm unable now to dissociate from the latrine. Round balls of millet, like porridge mixed with plasticine, form an impermeable bed on which is placed a sauce constituting the greatest gastronomic horror I've experienced to date – a gluey, dark-red sauce of baobab pulp and dung-cured fish. I look forward more than ever to the after-lunch cup of Nescafé, which I take without sugar. A visiting teacher squirms in disgust – can people really drink sugarless coffee?

In the late afternoon I always return with Ahmad to the Thiérry Sabine, the owner of which continues to promise the imminent arrival of the next shipment of drinks. At night, after Ahmad has left, and I'm back in the teenagers' quarters, I discover a less ascetic side to local life. Away from Ahmad's moralizing glance, and Hourria's nutritional concerns, Gamal and his friends reveal a passion for cigarettes and Western music. They switch on an antique ghetto-blaster (the current craze is salsa), and have a furtive smoke. Then the game can begin. The game 'has been all the rage in Timbuktu since 1989', according to Gamal. It is played on a pirate set with wooden pieces beautifully fashioned by Tuareg craftsmen. The game is Scrabble.

Domestic details such as these enable me to have a fuller and more balanced outlook on a town which had first appeared to me as a living chapter of history. But the more I uncover the everyday reality of the modern town, the further I seem to be diverted from the original purpose of my visit. It is to the town's Andalucían links that I eventually return in the hope of discovering what Mahmud had promised – something of the mysterious Timbuktu of fabled riches.

Unfortunately, the only person who can lead me to this Timbuktu is Mahmud himself. And Mahmud has become again the elusive Godot-like figure whose existence is open to question. Everyone is awaiting his return, the promised imminence of which is as illusory as the beer at the Thiérry Sabine. Everything seems dependent on him, even the running of an orphanage that he and Ahmad have founded together but which has not been functioning since he's been away. 'We have to wait for Mahmud,' sighs a stoic Ahmad, who goes back almost weekly to the airport to see if the flight from Bamako has brought any news of him.

There is no one to help me even at the local historical centre where Mahmud has undertaken so much of his research on Timbuktu. The jovial director of this institution speaks with an excited, incomprehensible speed as he shows me a handwritten list of manuscripts that have been rescued from private libraries sometimes as primitive as a wooden box suspended from a tree. Some of these works are undoubtedly very rare and precious, many appear to have come from al-Andalus, but I've no idea of their contents, I'll have to ask Mahmud.

The director leaves me in the hands of one of his assistants, who can barely be bothered to look up from the book he is reading. He brusquely demands 'specific questions', to which he gives unhelpfully succinct answers, his usual response being that 'Mahmud will know'. The most I learn is that the descendants of Yuder Pacha's army are known collectively as the 'Arma', and that the ones of Spanish origin are referred to as the 'Aluchis'. Is Mahmud an Aluchi? 'You should ask him yourself.'

The Spanish philosopher Ortega y Gasset, in an article of 1924 in which he drew attention to the Spanish-led conquest of Timbuktu, wondered why Spaniards hadn't visited the town in search of 'our noble relatives'. When I ask the assistant about the possibility of talking to someone of indisputable Spanish descent, he says a few words to Ahmad, who nods in agreement. Later that day I'm taken to the workshop of an old cobbler from the Dyingereyber district.

The bespectacled cobbler, in pale blue pantaloons and a white cap, sits squatting in a tiny room surrounded by scraps of leather, tools of medieval appearance, and a pot of baobab paste, which he uses for the glueing of soles. His ancestors are from Córdoba, the traditional Spanish centre of leatherwork. Continuing to work as he talks, he speaks about his son, who is one of the handful of people from Timbuktu accompanying the town's mayor to Granada. The son is a very close friend of Mahmud, 'who can tell you more about my past than I can'. I mention Mahmud's reference to the fifteenth-century Spanish origin of the footwear still made in Timbuktu. The cobbler thinks that Mahmud must have been talking about the local riding boots – 'but no one has been wearing those since the troubles, people no longer ride horses,' he notes. Today he has a new popular line in shoes – shoes with floral decorations and the name of the wearer. I commission from him a pair inscribed with the name of the Moorish Queen; next to her he persuades me to put in the epithet 'Tombouctou la mysterieuse'.

On another day I'm introduced to the family of cabinet-makers who continue to produce the tooled, metal-adorned doors that so impressed me on my arrival at Timbuktu. The smiling elder son gives me a demonstration of tools that have remained the same over the centuries even while the materials have changed: the wood is no longer as good as before, and the metal adornments of today are sometimes made from melted down cans. However, his work also includes the restoration of doors and cabinets originally made for distant ancestors of the present owners. Posing for a photograph, he and a boy assistant carry out into the street a door dating back 'at least to the seventeenth century'. It is not for sale.

A Muslim, he says, would never sell off the house of his forefathers: his own house and workshop, for instance, have been in his family's possession since the time when al-Saheli invited their cabinet-making ancestors to move from Spain to Timbuktu. He knows this from stories that have been passed down from one generation to another. The honesty of his smile and manner give me no cause to doubt him. As our hands clasp at the moment of my leaving, I become conscious that in this moment I've stretched out my arm across the centuries and have come closer to al-Andalus than I'm ever likely to get.

But the mysteries of Timbuktu have still to be revealed to me – mysteries that I've come to perceive in terms of a fabulously appointed Andalucían interior enriched with treasures smuggled out of Moorish Spain. The Andalucían detailing on some of the exteriors has given slightly more substance to this chimerical vision, but the few interiors I've seen so far have borne out more realistic expectations – unadorned spaces in mud. Ahmad keeps on promising to find me a richer interior, an interior of the kind Mahmud would certainly have taken me to see. But it is not until my last afternoon in Timbuktu, after considerable pestering on my part, that he does anything about this.

He proposes that we visit a 'palace' in the Sankore district that had belonged to the greatest of Timbuktu's scholars, Ahmet Baba – the man who had made sixteenth-century Timbuktu a place of pilgrimage for learned men from all over Africa.

Two female descendants of Ahmet Baba, one young and beautiful, lie in the shade of the threshold, bewildered by our arrival. Ahmad says a few words to them, the mother nods while the daughter suppresses a giggle. We're invited to show ourselves round; my heart quickens with excitement but soon slows down when I realize that the interior is exactly like the others I've visited.

Ahmad, as sombre as ever, senses my disappointment, and tries to console me as we walk back home in the sunset.

'You were hoping for too much from a first visit to Timbuktu. Now you've got no other choice, you'll have to come back here, not just once, but twice, three times, four times perhaps.'

He stops to stare at me with eyes as red as the rays of the sinking sun.

'Only after repeated visits do you stand any chance of finding what Mahmud had told you about – the mysteries of Timbuktu.'

I haven't the patience to await this future possibility, and decide to move further up the Niger in a final bid to fulfil my ever fading hope of uncovering some sensational legacy of the Andalucían presence. I decide to visit Djenné.

The army of Yuder Pacha, after conquering Timbuktu, had also headed west to Djenné, a town often described as Timbuktu's 'twin sister'. Its name might not have the latter's fabled resonance, but the place itself was even wealthier than Timbuktu during its fifteenth- and sixteenth-century heyday. Dubois called the town the 'jewel of the valley of the Niger', and even the cynical Caillié had been impressed – both by the splendour of its architecture, and by the sophistication and literacy of the people, who were well-read in the Koran, and differed from other Africans he had known by not roaring with laughter whenever he blew his nose into a handkerchief.

Djenné, in economic decline since the seventeenth century, and bypassed today by the main road running in between Bamako and Mopti, has apparently resisted change and tourism to remain an unspoilt medieval town whose architectural appearance corresponds perhaps more closely to the Western vision of Timbuktu than Timbuktu itself.

The plane from Timbuktu to Bamako makes a stop at Mopti, where I get off to be met by rumours of a cholera epidemic that has already claimed the lives of two hundred people. Within an hour I'm seated outside at a riverside bar, planning the speediest possible continuation of my journey to Djenné.

Helping me in this task is a boyish-looking twenty-year-old called Tall, a local guide of Timbuktu origin whom Gamal has recommended. 'You have in Mopti a petit frère called Tall,' Gamal had told me at Timbuktu airport, rightly predicting the pangs of nostalgia I would feel later in the day, away from my newly acquired family.

Tall, who has been living off his wits since the age of ten, is clearly someone whose success as a guide has been dependent on a combination of charm, strong-headedness and a talent for assessing instantly the weaknesses of tourists. While seated with him at the bar, he formalizes our brotherly relationship by writing out a contract that entails paying him a daily rate equivalent to a month's salary in Mali. Smiles are exchanged along with a hefty advance, and Tall rushes off to search for a taxi – apparently the only practical way of geting us to Djenné by nightfall.

After the quiet days in Timbuktu, my journey has acquired some of the frantic urgency that had characterized the last and ill-fated Niger trip of Mungo Park, who, in 1805, had sped past Mopti in his failed attempt to follow the river all the way to a sea. I think of Park and his obsessive quest while contemplating from the bar a view he would certainly have recognized – a confusion of black, cargo-laden canoes, a riverbank seething with merchants in flow-ing robes, bearers with hessian sacks, women alongside heaps of dried and fly-ridden fish.

Tall's hasty return speeds me away from this view and into a decrepit car that appears to be shaking off its remaining body parts as we hurtle towards Djenné across empty, pock-marked roads. Four hours later, in the mellow light of the late afternoon, we are being ferried over to the island bearing the medieval mirage that is our destination.

Laughing children are running in the cloud of dust stirred up by our car on its theatrical entry into the town. From this very moment of arrival I'm convinced that my quest is finally over. Djenné is less of a canvas than an operatic stage set – a haunting arrangement of streets and squares that await the acting out of a grand, oriental fantasy. Instead of a mud architecture of one-storeyed and near uniform humility, there are mud palaces with the genuine look of palaces – tall, bizarrely crenellated, proud of the wood and metalwork decorations that highlight their architectural features. And, above all this, exerting all the tricks of which such architecture is capable, rises a sandcastle mosque larger and more elaborate than any other of its kind in Africa.

Escaping briefly from Tall once we've found a roof-space for the night, I explore penumbral streets that murmur with hushed pres-ences now that evening prayers in the mosque are ending. A huge and over-excited dog, avoiding the crowd of worshippers, rushes at terrifying speed in my direction eventually to wrap his sandy paws around my body. I push him off, but he continues to follow me, and does so obstinately for the rest of my walk, mysteriously indifferent to the many onlookers we pass in the growing darkness. A young man who has noticed this, tells me not to worry. 'He latches on to all the *blancs* who come here. His mother's owner was a Frenchman.' In the dog's stubborn memories of his French ancestry I'm confronted once again with an emotion that has dogged me throughout my journey – a persistent, irrational attachment to the past.

The dawn that is breaking over the rooftops of Djenné is as special as my first night in Timbuktu. It heralds the arrival of the Imam of Mecca.

In the ochre warren that is slowly emerging into the soft, spreading light, a solitary boy is hurrying with a silver pail of water. A small group of robed men enters the street a short time later, followed by a further and much larger group, then a long line of boys walking Indian file behind a teacher. The boys, swathed in their best and most colourful robes, are holding small chalk boards marked with lines from the Koran. The sun rises, more groups appear, more lines of boys, the street becomes a steady stream of colours converging into other streams until finally the whole warren is flooded with brilliant yellows, ultramarines, vermilions, indigos, scarlets, purples, greens, whites.

The crowds flow into the sandy expanse of the main square, where they form into an avenue staking out the processional route that the Imam will follow on his way to the mosque. Boys, squatting at the front, start chanting the Koran when the news spreads around that the three cars bearing the Imam and his entourage have finally arrived. The Imam, in dark glasses, leaves his black car to walk between the lines of the faithful. 'How small he is,' Tall mutters.

When the estuary of colour begins emptying its waters into the great sea of the mosque, I embark with Tall on the mission that has brought me to Djenné. We re-enter the now abandoned stage set of the back streets, and make our way down a long, narrow alley towards a palace built by one of Yuder Pacha's generals. The elderly descendant who lives there now is still known as 'the Moroccan'.

The heavy green door of his palace is closed, but Tall knows that the Moroccan's wife and daughters will be in the courtyard of an adjoining building. 'No women are allowed today in the streets,' says Tall. 'They cannot be seen in public when the Imam of Mecca is in town.'

The womenfolk of the Moroccan's household are seated around an old well, which is said by Tall to have magical properties. Words in Songhai are exchanged with the wife, who tells us to return in the early evening to talk to her husband and see his palace. Tall suggests we spend the intervening hours touring the surrounding villages in a horse and cart.

The horse and cart, making me more conspicuous than ever, sets off at a gallop across swampland that has been turned dry by the long drought. A wind builds up, the landscape briefly disappears under sweeping clouds of sand. We visit villages inhabited by the descendants of slaves and Egyptian Jews; we meet Fulani women weighed down by mammoth earrings of gold; we are approached by fathers asking me to save their ill children; we hear from a holy man about the difficulties of finding ostrich eggs in times of desert war. When the evening approaches we're on the outskirts of Djenné, asking permission from an official to see the adjoining and much depleted ruins of ancient Jeno, capital of a near mythical civilization. By the time the official has taken down my particulars, the darkness is already so great that little can be seen.

We go back to the House of the Moroccan under a moonless black sky. The old man is waiting for us behind the now open door of his palace. But it is so dark that even after a few minutes of adjusting my eyes to the obscurity I'm unable to make out anything either of the interior or of the person who is talking to me in a slow, croaking voice. He speaks only in Songhai, his words lazily translated by Tall.

Yes, he confirms, he is indeed descended from a general who accompanied Yuder Pacha on his mission to conquer the Songhai kingdom. The army had set off from Fez, where his ancestor had been living. Did his ancestor form part of that town's large Andalucían community? Yes, he mumbles before throwing doubt on the reliability of his story by claiming that 'all Moroccans are of Andalucían origin'. Then he says that I'm asking questions to which only members of his family are entitled to an answer.

He prefers to talk about his house and its 800-year-old magic well. The well, he emphasizes, is his house's only treasure, and it's inhabited by spirits who have always informed his ancestors about any plots against them.

Tall is getting bored. He asks me to slip a few notes into the old man's hand. I agree that there is little point in continuing the interview, and get up to leave. The croaking voice holds me back for a moment. The old man is wondering if I know of a certain Mahmud Zakari, who has often been to see him in Djenné.

'Mahmud,' the voice continues, 'is always talking to me about this extraordinary place in Spain called the Alhambra.' The glow from Granada, and all the delusions it has sustained, has finally begun to flicker.

'But what is this Alhambra?' the voice persists. 'Is it a public park, a fun-fair, a zoo?'

ACKNOWLEDGEMENTS

My thanks to Fernando Olmedo, who first suggested this book; to Jerónimo Paéz, who commissioned it; to Chelo Beltrán, who translated it into Spanish; to Alexander Fyjis-Walker, who has bravely published it in English; and to the staff of the Legado Andalusí and the Equipo 28, who have supported it throughout.

My thanks also to Richard Cowan, David Godwin, Bob Goodwin, Ian McAndless, Carmen Llanos, my friends in Granada, Morocco and Timbuktu, the many other people who have helped me at different stages of my journey, and, as always, to Jackie.

I hope that those who think they have been portrayed in the book will forgive the many liberties with plot and character, and accept this essentially as a work of fiction.

The Koutoubia

FURTHER READING

A good starting-point for those wishing to undertake themselves an Islamic journey through Spain is perhaps Richard Fletcher's *Moorish Spain* (London, 1999), which is also the only work to tackle, albeit briefly, the many romantic distortions of Spain's Islamic history. Among the more detailed general works are Anwar Chejne's encyclopaedic *Muslim Spain, Its History and Culture* (Minneapolis, 1974), and the two volumes of widely varied essays comprising Salma Khadra Jayyus' anthology, *The Legacy of Muslim Spain* (Leiden, 1994).

The history and everyday life of Islamic Granada are vividly and fulsomely related in Miguel Ángel Ladero Quesada's *Granada: Historia de un país Islámico, 1939-1571* (Madrid, 1989), and Rachel Arié's *L'Espagne musulmane au temps des Nasrides, 1939 à 1499* (Paris, 1990). Two other indispensable works on the later history of Islamic Spain are L. P. Harvey's *Islamic Spain, 1950-1500* (Chicago and London, 1990), and Julio Caro Baroja's *Los moriscos del reino de Granada* (Madrid, 1976).

Most of the liveliest contemporary accounts of al-Andalus are from Granada, notably the startlingly immediate *The Tibyan: Memoirs of 'Abd Allah ibn Buluggin, last Zirid amir of Granada* (translated and edited by Amin. T. Tibi, Leiden, 1986) and Ibn al-Khatib's description of Nasrid Granada and its rulers, *Al-Lamha al-badriyya* (The Shining Rays of the Full Moon), which was recently edited by Emilio Molina and José María Casciaro as *Historia de los Reyes de la Alhambra* (Granada, 1998). Extracts from the works of Ibn al-Khatib and other early writers can be found in Francisco Javier Simonet's *Descripción del reino de Granada* (Granada, 1989).

The poems from al-Andalus collected by the Loja-born Ibn Saïd are the subject of A. J. Arberry's *Moorish Poetry: A Translation of 'The Pennants'*, an anthology compiled in 1943 by the Andalucían Ibn Saïd (Cambridge, 1953), while a short selection of the writings of the Murcian mystic Ibn al'Arabi has been brought together by the Editora Regional de Murcia as *Ibn al-Arabi, guía espiritual* (Murcia, 1990). A good idea of morisco literature, with its extraordinary blend of western and eastern influences, can be had by reading Luce López-Baralt's *Un Kama Sutra español* (Madrid, 1999), a magnificently edited edition of a pioneering sexual treatise written by the anonymous 'refugiado de Túnez' ('refugee from Tunis').

Anyone interested in the art and architecture of Islamic Spain, and the impact of this culture on North Africa, should turn to the weighty exhibition catalogue, *Al-Andalus, The Arts of Islamic Spain* (The Metropolitan Museum of Art, New York, and the Alhambra, Granada, 1999); a good if less demanding read is Marianne Berruand and Achim Bednorz's excellently illustrated *Moorish Architecture in Andalusia* (Cologne, 1999).

The vast and often unrewarding literature on what I have called here the 'Phantom Palace' is dominated by Oleg Grabar's stimulating and very controversial *The Alhambra* (London, 1978), and Antonio Fernández-Puertas's massively researched if also occasionally impenetrable work of the same title (London, 1997); the romantic vision of the monument is brilliantly assessed in Tania Raquejo's *El Palacio encantado: La Alhambra y el arte Británico* (Madrid, 1990).

Three specialist guides to Spain's Islamic remains are Godfrey Goodwin's *Islamic Spain* (London, 1990), the Editora Regional de Murcia's *Guía Islámica de la Región de Murcia* (Murcia, 1999), and El Legado Andalusí's *Las rutas de Al Andalus* (Seville, 1995). El Legado Andalusí have also recently brought out the outstanding *Itinerario cultural de Almorávides y Almohadesi* (Seville, 1999), which covers not only Spain but North Africa.

Those wishing to trace the history of Moorish Spain across the Sahara should turn to E. W. Bovill's immensely readable *The Golden Trade of the Moors* (Oxford University Press, 1970), and to Ismael Diadié Haidara's specialist study *El Bajá Yawdah y la conquista saadí del Songhay, 1591-1599* (Cuevas de Almanzora, 1993). For the description of Timbuktu by Leo Africanus (Juan León Africano) see the sumptuous edition of the latter's book on Africa brought out by El Legado Andalusí under the title *Descripción general del África y de las cosas peregrinas que allí hay* (Granada, 1995).

Works belonging to the often interchangeable categories of fiction and travel literature have of course played an especially important role in my own Spanish and African wanderings. *The Travels of Ibn Battuta*, which provided this book with its essential structure, have been edited in English by H. A. R. Gibb (Cambridge, 1958, 4 vols.). Other early travel accounts on Islamic Spain are featured in García Mercedal's three-volumed *Viajes de extranjeros por España y Portugal desde los tiempos más remotos hasta finales del siglo XV* (Madrid, 1959).

With the major exception of the perennially perverse George Borrow, most foreign travellers to Spain in the 19th-century wrote lengthy and usually ecstatic passages about the country's Islamic monuments. Some of the greatest prose of this kind is contained in Richard Ford's *Handbook for Travellers in Spain* (London, 1845), a work in which passion, erudition, and occasional flights of fantasy are balanced by a down-to-earth sense of humour. Little such humour can be detected in Washington Irving's constantly reprinted *Legends of the Alhambra* (1st edition, London 1839), which, together with Gautier's *Voyage en Espagne* (Paris, 1846; translated C. A. Phillips as *A Romantic in Spain*, London, 1996) and Edmondo de Amicis's *Spain and the Spaniards* (London, 1885), can take much of the blame for the promotion of an absurdly sentimental vision of Spain's Islamic legacy. This vision has been extensively perpetuated by 90th-century travel-writers on Spain, though not by Gerald Brenan, whose *South from Granada* (London, 1957) offered instead an alternative exoticism based on the lost world of the Alpujarras.

Many of the writers who wrote so gushingly on Spain became afterwards similarly effusive about Morocco, for instance de Amicis, who went on to write the characteristically far-fetched if very entertaining *Morocco, its People and Places* (most recent English edition, London, 1985). In complete contrast to this is Charles de Foucauld's *Reconnaissance au Maroc* (Paris, 1888) which recounts the author's extraordinary adventures into forbidden territory with considerable restraint and scholarship. Two of the more notable twentieth-century travel books on Morocco are Walter Harris's hilarious if at times scarcely believable *Morocco that Was* (1991), and Elias Canetti's haunting and stylistically memorable *Voices of Marrakesh* (1967, English translation 1978). The most evocative book as yet written on Timbuktu is A. Dubois's *Tombouctou la mystérieuse* (Paris, 1897).

Romantic imaginings of the Orient, and of Granada in particular, have been an especially rich source of fiction since the time of Chateaubriand's *Last of the Abencerrages* (first English edition, London, 1830). Though this Orientalist pot-boiler by Chateaubriand is little read today, recent novels in a similar vein have enjoyed enormous popularity, including Tariq Ali's *Shadows of the Pomegranate Tree* (London, 1999), Antonio Gala's fictitious Boabdil manuscript, *El manuscrito Carmesí* (Barcelona, 1990), and Amin Malouf's wonderful *Leo the African* (English translation, 1988). Salman Rushdie's *The Moor's Last Sigh* (London, 1995), though not an historical novel at all, is an excellent example of the imaginative transformation of the many myths surrounding the final days of Moorish Spain.

© Michael Jacobs 2000

The moral right of the author has been asserted

This edition published by Pallas Athene 2000
If you would like further information about titles published in the
Pallas Athene Editions series, please write to:
Dept. T, Pallas Athene, 59 Linden Gardens, London W2 4HJ

Series editor: Alexander Fyjis-Walker
Series assistant: Jenny Wilson
Series designer: James Sutton

Cover illustration: Capital in the Alhambra,
Pallas Athene
Author photograph: Bob Goodwin

ISBN 1 873429 36 3

Printed in Italy